Managing Cultural Diversity in Technical Professions

D1007737

Uniting North American Business: NAFTA Best Practices
Jeffrey D. Abbott and Robert T. Moran

EuroDiversity: A Business Guide to Managing Difference
George Simons

**Global Strategic Planning: Cultural Perspectives for Profit and
Non-Profit Organizations**
Marios I. Katsioloudes

**Succeeding in Business in Central and Eastern Europe: A Guide to Cultures,
Markets, and Practices**
Woodrow H. Sears and Audrone Tamulionyte-Lentz

Competing Globally: Mastering Multicultural Management and Negotiations
Farid Elashmawi

Intercultural Services: A Worldwide Buyer's Guide and Sourcebook
Gary Wederspahn

Managing Cultural Differences, Fifth Edition
Philip R. Harris and Robert T. Moran

**Multicultural Management 2000: Essential Cultural Insights for
Global Business Success**
Farid Elashmawi and Philip R. Harris

International Directory of Multicultural Resources
Robert T. Moran and David O. Braaten

International Business Case Studies for the Multicultural Marketplace
Robert T. Moran, David O. Braaten, and John E. Walsh

**Developing the Global Organization: Strategies for Human
Resource Professionals**
Robert T. Moran, Philip R. Harris, and William G. Stripp

Transcultural Leadership: Empowering the Diverse Workforce
George F. Simons, Carmen Vazquez, and Philip R. Harris

Dynamics of Successful International Business Negotiations
William G. Stripp and Robert T. Moran

RELATED TITLES

Diversity Success Strategies
Norma Carr-Rufino

Mentoring and Diversity
Belle Rose Ragins and David Clutterbuck

Managing Cultural Diversity in Technical Professions

Lionel Laroche, Ph.D., P.Eng.

An *Imprint of Elsevier*

Amsterdam Boston London New York Oxford Paris
San Diego San Francisco Singapore Sydney Tokyo

Butterworth-Heinemann is an imprint of Elsevier.

Library of Congress Cataloging-in-Publication Data
Laroche, Lionel.
  Managing cultural diversity in technical professions / Lionel Laroche.
    p. cm.—(The managing cultural differences series)
  Includes bibliographical references and index.
  ISBN-13: 978-0-7506-7581-9 ISBN-10: 0-7506-7581-0 (pbk.: alk. paper)
  1. Diversity in the workplace. 2. Intercultural communication.
3. Professional corporations—Management. 4. High technology
industries—Management. I. Title. II. Series.

HF5549.5.M5 L37 2003
658.3'0089—dc21   2002027836
ISBN-13: 978-0-7506-7581-9
ISBN-10: 0-7506-7581-0
British Library Cataloguing-in-Publication Data
A catalogue record for this book is available from the British Library.

The publisher offers special discounts on bulk orders of this book.
For information, please contact:

Manager of Special Sales
Elsevier
200 Wheeler Road
Burlington, MA 01803
Tel: 781-313-4700
Fax: 781-313-4880

For information on all Butterworth-Heinemann publications available, contact our World Wide Web home page at: http://www.bh.com

Transferred to Digital Printing 2010.

*To my parents, Gilles and Annie Laroche, who gave
me the desire to travel;*

*To my wife, Diane Michelangeli, who helped me make sense
of my experience in North America;*

*To my children, Carolyn and Daniel. May they live in a
world where cultural differences are truly seen as opportunities
rather than issues or challenges.*

Contents

1

Culture and Cultural Differences 1

2

Managing Technical Professionals 21

3

4

5

6

Foreword

Engineers and scientists born outside of North America are an essential and growing part of many technology-based organizations in Canada and the United States. We often bring fresh perspectives and new ways of doing things, which, if managed effectively, can generate tremendous benefits for the long-term success of our organizations. Such cultural diversity can be a great asset for any research organization. The challenge is to build a synergistic management environment where creativity and inventiveness can flourish among people with diverse cultural backgrounds. I believe this book will help managers and team leaders in multicultural research organizations to meet that challenge.

Because it is written by a technical professional for technical professionals, *Managing Cultural Diversity in Technical Professions* provides much-needed answers to many of the questions we ask ourselves about how to manage effectively in a culturally diverse environment. For example, the description and diagrammatic representation of cross-cultural feedback give invaluable insights into complex socio-technical interactions. Although many books have been written on cultural differences, this book stands out because of the depth of analysis that it provides. Lionel analyzes cross-cultural reporting relationships, multicultural team dynamics, and career management in great depth and explains these ideas in simple, yet powerful terms. Well-designed sketches and diagrams complement the text and will help technical professionals visualize any unfamiliar concepts. The end result is a set of practical recommendations that any technical professional can readily implement.

In addition to providing these insights and information, Lionel is an engaging writer. He brings interesting concepts and ideas to life through anecdotes both from his own experience as an engineer and from the experiences of other technical professionals. Based on my own experience of Lionel's work from the training and coaching he provided us at Syncrude, this book should "hit home" with technical professionals.

Maja Veljkovic
Senior Research Advisor
Syncrude Canada Ltd.

Series Preface

Culture is a fascinating concept. It has so many applications, whether between nations, organizations, or peoples. Communicating effectively across cultures, negotiating on a global scale, and conducting international business are always challenging. To thrive, and in many cases to survive, in the 21st century, individuals and institutions must incorporate cultural sensitivity and skills into their relations, strategies, and structures. Inability to deal with differences or diversity in human cultures is a sign of weakness and obsolescence in persons and groups. The new millennium has no tolerance for "ethnic cleansing," anti-Semitism, or any other form of religious, racial, or gender discrimination.

As originally conceived, our book, *Managing Cultural Differences*, was intended to increase human effectiveness with people who differ in cultural backgrounds. With the new century, our "flagship" sails into her fifth edition. We are particularly gratified that not only have business organizations found the book useful, but in academia, more than 200 universities worldwide have adopted our work as a textbook. This pioneering publication has also spawned many "offspring," so the *Managing Cultural Differences Series* was launched and has subsequently grown into more than a dozen titles.

As series editors, we are pleased with these outstanding products. We trust that you will continue to find our literary efforts helpful as you seek to address transcultural challenges in our rapidly changing, highly interdependent communities!

We hope you will visit the website of our publisher, Butterworth–Heinemann, for continuing updates on the MCD Series (www.bh.com). To make inquiries about the availability of our Authors' Network for consulting or training, contact by e-mail, k.maloney@elsevier.com.

Philip R. Harris, Ph.D.
LaJolla, California
Robert T. Moran, Ph.D.
Scottsdale, Arizona

Prologue

As a chemical engineer, I worked on several international projects with engineers and scientists from all over the world. Even though we were all technical professionals who spoke English fairly well, we were not getting anywhere. I had this experience first when working at Procter & Gamble, then at Xerox; the same kinds of cross-cultural issues could be observed at both companies. Having some personal interest in this area, I researched it further and realized that:

- *Most technical professionals do not recognize the impact of cultural differences in their work*. They are trained to focus on data, experimental results, and quantified information. Because the laws of physics are the same the world over, how could cultural differences play a role in their work?

- *Cross-cultural issues lead to a significant underutilization of talent*. Many immigrants who come to North America with significant technical education (many have Masters or Ph.D.s) and experience end up operating a dry cleaning business or driving a cab. Many others work in positions where their skills are not fully used (Ph.D.s working as technicians or IT specialists entering information in databases) or go from one short-term contract to another.

These two observations are the basis for this book. By educating technical professionals on the impact of cultural differences, I hope this book can help American and Canadian technical organizations make use of this unused or underused talent. Tremendous benefits can be derived by merging synergistically the techniques, approaches, and knowledge of people coming from a wide range of cultural backgrounds.

Numerous books examine the impact of cultural differences on organizations as a whole, on specific parts of organizations (like sales), or on particular responsibilities (like negotiations or strategic planning), and readers are referred to the bibliography for further reading. I believe, however, that this book is the first to examine in detail the impact of cultural differences specifically on technical professionals.

This book is written with two audiences in mind:

- Technical professionals (e.g., engineers, scientists, technologists, technicians) who were born and educated in Canada or in the United States, who are dealing with cultural differences in their workplace. They may be members of a global team, work in an organization that employs many people born outside North America, or be employed by the North American subsidiary of a multinational organization.

- Technical professionals who were born outside North America, who came to North America as teenagers or adults, and who have worked in North American organizations for a couple of years or more. These people may be immigrants (mostly) or expatriates (sometimes) from other parts of the world.

This book examines the impact of cultural differences on these people at the individual and organizational levels. It focuses on the interactions among culturally different people and describes the consequences on the organization as a whole. It is based on the questions, concerns, and suggestions of numerous technical professionals, and it is written from their perspective, considering how they have experienced these cross-cultural situations.

This work is the extension of a course provided to numerous technical professionals throughout Canada and the United States; as such, it can readily be used as a textbook for cross-cultural training programs delivered either in the workplace or in a university setting. Technical professionals who are facing specific cross-cultural issues in the workplace can also use this book as a self-study guide, by looking up the specific issue of concern to them and implementing the corresponding suggestions contained here.

The material presented in this book comes from a variety of sources:

- Some is based on the work of cross-cultural management experts such as Geert Hofstede, Fons Trompeaars, Edward T. Hall, Phil Harris, and Robert Moran.

- The experience of numerous technical professionals with whom I have interacted. As an engineer and a trainer, I have interacted with professionals from more than 50 countries. Because many of the concepts presented in this book are more easily understood when they are illustrated with anecdotes, this book describes many situations (cross-cultural specialists call them "critical incidents") involving people from many different parts of the world.

- My own experience and observations. In this respect, people who know me are likely to recognize some of the situations in which they have been involved. I hope they will forgive me for using these situations and adapting them to the format of this book.

This book is designed to help technical professionals overcome the challenges and reap the benefits of cultural differences in the following manner:

- Chapter 1 provides an *introduction* to the topic. It defines what cultural differences are and examines the relationship among culture, personality, and human nature. It also examines the types of impact that technical professionals are most likely to observe in their everyday professional activities.

- Chapter 2 examines *management* and the interactions and relationships between a manager and his or her employee when they come from different cultural backgrounds. Everyone wants to work for or to be a good manager; however, being "good managers" requires different approaches in different countries.

- Chapter 3 examines *teamwork* when team members come from different cultural backgrounds. Unknown to most technical professionals, the definition of "good team players" and what they are expected to do, say, and be varies significantly from country to country.

- Chapter 4 examines *communication* in the workplace, with particular emphasis on technical presentations and meetings. This chapter focuses on ways to communicate effectively with people who come from different cultural backgrounds.

- Chapter 5 examines the *career management* process for technical professionals in North America and compares it with the career management process in other countries. It contains advice for technical professionals who are managing their careers in a culturally different environment.

- Chapter 6 *looks ahead* and examines how the impact of cultural differences is likely to evolve. It concludes this work with general recommendations.

Because most people infer other people's motivations and values from their actions and behaviors, this book takes a behavior-based approach to cultural differences. With the exception of the first and last, all chapters are structured in the following manner:

- They start from what most technical professionals observe and think when they are dealing with culturally different people. In most cases, this reaction can be summarized by: "I do not understand this person's actions or reactions." In some cases, these actions or reactions are considered strange; in others, they are interpreted as resulting from negative intentions (this person is hungry for power, does not trust me, is selfish, etc.).

- The next step consists of analyzing these observations and the corresponding thoughts of the people involved and examining their cultural components. Many misunderstandings occur because people are unaware of the differences in expectations related to careers, teamwork, management, and so on that exist between different cultures.

- This analysis of cultural differences becomes the basis for suggestions and recommendations on how to bridge the gap between the different expectations and attitudes of various cultures.

- A brief summary of suggestions and recommendations is provided at the end of each chapter.

This book can be read in three different manners:

- *Start to finish.* Readers who want to understand in depth the challenges and opportunities related to cultural differences are advised to read this book in sequence. Each chapter contains just enough information about cross-cultural concepts to understand the dynamics underpinning the issues at hand. Readers who want to learn more about these cross-cultural concepts can use the references listed at the end of each chapter.

- *Individual chapters.* Readers who need to understand and determine quickly what to do in a specific situation would go directly to the chapter that deals with this kind of situation.

- *Training focus.* Human resources managers and diversity trainers who work with technical professionals are advised to start with Chapter 1, then go to Appendix A, then go back to the chapters that cover the topics of interest to them. Appendix A is designed to help them put themselves in the shoes and minds of technical professionals.

Because different readers have different interests and face different situations, each chapter has been written as a self-contained whole. If you are not interested in teamwork, for example, you can skip the corresponding chapter without loss of understanding in other chapters.

As a result, this book can be easily read one chapter at a time—as time permits.

It is important to note that many ideas and themes recur throughout the book. Therefore, readers are encouraged to take advantage of the cross-chapter references, which are a guide to the places in the book where each key concept is fully explained.

Finally, the appendices contain information that may be helpful to put some of the material presented in this book in context:

- Appendix A contains advice for diversity trainers and human resources managers who work extensively with technical professionals. It is designed to help them understand better how to approach and present their message to technical professionals.

- Appendix B provides information on the demographics of immigration in the United States and Canada.

- Appendix C illustrates the diversity of technical studies around the world by comparing the undergraduate education required in order to become a mechanical engineer in various countries.

- Appendix D describes technical professional associations that people can join in North America.

- Appendix E contains a glossary of U.S. and Canadian expressions that may be unfamiliar to technical professionals who were educated in other countries. This appendix includes explanations of the idiomatic expressions used in this book as well as some of the most common "sports English phrases" that may be confusing if you do not know baseball, football, or hockey.

I hope that readers will find the insights presented in this book a useful resource in their careers. Within these pages, I could not cover every aspect of culture that impacts the daily professional lives of technical professionals. Because this text is part of the Managing Cultural Differences Series, readers will find ample supplementary materials in the other Butterworth–Heinemann publications listed in the frontmatter.

Lionel F. Laroche, Ph.D., P.Eng.

Acknowledgments

This book represents the combination of 15 years of experience as a chemical engineer and 5 years as a cross-cultural trainer and consultant. In both fields, I have received extensive help from numerous people who have supported me over the years, and I would like to thank them all for their help.

Some people have contributed very directly to the creation of this book: Phil Harris patiently encouraged me to put forward a proposal and reviewed my manuscript, while Karen Maloney coached me throughout the writing process. This book would not exist without them. I also want to thank Maja Veljkovic for accepting my invitation to write a foreword for this book, for her continuous support, and for her friendship.

Many people have also contributed indirectly to the contents of this book:

- Clients, through their expectations and needs, have led me to continuously dig deeper into cultural differences and their impact in the workplace. In particular, I would like to thank Mike Noon and Edith Cook (Syncrude), Eran Schwartz and Sanjay Verma (Procter & Gamble), Dawn Comfort (AEAT Hyprotech), Jean Brice Guerin (Rexel), Bob Anderson (TRW), and Wilf Flagler (Ontario Society of Professional Engineers), who have taught me so much by working closely with me on customized programs. I would also like to thank Alma Farias for expanding my horizons into Latin America.

- Other cross-cultural trainers and consultants. The numerous conversations I have had with David Boyle, Cliff Clarke, John Bing, and Leonore Clauss have helped shape the ideas presented in this book.

- Former colleagues at Xerox and Procter & Gamble who have helped me understand the unwritten rules of the North American workplace in a concrete manner. In particular, I want to thank Brian Gray (Procter & Gamble) and George Liebermann, Daniele Boils-Boissier, and Marko Saban (Xerox) for their support and their friendship.

- My relatives and friends, who represent a wide range of cultural backgrounds. They are living proof that cultural differences enrich our lives and make the enterprise worthwhile.

Lionel F. Laroche, Ph.D., P.Eng.
Toronto, Ontario
Canada

Culture and Cultural Differences

When the German-based supplier of one of our critical chemical components announced that it would not fulfill the order I had placed six weeks ago, I asked them to make me one more batch. Qualifying another supplier required much time and money and I had no material left, so I was quite keen to have them do that. I first offered to purchase one year worth of their production, then two years worth of production, then two years worth of production at a 25 percent premium. The answer always came back "Nein," and I had to look for an alternate supply source. I could not believe it! When I talked with my Canadian and American colleagues about this, they could not believe it either. Eventually, I found out that the supplier had decided to stop making this chemical because of the emergence of a new Chinese manufacturer who was selling the same material at a fraction of the price. Clearly, the fact that I was willing to buy a large quantity from them at a premium did not enter their market force analysis.

—Canadian chemical engineer

What Is Culture?

Because culture is a complex concept, it has been defined in many ways. The definition proposed by Kluckhohn, which is often used in anthropology literature, states that:

> Culture consists in patterned ways of thinking, feeling and reacting, acquired and transmitted mainly by symbols, constituting the

distinctive achievements of human groups, including their embodiments in artifacts; the essential core of culture consists of traditional (i.e., historically derived and selected) ideas and especially their attached values. (Kluckhohn, 1951)

Most definitions of culture include the following points:

- *Culture is a distinctly human feature.* There is no equivalent of culture in the animal world. Within a given species, groups of social animals (like bees or monkeys) all use the same rules for interactions within the group or among groups.

- *Culture is a group phenomenon.* It is associated with a specific society or people. Culture is to this society or people what personality is to an individual. It distinguishes one society or people from another.

- *Culture is something we have in common with some people and not with others.* For example, Mexicans have a common culture (the Mexican culture); non-Mexicans visiting Mexico do not have this culture in common with locals. This commonality is what enables us to spot compatriots easily when we travel abroad.

- *Culture is inherited.* It is transmitted from one generation to the next through a variety of means, such as arts, stories, tales, novels, movies, and education. The transmission of cultural values from one generation to the next is both active and passive: Children learn both from the rules, guidelines, and insights provided by their parents and teachers as well as from the observation of how adults handle specific situations.

- *Culture specifies a range of attitudes and behaviors that are considered acceptable in specific situations.* It also attaches meaning to specific reactions and behaviors and enables us to infer people's thoughts and feelings based on their deeds and words.

In some ways, we are (Exhibit 1.1):

- *Like all others*: We are all humans; we all need food, shelter, clothing, and affection in order to survive and grow. *Human nature* is common to all of us. It represents what we bring to the world at birth as a human being. Think of it as our hardware.

- *Like no other*: Each person is unique in his or her own rights. *Personality* is a person's unique set of mental programs that belong exclusively to him or her, developed through his or her personal experiences. The fact that each person is unique and

Exhibit 1.1

Each person's actions and words are built on three levels.

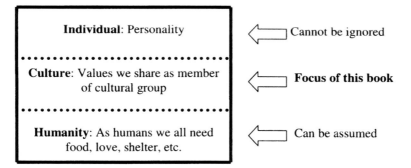

should be considered, in the end, as a unique individual can never be overemphasized.

- *Like some others*: This is our *culture*. We share it with some people, but not with all other people. *Culture* is the shared learning within a given social environment. Think of it as our operating system. Just like some tasks are much easier to accomplish with one operating system than with another, some objectives are easier to accomplish in some cultures than they are in others.

Culture is often represented as an iceberg (Exhibit 1.2). Like an iceberg, culture contains a small, visible part made of the *tangible or exterior manifestations* of a culture, which we perceive through our senses. For most North Americans, tasting sushi, dressing in *saris* or *djellabas*, watching foreign movies, playing *mah-jong*, speaking Russian, or listening to Indian music all represent cross-cultural experiences. In the business world, tangible manifestations of a culture include the following:

- Reports, documents, presentations, etc.
- Procedures
- Organizational structure
- Architecture of buildings and layout of offices inside
- Dress and appearance
- Communication and language

Exhibit 1.2

The iceberg representation of culture. Parts of culture are visible, whereas others are deeply submerged.

arts, literature, language, food, dress, games

concepts of time, beauty, sin, disease,
socially accepted behaviors,
friendship, change, privacy,
relationships between men/women,
relationship between mankind/nature,
role of people in society, education,
approach to problem-solving/logic,
motivations, preferences, values,
and many more....

As we will see throughout this book, you can actually gather a fair amount of information about an organization by merely observing the workplace and the interactions among employees. Also like an iceberg, culture contains a large, invisible part, which consists of the *values and thought patterns* that each culture has created over time; it includes many aspects of societal life. It ranges from the way people handle time to their motivations and the meaning they attribute to their existence. Because it cannot be observed, this part of a culture needs to be inferred from what people say and do. In the business world, the invisible part of the iceberg includes the following:

- Time and time consciousness
- Relationships
- Values and norms
- Mental processes and learning
- Work habits and practices, including concepts of teamwork, management, performance, hierarchy, etc.

Which Culture Are We Talking About?

Culture can be considered and analyzed at several levels:

- *Organizational level.* Comparing one industry to another (e.g., dot-com startups with established, brick-and-mortar companies) provides insight into corporate cultures. Similarly, studies that compare companies within a given sector help us understand the unwritten rules of an organization. Corporate culture has a significant impact on major business processes, notably strategy and mergers and acquisitions.

- *Trading bloc level* (e.g., Far East, Latin America, European Union). Although this level is interesting from a macroeconomic perspective, it is relatively difficult to draw general conclusions about members within one trading bloc versus people in another. For example, both North American Free Trade Agreement (NAFTA) members and the European Union are far from being culturally homogeneous groups. Because there are more variations within one bloc than among blocs, this level of analysis is usually of little help to individual technical professionals.

- *Society or people level.* For many societies or people, this level is the same as nations; for example, Japan is the nation populated by the Japanese. This correspondence is not entirely one-to-one; for example, Yugoslavia and the U.S.S.R. used to be nations made of numerous cultures.

- *Professional level.* There are common characteristics of members of certain professions, as jokes about lawyers and engineers underline. In the professional world, technical professionals can usually differentiate between sales representatives and other technical professionals. As discussed later in this book, different professions are perceived differently in different countries; this applies to technical professionals, who enjoy a much higher social status in developing countries than they do in Canada and the United States.

- *Regional level.* Many countries are made of regions that have their own distinctive cultures. Differences between English Canada and French Canada (the two "Canadian solitudes") are well known and much publicized whenever there is a referendum regarding Quebec separation. In the U.S., the South and the Northeast (the North of the Civil War) are also quite different. In Europe, most countries are also divided in regions that have their own accents and foods.

This book examines culture at the society/people level. It compares how technical professionals in different countries do their jobs in order to explain what happens when technical professionals from different countries work together. It also provides suggestions on how they can be most effective together. While regional cultural variations of these countries are very important to technical professionals who are dealing with them, they are beyond the scope of this book. Readers are encouraged to look for books that examine specific cultural variations within the part of the world that is of interest to them.

What Is the Function of Culture?

Having culture as a default mode of operation makes everyday life much simpler. Indeed, culture includes an implicit list of standard operating procedures (SOPs) for daily activities and interactions. For example, culture tells us how to greet one another, when it is appropriate to call someone on the phone, and what topics we should avoid in conversations. In the professional world, culture tells us what time people will likely come to work and leave, what we should do to help others, when it is appropriate to ask for help, what we should do to achieve our professional goals, and so on.

What Are Cultural Differences?

Cultural differences are differences in either the visible or invisible part of the iceberg between two cultures. They include differences at all levels, from the clothes people wear to their motivations and religious beliefs. Cultural differences include differences in everyday SOPs; for example, do we shake hands or bow to greet one another? When we say we meet at 9 a.m., do we mean 9 a.m. sharp or anywhere between 9 and 9:30 a.m.?

Obviously, differences in the visible part of the iceberg are much easier to notice and identify than differences in the invisible part of the iceberg. An analysis of visible differences can be used as a starting point to understand invisible differences, but there might be a significant gap between the two. For example, recognizing differences in the way religious buildings are built, structured, and decorated help us understand differences in religious beliefs, but comparing mosques and churches gives us only a glimpse of the differences between Islam and Christianity.

Culture is created by human beings. As such, any observer of culture is part of a society and has his or her own cultural background. Therefore, culture does not exist in isolation and cannot be observed by itself, like the physical phenomena that technical professionals are so familiar with; the observer cannot be fully neutral. We can only define a culture relative to another culture, by comparing what members of one people or society do, say, or think to what members of another people or society do, say, or think.

As a result, the same culture can be seen differently by people from different cultural backgrounds. To some extent, cultural characteristics are in the eyes of the beholder and reveal something about observers as they make their observations. For example, many Japanese consider that most Americans take too much time off (taking a couple of days off is usual in Japan, but a whole week?). By contrast, most Europeans consider that the average American does not take enough time off (by law, French people get five weeks of vacation every year, regardless of seniority, three of which they have to take at one time). When we speak about culture and cultural differences, we need to specify both what is observed and the vantage point from which we are observing.

Like all differences, cultural differences can be reversed and looked on from the opposite vantage point. For example, the previous paragraph looked at Americans from a Japanese and French perspective. If we look at Japanese and French people from an American perspective, we can say that many Americans consider that the average Japanese does not take enough vacations and that the average French person takes too much.

Within the submerged part of the iceberg, some aspects are deeper below the water line than others. For example, time and time consciousness is just below the water line; differences in this area are usually quickly identified. A short business trip in Latin America is sufficient to realize that time is perceived and handled differently there and in the United States and Canada. These different concepts of time have become part of the language: When Americans and Canadians use the word *mañana* in English, they often mean "tomorrow, maybe," even though the word means tomorrow in Spanish. In Argentina, people who want to specify that a meeting will start at 9 a.m. sharp (as opposed to between 9 and 9:30 a.m.) will say *a la Americana or a la gringa*. By contrast, the concept of teamwork is way below the water line and requires much more observation and time working in a different culture to identify. Some people who emigrated to Canada or the United States from parts of the world that are culturally very different may work here for 20 years without identifying this critical cultural difference.

How Can We Tell That We Are Dealing with Cultural Differences?

Culture does not dictate the behavior that we are supposed to choose in a specific situation; rather, it determines the implications and consequences of each option. For example, you may choose to disagree publicly with the CEO of your company; regardless of the culture in which you work, that option is always available to you. However, the consequences of such a choice are different depending on whether you do it in India, where it will likely put a stop to your career in that organization, or in Sweden, where it will have comparatively little consequence. Twenty years ago, disagreeing publicly with senior officials of the Communist Party would have had even more negative consequences in Eastern Bloc countries.

As a result, people from a particular culture may overwhelmingly choose one option over others in a particular situation. This trend helps us recognize cultural differences. If, in a given situation, I know that most people from my culture would choose option A and I find that most people from a different culture choose option B, then I am clearly facing a cultural difference. For example, consider the choice between lieu time (i.e., time off given to the employees to compensate them for their overtime) and extra pay for overtime. The proportion of employees opting for lieu time will be much higher in France than in the United States; there is a clear cultural difference in this respect.

Where Is the Boundary between Culture and Personality?

For technical professionals working in multicultural environments, one of the key issues to contend with is differentiating between culture and personality. When Donatella reacts to one of my comments in a way I do not anticipate, is it because of her personality or because of her Italian cultural background?

The answer to this question is rarely black or white; it often comes in shades of gray. Although Exhibit 1.1 represents the boundary between personality and culture as a straight line, this boundary is in reality blurred as shown in Exhibit 1.3, and there can be a significant overlap between the two. Rather than a cliff separating land from the ocean, this boundary is much more like a marsh where salt

Exhibit 1.3

The boundaries between personality and culture, and between culture and humanity, are often blurred. For example, we all need food to survive and thrive, yet different cultures tend to favor some foods more than others; at the individual level, we all have our own particular tastes, likes, and dislikes.

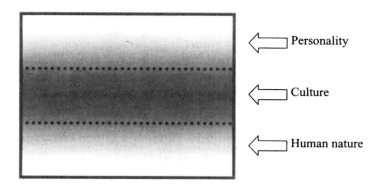

water and fresh water mix to varying degrees as one moves from land to sea.

Although people from a given cultural background may overwhelmingly choose a given option, unanimity is unusual. A person's actions and words depend on both culture and personality. Two people may grow up in the same culture but behave differently. If we represent culture by a bell curve, some people in the same culture may have developed personalities on either side of the bell curve; however, the culture as a whole has a mean centered on certain core values held by most people within that culture. By comparing the mean averages of bell curves of various cultures, we can start to quantify cultural differences systematically. For example, consider the alternative shown in Exhibit 1.4 between working individually and working in teams.

As Exhibit 1.5 shows, a range of opinions exists in both Sweden and Canada; it also shows that a clear difference in means exists between Swedes and Canadians with respect to teamwork.

How Can We Avoid Stereotyping People?

As Exhibit 1.5 shows, there is often an overlap between the bell curves that represent the answers of people in different countries. It is

Exhibit 1.4

Respondents to this question are asked to choose where they lie on the spectrum between working by themselves and working in teams.

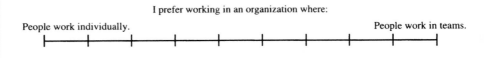

Exhibit 1.5

Distribution of the people from Sweden (dashed line) and Canada (solid line) regarding work preferences.

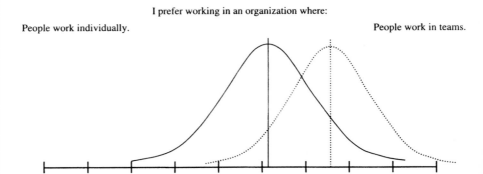

virtually impossible, therefore, to make statements that cast everyone from a particular culture in the same light; such statements tend to be stereotypical and usually do more harm than good. At the same time, Exhibit 1.5 clearly shows that Swedes have a higher probability to prefer working in teams than Canadians. Such a statement is a generalization; knowing that such preference exists can be helpful when Swedes and Canadians are working together because they know they can expect a difference in their actions and words in this area.

Although stereotypes and generalizations are often considered the same, some key differences need to be kept in mind, as demonstrated by Exhibit 1.6. This point illustrates the challenge of dealing with cultural differences. In order to say something meaningful, we need to make generalizations. At the same time, we need to avoid stereotypes: "Generalizations are useful when trying to describe the overall form of the forest without getting lost in the individual trees" (Nees, 2000).

Exhibit 1.6

Contrasting generalizations and stereotypes.

Stereotypes	Generalizations
• Present a fixed and inflexible image of a group. • Ignore exceptions and focus on behaviors that support the image they present. • Are ethnocentric or racial. • Put both insiders and outsiders on the defensive.	• Are based on a large sample of a group. • Provide general characteristics based on cultural and social factors. • Assume that individuals within groups vary in their compliance. • Inform rather than prescribe. • Help outsiders identify topics that are likely to be sensitive and should be handled with care.
Examples: • All French people like wine. • Americans love fast food.	*Examples:* • Wine is an important aspect of French culture. • When eating, convenience and speed are important for Americans.

The key lies in the application and use of this work. Remember that various factors affect individual behavior. Ultimately, how you apply the suggestions contained in this book needs to be based on your own evaluation of the individuals and the situation.

Does Different Imply Better?

The study of cultural differences is based on the fact that people in different societies do things differently. Because the word *comparison* covers both comparative studies, where two objects of study are put side-by-side in order to identify similarities and differences, and evaluation, where one object is considered "better" than the other, comparisons of cultures often lead to the question: "Which one is better?" This question calls for an important caveat. The fact that two cultures are different by no means implies that one culture is better than another. In this respect, culture is like personality; saying that one person is better than another does not make much sense. Making such judgments requires an absolute scale for people or culture (i.e., a scale that is universal, upon which everyone would agree). Because people and cultures value different things, creating such a scale is virtually impossible.

On the other hand, we routinely say that one person accomplishes certain tasks more effectively than another. This is clear in sporting events, where one person or team receives a gold medal and is hailed as "the winner" and "the best." Similarly, we can say that certain cultures are better suited for some tasks than others. To some extent, individuals tend to develop greater expertise in the areas they value. Like individuals, people in a cultural group tend to optimize their actions and processes to obtain more of what they consider important.

For example, the Australian culture values sports and athletic achievements more than the French culture. As a result, Australia obtains more medals at the Olympic Games than does France. In this specific area, one may say that the Australian culture has an edge over the French culture (Bryson, 2001). Conversely, the French culture emphasizes food and meal enjoyment more than the Australian culture. As a result, French people invest more of their time, money, and efforts into preparing and enjoying meals. In this specific area, one may say that the French culture has an edge over the Australian culture.

As discussed previously, the collective edge that the French culture has relative to the Australian culture with respect to food and meal enjoyment and the edge that the Australian culture has relative to the French culture with respect to sports cannot be extrapolated to the individual level. It only applies on average. The average French meal lasts longer than the average Australian meal; the average Australian practices and watches more sports than the average French person; however, some French athletes obtain gold medals at the Olympic Games and there are internationally acclaimed Australian chefs. Technical professionals need to keep both aspects in mind when extrapolating the content of this book to their situations.

Do Cultural Differences Really Have an Impact on Technical Professionals?

For many technical professionals, the fact that cultural differences may have an impact on their work is far from obvious. After all, a distillation column or an electronic circuit operates according to the same scientific laws, regardless of where it is used. Contrary to food and consumer products, which have to be adapted to the tastes and preferences of their purchasers, technical products and services are designed to fulfill a specific function. The only adaptation required for many technical goods, such as valves and fiber-optic cables, consists in meeting local codes and regulations.

In addition, technical professionals are trained to focus on data, hard facts, and technical information and to examine these objectively, in a scientific manner. The scientific method is considered universal, and experiments performed in one country are expected to be reproducible in other countries. Yet cultural differences have a much more significant impact on the work of technical professionals than most people realize, as the following situations (and the opening quote at the beginning of this chapter) illustrate:

> Situation #1: In a car, how should interior space be allocated? Should there be more space in the front or in the back? The answer depends on where the car is sold. In the United States and Canada, the buyer of a car is usually its driver, so interior space tends to be allocated to the front of the car. In India, anyone who can afford a car can also afford a chauffeur and usually will; as a result, interior space is allocated to the back of the car.   ~

> Situation #2: The engineers of an American car parts manufacturer were confounded when their Japanese clients returned a shipment without opening the boxes, claiming that the parts were inadequate. The Americans wondered how the Japanese could determine whether parts are good or bad without looking at them. Upon follow-up, they found out that the Japanese had looked at the shipment packing slip and found that it was completed improperly; because they believed that a company that cannot complete a packing slip properly cannot make a good car part, they sent the shipment back on the spot.

Physical phenomena and technical data are indeed unaffected by cultural differences. The speed of light is 3×10^8 m.s^{-1} everywhere in the world and all optical systems make use of the same physics; however, the interpretation and representation of technical data are performed by people. People all have their cultural background, which they bring to any of their professional activities, most of the time without being aware of it.

A simple example of how culture is included in the representation of technical data is the choice of units. For the speed of light, I have used m.s^{-1} because I studied physics in France, where the default unit system is the International System of Units or SI (e.g., kg, m, s). This system is used in many countries, whereas U.S. technical professionals use mostly British units (e.g., miles, inches, gallons, psi).

Which Technical Professionals Are Most Likely to Experience These Differences?

Cultural differences have a greater impact on some technical professionals than on others. Obviously, experiencing cultural differences requires interaction with culturally different people; the closer the interaction, the larger this impact is likely to be. As a general rule, cultural differences are likely to have a particularly strong impact in the following areas:

- *Science and engineering departments in Canadian and American universities.* Scientific and engineering departments of American and Canadian universities attract many students from around the world. In many universities, foreign students are a majority, particularly at the graduate level. Many continue doing research beyond their Ph.D.s and become postdoctoral fellows, research associates, and professors in Canada or the United States. In this respect, Canadian and American universities are some of the most culturally diverse work units.

- *Research centers.* The predominance of foreign students in scientific and technical programs is also reflected in research centers throughout Canada and the United States, which tend to have fairly culturally diverse staffs. This is particularly true in some Canadian research centers, where the staff often consists of mostly technical professionals born and raised outside Canada.

- *Information technology and high-tech organizations.* The shortage of qualified technical professionals experienced in the 1990s by the information technology (IT) and high-tech sectors throughout Canada and the United States led to the immigration and hiring of numerous technical professionals in these sectors. As a result, many of these organizations have staffs that are culturally diverse. As of 1996, 38 percent of computer engineers working in Canada were immigrants; the percentage has likely increased since then (see Appendix B for details).

- *Multinational companies.* Large companies with offices around the world derive much competitive advantage from their ability to combine resources from around the world. This can be done through global project teams (teams that include members from various subsidiaries) or through expatriation of key human resources.

Within these organizations, some people are more likely to experience the impact of cultural differences than are others:

- People who are working in a country other than the one where they were born and educated usually feel the impact of cultural differences more than "locals." In this respect, expatriates and immigrants experience this impact quite strongly.
- People working in positions where they need to influence others or coordinate the work of others to achieve specific objectives usually feel the impact of cultural differences more than individual contributors. Managers of culturally diverse departments and leaders of culturally diverse teams experience this impact much more strongly than programmers or technicians, for example.
- Distance and time differences compound cultural differences. Members of global teams (i.e., teams made of people located in different countries or parts of the world working together on a single project) are particularly likely to experience the impact of cultural differences.

What Should Technical Professionals Be Looking For?

Most technical professionals, who have limited training in cross-cultural communication and management, tend to observe and identify cultural differences from empirical observations. They notice that, in a given situation, most Americans do or say X, whereas most Chinese do or say Y. This observation is often coupled with an incomplete understanding of the motivations and reactions of culturally different people.

Following are some of the most common "symptoms" of cross-cultural issues and misunderstandings. These issues are classified by situations in which they are most likely to occur. The chapter under which each symptom is listed contains a "diagnosis" of this issue, suggestions for "cures," and a description of the benefits that can be achieved through synergies among culturally different people.

Manager–Employee Relationship

Managerial issues related to cross-cultural differences may yield tense relationships between managers and their direct reports. In these situations, culturally different managers and employees perceive these issues differently. Managers who have people coming from different cultural backgrounds reporting to them should look for the following signs:

- Lack of initiative and technical knowledge
- "Loose cannons"
- Lack of response or overreaction to feedback
- Excessive defensiveness and negativity
- Excessive deference toward managers and higher-ups

People who report to managers coming from different cultural backgrounds should look for the following signs:

- "Micromanagers"
- Managers who appear technically incompetent
- Unexpected feedback
- Managers who continuously put them "on the spot"

Managerial issues resulting from cross-cultural differences are examined in detail in Chapter 2.

Teamwork

Here are signs that cultural differences may be playing an important role in your multicultural team:

- Some team members are getting involved and interfering in their teammates' areas of responsibility.
- Some team members consider that their teammates are not providing the support they should provide.
- Teams are polarized between those who want the team to move forward quickly and those who want to make sure that the team moves in the right direction.
- Teams break down and operate as a collection of subteams or one culturally different member is ostracized because of "personality problems."
- Team members are confused with respect to decisions. Has the decision been made or is it still open for discussion? Who is making the decision and based on what information?

- Teams start on the wrong foot; the first interaction among team members leaves a poor first impression.

The impact of cultural differences on teams is examined in detail in Chapter 3.

Communication

Cross-cultural communication issues come in many shapes and sizes, but they all boil down to the fact that the message did not get across. In the best cases, the recipient of the message did not understand the meaning of that message. In the worst situations, the recipient has understood something totally different than what was meant. Chapter 4 lists and analyzes the most common issues and suggests steps that people can take to deal with these issues.

Career Management

The following situations may indicate that cultural differences are playing an important role in the careers of New North American technical professionals in your organization:

- A position at the next level has opened, and the best candidate got the job. A New North American employee seems to think that he or she was suited for that position, whereas management considered that he or she did not even come close to qualifying for the promotion.
- Some New North American employees who have been given many forms of recognition appear continuously dissatisfied and comment about a lack of recognition.
- Some New North American employees apply for transfers within the organization that do not make any sense (i.e., the two positions are totally unrelated and the transfer is too big of a jump) by management's standards. They may also apply for positions for which they are not qualified.
- Some New North Americans appear to "expect that managers can do miracles." For example, they appear to expect them to be able to create positions for themselves or for their relatives.

Conversely, the approach that New North American employees take to manage their careers in North America may not be adapted to this environment. In these cases, they may experience the following:

- They have been bypassed for a promotion they rightfully deserved.
- Their work does not receive proper recognition.
- They are not considered for positions for which they consider themselves qualified.
- They do not receive much support from managers and colleagues when it comes to career management.

The impact of cultural differences on career management is analyzed in detail in Chapter 5.

Creating Synergy

For many people, cultural differences initially create issues that make life significantly more complicated and less fun. Things these people know how to do in a snap in their own culture now become difficult and take much longer than anticipated. For example, an expatriate who has been driving for many years in his or her own country may fail the driving test in another country, leading to some wasted time and frustration.

Over time, cultural differences can become a source of learning and personal growth. By working with people who have a different frame of reference, one can learn to look at problems from a different point of view, learn new ways of solving problems, and create new approaches that blend those used in different cultures. In this book, we refer to this process of learning from other cultures and creating new approaches as "creating synergy" among various cultures. Such synergies can be powerful; from a business standpoint, they turn cultural differences into an organizational asset that is difficult to duplicate.

Clarifying Terminology

I will close this introduction by defining the vantage point from which this book is written and a few terms that are used throughout this book. This book is centered on North America, which I define in a cultural sense rather than a geographic sense. In this book, North America refers to Canada and the United States, while Mexico is considered here as part of Latin America.

For simplicity, I will reserve the terms *American* and *Americans* for citizens and permanent residents of the United States. People living in Canada, Mexico, and South and Central America are also "Americans," but using this term in this broad sense leaves no specific word for people living in the United States.

Also for simplicity's sake, the cultures to which this book refers are the mainstream cultures in each of the countries mentioned. For example, any reference to the French culture refers to the mainstream French culture, shared by most French technical professionals in large cities or multinational companies. Similarly, references to the American culture correspond to mainstream, white Anglo-Saxon, middle-class America. In the case of Canada, the word "Canadian" makes reference to both English Canada and French Canada, unless otherwise specified. Finally, "French Canadians" refers to Canadians who speak French, while "French" refers to people from France. Cultural variations within each country (like the differences between Black and White America, or between the various regions and social classes in France) are beyond the scope of this book.

This book examines interactions in the North American workplace that take place among technical professionals coming from different cultural backgrounds. These interactions often involve people who have emigrated to Canada or the United States as adults, when many of their values and beliefs were formed. Many have already acquired American or Canadian citizenship, whereas others are "permanent residents" of the United States or "landed immigrants" in Canada. Throughout this book, I refer to these people as "New Americans," "New Canadians," or "New North Americans," as the case may be. I wish to emphasize the fact that this term does not contain any value judgment. I am a New Canadian because I immigrated to Canada in 1991 at the age of 25; this is the only criterion used in defining "New Canadian." I shall use the term "recent immigrants" in the case of people who have immigrated to North America in the last five years. In order to make this book as accessible to New North Americans as possible, I have limited the use of colloquial expressions to those that New North Americans are most likely to hear in challenging cross-cultural situations, like "loose cannon" and "shooting from the hip." These expressions are explained in Appendix E.

Although this book centers on North America and uses numerous anecdotes and situations taking place in North American technical organizations, it is not limited to this environment. Many examples in this book are taken from other cross-cultural experiences, such as Westerners living and working in Hong Kong or in Japan, North Americans living and working in Europe or Latin America, and so on.

In all cases, these examples help illustrate points that apply to North American technical professionals working in a multicultural environment.

References

Bryson, B. 2001. *Down under*, London: Black Swan Books, p. 146.

Elashmawi, F. 2001. *Competing globally: mastering multicultural management and negotiations*, Woburn, MA: Butterworth–Heinemann.

Harris, P.R., and Moran, R.T. 1999. *Managing cultural differences. Leadership strategies for a new world of business*, 5th ed. Woburn, MA: Butterworth–Heinemann.

Kluckhohn, C. 1951. *The study of culture*. In D. Lerner and H.D. Lasswell, Eds., *The Policy Sciences*. Stanford, CA: Stanford University Press.

Nees, G. 2000. *Germany: Unraveling an enigma*. Yarmouth, MA: Intercultural Press, p. 5.

Managing Technical Professionals

During one of our meetings, there were four Italian pilot plant engineers and technicians and three Canadian engineers in the office of the pilot plant manager. The pilot plant manager proceeded to give feedback to his people. He did it all in Italian, but you did not really need subtitles. He was taking them one by one, telling them how bad a job they were doing, using all kinds of names of rare birds and dragging them through mud. This went on for about half an hour, then we all went for lunch together.

—Canadian engineer working in Italy

Everyone wants to work for a good manager and every manager wants to be a good manager. Yet cross-cultural management is a difficult task because the definition of "good managers" and what they are expected to do, say, and be varies significantly from country to country—a fact unknown to most technical professionals.

This chapter examines the interactions and relationships between managers and employees when they come from different cultural backgrounds. It focuses specifically on manager–employee relationships between two technical professionals, where one is North American and the other is a New North American (or a foreign expatriate). It assumes that the employee reports directly to the manager and that the manager is the person responsible for the performance evaluation of the employee. The special case where these two people are located in different parts of the world is examined at the end of this chapter.

What Are the Signs of Cross-Cultural Management Issues?

When managers and their employees come from different cultural backgrounds, issues are likely to arise around initiative, competence, and feedback (to name a few). This chapter examines some of the most common cross-cultural issues related to the relationships between managers and employees. These issues are often perceived simultaneously by both manager and employee; however, in many cases, these people experience the same cross-cultural issue in different manners.

Manager's Perspective

Let's look at the manager's perspective first, before examining cross-cultural management issues from the employee's perspective. Issues may arise when New North American employees report to North American managers, or vice versa.

Lack of Initiative and Technical Knowledge

This is one of the most common issues experienced by North American managers, particularly those who manage employees coming from the Far East (including India), Eastern Europe, or Latin America. From a manager's perspective, lack of initiative manifests itself in the following manner:

- These employees are known to be competent, but they rarely put their ideas forward. In particular, they do not offer to take on parts of a project in which they are clearly the organization's experts.

- They rarely "speak out"; they may have concerns about the direction taken or the choices made in a particular project, but they do not express these concerns to anyone other than their cultural peers.

- They may keep running to the manager's office in order to ask for the manager's opinion or permission. As one Canadian manager puts it: "Whenever my Iranian employee has a problem, she comes running into my office and asks me to solve it." As a result, some managers start to avoid these people (sometimes subconsciously, sometimes deliberately). Managers often start questioning the technical competence of such employees ("They would not need to run to my office at the first sign of trouble if they knew how to handle these problems").

Loose Cannon

This issue, which is partly the opposite of the previous one, is more commonly observed in the case of New North American managers who have North American employees, or North American managers who have Scandinavian employees. In this case, employees take too many initiatives to the manager's liking. From the manager's perspective, employees who take too much initiative are "loose cannons." This translates into the following situation:

- Loose cannon employees initiate or get involved in projects without consulting the manager. The managers find out about this involvement later on, often through a third party.

- They make and act on decisions that the managers consider theirs to make. In many cases, these decisions are made based on criteria that do not match the manager's priorities. In some cases, this leads to significant disagreements between manager and employees, where the manager needs to have the employees redo an important piece of work.

- They consult with the managers on their progress less often than the managers would expect. By the manager's standards, loose cannons do not provide enough information during these progress report discussions; in particular, they may not describe fully the issues they are currently facing.

- Loose cannon employees appear to managers as having a mind of their own. Because of their unpredictability, managers avoid putting these people in high-profile situations (e.g., making presentations to higher-ups) because they may say something they shouldn't or answer a question inappropriately.

- In extreme cases, the decisions and reactions of loose cannon employees may be considered as insubordination by the managers. Here is what a Middle Eastern IT manager said of one of his Canadian employees:

  In one of our first meetings, I made some suggestions for one of his projects. He answered that these ideas would never work. He said that he was the project manager and that he knew what he was doing. I stared at him; I could not believe how disrespectful he was. He stared back. I never got anywhere with him.

Unexpected Reactions to Feedback

New North American employees may have unexpected reactions to feedback provided by North American managers. Here is how this translates in practice:

- Some employees may not respond to the feedback they are given by the managers. For example, a Romanian engineer had to be placed on a Performance Improvement Plan by his manager in order for him to realize that his behavior did not meet expectations.

- Other employees may overreact by the manager's standards. A Mexican engineer who was given some negative feedback by his American manager in front of his colleagues resigned the next day. In his manager's mind, this reaction was not warranted; the initial issue was not major and certainly would not have prompted the average American engineer to resign.

- Some New North American employees appear not to appreciate the positive feedback that the managers give them. For example, a Polish engineer who had received all the technical and merit awards that the company had to offer considered quitting the organization because his skills were not given proper recognition.

Excessive Defensiveness and Negativity

Culturally determined defensiveness and negativity generate significant issues in the North American workplace:

- Some New North American employees may respond with excessive defensiveness when undesirable events occur. For example, a Russian IT specialist often answers that the problem is not his fault and that someone else created the current mess. He even has the documents to prove it, because he has saved the e-mail messages, letters, and reports that show that someone else is to blame. From his North American manager's perspective, his time and energy would be better spent working on fixing problems and improving the situation rather than assigning blame and responsibility to others.

- This defensiveness may carry over to instructions provided by managers. For example, a French engineer often finds reasons why he will not be able to meet his Canadian manager's requests, no matter how simple these requests are. In one case, his manager pointed out that they spent more time discussing why it may not work than it would take the engineer to try it.

- Some New North American employees may continuously express reservations about projects and tasks, finding reasons why the targeted results cannot and will not be achieved. This negativity takes a lot of energy from the managers (and their colleagues, as discussed in the next chapter).

Excessive Deference Toward Managers and Higher-ups

The deference that some New North American employees show to managers and higher-ups is excessive by North American standards. This tends to occur more often with North American managers and employees from the Far East, Eastern Europe, or Latin America. In practice, this translates into the following situations:

- *Greetings that may make North American managers uncomfortable.* For example, a Canadian IT manager mentioned that he was frustrated with the way one of his Korean employees greeted him. Every morning, he would be greeted with "Good morning, sir," despite his repeated attempts to make his Korean employee switch to first names.

- *Too much weight given to any suggestion made by managers or higher-ups.* Any opinion they express or any suggestion they make about the project of their New North American employees are immediately incorporated into the project plan, no matter how much or how little thought the managers have put into it.

- *Gestures that are considered inappropriate in the North American workplace.* For example, a Russian programmer bringing music CDs to her manager; an Indian engineer bringing small gifts from India for his manager and his manager's manager; or an Italian technician paying compliments to his female manager about the way she dresses. In extreme cases, these gestures may be construed as "sucking up" to managers.

- *Too much information provided to management.* Some New North American employees copy managers on e-mails and documents more often than their North American managers think is appropriate, resulting in significant frustration for these managers ("This is a waste of my time. I do not need to know all this."). Managers often react to this glut of information by skipping or deleting without reading any message coming from these employees; as a result, they may not notice the truly important and urgent messages sent by these employees.

Employee's Perspective

Employees also experience cross-cultural management issues. In most cases, the descriptions they give of the same situation are different from the description provided by the managers. Here are some of the most common issues.

Micromanagers

This issue is more likely to be reported by North American employees who report to a New North American manager coming from the Far East, Latin America, or Eastern Europe, or by Scandinavian employees reporting to North American managers. Here is what employees experience:

- The managers do not provide them with enough freedom in their job. The managers are asking for updates and progress reports more frequently than employees would consider reasonable. During progress report discussions, the managers go over their action plan and next steps in more detail than the employees would like.

- Micromanagers tend to direct the activities of employees at a detailed level. By reviewing their progress frequently and continuously assigning tasks to them, micromanagers have an extensive control of their time.

- The managers are excessively involved in the decision-making process, even in the case of relatively minor decisions. In many cases, they end up making decisions that employees believe they can make by themselves. This usually results in significant frustration for the employees.

- When employees make decisions, the managers expect that employees will give a lot more weight to their opinions and suggestions. Here is the experience of a French engineer reporting to an Iranian manager:

  I was writing a paper on a topic that was not related to my work. When I mentioned it to my manager, he asked me to change the topic to bring it in line with internal company objectives. I replied that this topic did not fit the theme of the magazine issue in which it was supposed to appear and that I had made a commitment to my client, the editor, on this point. He did not answer, but his reaction clearly showed that he considered himself as the only client that should matter to me. I was transferred out of his department within two weeks.

Technically Incompetent Managers

This issue is more likely to be reported by New North American employees coming from the Far East, Latin America, or Eastern Europe who report to a North American manager. Here is what employees experience:

- When they ask the managers for advice or suggestions, the managers often respond: "I don't know; you figure out what is best in this case." After hearing this answer repeatedly, they end up wondering whether the managers have the necessary technical skills to do their jobs as managers. They think to themselves: "How was he or she promoted?"
- The managers seem interested only in discussing the "political" implications of the decisions to be made. The managers start progress meetings by discussing these items and leave the room as soon as the discussion turns to the technical aspects of the project.
- The managers may be hard to reach. Employees may not receive any response to their e-mail or voice-mail messages; meetings may be frequently postponed. Employees find it difficult to get the manager's attention.

Unexpected Feedback

New North American employees sometimes experience surprise and shock when they receive unexpected feedback from the managers:

- In some cases, strongly negative feedback seems to come out of the blue. Everything seemed to be going reasonably well, with some minor issues here and there, when suddenly they find themselves on a Performance Improvement Plan.
- In other cases, New North American employees receive feedback from the managers in a way that makes them lose face in front of their colleagues. Their honor is put at stake.
- During their Performance Appraisal sessions, the managers ask them to act in ways that do not show the appropriate respect for clients, co-workers, or higher-ups.

Put on the Spot

New North American employees may find that the managers are routinely putting them on the spot. Here is how they perceive these situations:

- They are constantly asked to make commitments and to deliver results over which they have no control. For example, they are asked to gather data from experiments performed by some of their colleagues by the end of the day, but these colleagues are often traveling or rarely respond to e-mail or telephone requests in a timely manner.

- The managers routinely ask them to work on technical problems that belong to others. In many cases, they foresaw these issues and expressed their concerns, which were clearly ignored or over-ruled, and are now asked to fix them afterward.

- The managers ask them tough questions in front of others. They believe that any interaction with the managers may put them on the spot. As a result, these employees experience continuously high levels of stress and have a hard time communicating effectively with the managers.

Correlation between These Issues

Clearly, managers and employees do not experience a given cross-cultural management issue in the same manner. There are common correlations, even though they do not apply all the time:

- Managers who consider their culturally different employees as loose cannons are often perceived as micromanagers by these employees.

- Employees who perceive their culturally different managers as lacking the technical knowledge to be good managers are often perceived by these managers as lacking initiative. These employees are also likely to show excessive deference to the managers or higher-ups.

- Employees who believe that they are often put on the spot by the managers are often perceived by the managers to be excessively defensive and negative.

As these situations illustrate, cross-cultural managerial issues often translate into a questioning of the competence and skills of others. For example, New North American employees who go regularly to the manager's office to get advice or discuss ideas may be quickly considered as lacking technical knowledge by their North American managers. Why else would they keep running to the manager's office? Similarly, North American managers who keep answering "I don't know. I want you to figure it out" are quickly considered technically incompetent by their New North American employees. Why else would they answer, "I don't know"?

What Is Going On?

In many cases, these reactions come from the fact that different cultures have different concepts of management. Being a good manager or a good employee requires different behaviors in different countries; behaviors that are considered positive in some countries are viewed negatively in North America, and vice versa. In this section, we examine how the concept of power distance affects cross-cultural manager–employee relationships; we also examine the dynamics of cross-cultural feedback.

Power Distance

Power distance is a measure of hierarchy (Hofstede, 1980). It represents the psychological distance between people and the managers in a given country or organization and the extent to which inequalities between those who have power and those who don't are accepted. A society with a high power distance leans toward a tight hierarchical structure in which individuals know their place and the limit of their roles. A society with a low power distance seeks status equality and interdependence among different layers of power.

Manager–Employee Relationships as a Function of Power Distance

Should powerful people be treated differently than others? Consider the following situation:

> On December 23, 1988, the following news item appeared in the press: The Swedish king Carl Gustav experienced considerable delay while shopping for Christmas presents for his children, when he wanted to pay by check but could not show his check card. The salesperson refused to accept the check without ID. Only when helpful bystanders dug into their pockets for one-crown coins showing the face of the king, did the salesperson decide to accept

this for ID, not, however, without testing the check thoroughly for authenticity and noting the name and address of the holder. (Hofstede, 1991)

Sweden is one of the least hierarchical countries in the world (see Exhibit 2.1). In more hierarchical countries, heads of state never have to worry about shopping; their staff does. These leaders consider themselves as having to abide by a different set of rules than the majority. More important, the majority of their countrymen and women consider them as having to abide by different rules and accept this point as a fact, like one accepts rain. Contrast the difficulties experienced by the King of Sweden while shopping with the experience of other heads of state:

- The former Russian President Boris Yeltsin resigned once he had secured immunity from prosecution for himself and his family on charges of bribery and embezzlement.
- The former French President François Mitterand never had to answer to charges of insider trading.
- The Queen of England is the "only person for whom Harrods used to close its doors to the public for one day a year so she could do her Christmas shopping." (Tan, 1992)

In his study of IBM subsidiaries around the world, Hofstede (1980) created a measure of power distance, thereby enabling a comparison of 40 national cultures on this scale. The power distance score of each country is obtained from the country average answer to questions related to authority and decision-making styles. Exhibit 2.1 represents graphically the power distance scores of the 40 countries covered by Hofstede's study.

Exhibit 2.1 shows that attitudes towards hierarchy vary greatly around the world. There is no absolute right or wrong on this scale: A country with a score of 80 is not better or worse than a country with a score of 20; it is simply different. There is, however, a relative right and wrong: Using the American style of management in Russia will usually not yield much result, and vice versa.

On this scale, a difference of 20 can be considered meaningful: For example, most Americans who go on expatriate assignments in countries that have scores higher than 60 (like Mexico) or lower than 20 (like Denmark) will notice a significant difference in this area. In most cases, they will need to modify their managerial style to some extent in order to achieve their professional objectives in these countries.

Exhibit 2.1

Power distance scores of 40 countries. High scores correspond
to hierarchical countries. Conversely, nonhierarchical/
participative countries have low scores on this chart.
Adapted from Hofstede (1980).

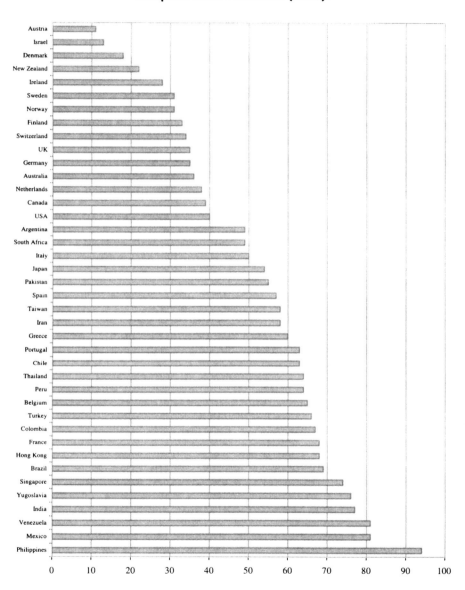

The power distance scale can be roughly divided into three ranges (below 35, between 35 and 50, and above 50), with Canada and the United States falling in the middle of the scale. In each range, corporations share broad common characteristics about the way they are organized, the way managers make decisions, and the approaches toward delegation (Exhibit 2.2).

The difference in managerial style between participative, mildly hierarchical, and highly hierarchical countries can be illustrated in the following manner. Consider the situation where a manager needs a picture of a horse (this "picture of a horse" is meant to represent any task or project that a manager may delegate to a technical professional, such as the design of a pump, an electronic component, part of a building, etc.):

- In participative countries, a manager is likely to say simply: "Draw me a horse." Employees expect and are expected to handle responsibilities by themselves and "take it from there."

- In mildly hierarchical countries, a manager is likely to say: "Here is a picture of a horse. I want something that looks like this." A mildly hierarchical manager narrows down the range of options compared with a participative manager and provides this information upfront.

- In highly hierarchical countries, a manager is likely to say: "Here is a paint-by-number picture of a horse, you go and fill it in." Highly hierarchical managers provide explicit directives to employees. Staff members are expected to implement the decisions made by managers as stated.

The amount of initiative that employees can take is also correlated with power distance: As power distance decreases, employees are expected to take more and more initiatives. In Scandinavian organizations (Sweden, Norway, Denmark, and Finland are on the low end of the power-distance spectrum), employees at low levels of the organization may initiate projects. As a Swedish sales engineer puts it:

> When I sell to Swedish telecom companies, I have a hard time determining who is making the final purchasing decision. Often, the manager implements the decision made by the technical expert.

By contrast, in hierarchical countries, initiative is something that is reserved for people who occupy high-level positions in the hierarchy. This is particularly true in countries that have experienced

Exhibit 2.2

Delegation, decision making, organization form, and the role of manager as a function of power distance score.

	Participative	Mildly Hierarchical	Highly Hierarchical
Power distance score	Below 35	Between 35 and 50	Above 50
Most common form of organization	Decentralized Self-empowered teams	Hubs and spokes Matrices, combining project teams and functional departments	Pyramid Departments
Manager's role	Coach Managers have influence primarily through their ability to influence and convince team members. They usually have little disciplinary leverage over their subordinates.	Manager Managers give a fair amount of freedom to their subordinates, but keep the right to make the final decision.	The boss is the boss is the boss He or she plays a pivotal role in a subordinate's activities.
Typical decision-making process	The team usually makes decisions, with input from the manager.	Managers get input from all their subordinates about the decision they need to make. They make their decision and expect everyone to implement it without further discussion.	Managers make decisions primarily based on their own experience, then communicate their decisions to their subordinates.
Delegation	Managers delegate responsibilities; subordinates also delegate upward.	Managers delegate responsibilities.	Managers delegate tasks.

authoritative political systems in recent years (like Eastern Europe or parts of Latin America); in these countries, taking the wrong initiative could have unpleasant consequences. As a result, decisions are made at a much higher level than in nonhierarchical countries. For example, in the case of the creation of Euro Disney, the French Prime Minister was involved in the negotiations between Disney and the French government (Laroche, 2000).

The way people refer to the managers also reflects their concept of hierarchy. Employees in highly hierarchical countries expect and place a significant distance between themselves and the managers; as a result, they often address managers according to their position in the organization. Expressions like "Monsieur le Directeur" or "Madame la Ministre" indicate a significant amount of deference toward higher-ups. The use of first names does not come naturally to highly hierarchical people, as indicated by the example of the Korean IT specialist mentioned earlier.

Deference to higher-ups is expressed in hierarchical countries in a number of practical ways: Opening the door and letting higher-ups go first, paying attention to every word they say, trying to anticipate their needs, speaking to them when making a presentation (even when the audience includes many other people), etc. The psychological distance between manager and employee becomes physically obvious in some situations; as one Korean engineer put it: "In Korea, if I met my manager in the stairs and we started a conversation, I was expected to stand one step below him to demonstrate my respect for him."

An important aspect of power distance is the fact that, if hierarchy is important to you, you tend to see hierarchy everywhere: In highly hierarchical countries, things and people are ranked according to criteria that are generally widely accepted within the country. Universities are ranked; for example, Japanese consider that graduating from the University of Tokyo is clearly better than graduating from any other university. For French people, graduates of the Ecole Polytechnique de Paris are clearly better than graduates from any other engineering institution. French engineering students are continuously ranked from first to last throughout their undergraduate studies. People also know their hierarchical position with precision: A French engineer was proud to say that he was 162nd in an organization of 150,000 when he retired. As discussed in Chapter 6, the rank attributed to a company or an institution plays a significant role in the career choices that hierarchical people make.

In mildly hierarchical countries, one can say, to paraphrase George Orwell, that "all employees are equal, but some are more equal than others." Rankings exist, but they are far less precise than in hierarchical countries. For example, a North American student is classified as "being in the top 10 percent," whereas the same student in France might be 45th out of 500. There are general tiers: On the engineering and science side, universities like MIT, Caltech, Stanford, and other similar institutions are considered as being part of the first tier, whereas other, less well-known institutions are considered as second tier.

In nonhierarchical countries (like Sweden), people are considered as equals to first approximation. There, asking people to rank universities draws vague responses; nonhierarchical people simply do not think in these terms.

As power distance increases, employees increasingly expect that they will have to provide more information more often to the managers. Hierarchical managers expect to know what is going on in projects within their jurisdiction in more detail than do nonhierarchical managers. As a result, hierarchical employees provide more information to the managers than nonhierarchical employees; in particular, they copy the managers on more e-mail messages, meet more often, and provide more detail about their work when they meet with the managers.

Employees also expect that the managers will tell them what to do to a much greater extent; in particular, the managers will give more detailed instructions when delegating tasks or responsibilities. They also question decisions made by the managers less often and to a lesser extent. One American pharmaceutical researcher working in Latin America described:

> Basically, whatever the boss says goes, period. Latin Americans put little value on what employees do or say as compared to the boss. Many of the Latin American members of our team expect to ask the managers for permission before doing anything.

With increasing power distance, the relationship with the managers will be less trusting and more adversarial in nature. When things do not work out, people in hierarchical countries have a much stronger tendency to see mistakes and assign blame to people, whereas people in less hierarchical countries tend to see learning opportunities and look for solutions. As a result, employees coming from highly hierarchical countries may have learned defense mechanisms that include the following:

- Copying people on e-mail messages so they can prove they sent the requested information on time and as specified

- Saving correspondence, memos, and e-mails so they can prove they did everything as expected

- Warning the managers about the risks of failure related to their projects (In their minds, this transfers the responsibility of failure to the managers.)

When Managers Have Significantly More Hierarchical Employees

As described in Appendix B, most immigrants to North America come from Latin America, Eastern Europe, and the Far East—all parts of the world that are more hierarchical than North America (see Exhibit 2.1). Therefore, they are usually accustomed to management styles that are significantly more hierarchical than what they experience when they join North American organizations.

This situation, where managers are noticeably less hierarchical than employees, can result in miscommunication, missed opportunities, and significant frustration on both sides. For instance, when managers delegate tasks or responsibilities, they usually do not provide enough information, according to employees' standards, for them to know what they need to do. For example, managers may say, "Draw me a horse," whereas employees are used to being handed paint-by-number pictures of horses.

Because they have insufficient information to do their job properly, employees come back to the managers with questions. They may say things like: "You asked me to draw you a horse. What kind of horse do you want? Male or female? Should that horse be white, black, brown, striped like a zebra, spotted, etc.? Do you want a plough horse or a racing horse?" As far as hierarchical employees are concerned, it is obvious that the managers already have the answers to these questions; they just have not communicated them yet.

To the employees' surprise and dismay, their less hierarchical managers do not provide specific answers to their questions. They often answer something like: "I don't know what kind of horse is best in this case. You figure it out." One Swedish manager working in Canada told his Canadian employee: "I pay you to figure that out" (Berg, 2002). In the minds of these managers, it is clear that they expect employees to determine for themselves the best kind of horse needed. They do not have the answers. They could figure it out, but they consider that this task is not the best use of their time—it simply is part of employees' responsibilities, as far as they are concerned.

For employees, this response usually generates a high level of stress. In their minds, the managers know the answer to their question, but refuse to give it to them. They think they are in a bind: They have to guess what answers the manager wants. Any hint that the manager prefers one option over another will be taken as direction. If they come up with the wrong answer, they expect to suffer humiliation in front of the managers.

The experience of a Swedish expatriate managing the Canadian subsidiary of a large Swedish company illustrates these points (Berg, 2002):

> I wanted to create a procedure taking care of visitors. To me, the receptionist was clearly the most qualified person for this task—she was handling most of our visitors. My idea was simply to ask her to write it, and I would then have a quick look at it. When I talked to her, she was clearly very reluctant; she seemed to become both defensive and nervous when I insisted on her doing it. I had to insist on her doing it on her own, without consulting me.
>
> The receptionist dwelled on this procedure for a couple of days until she finally burst into my office. She was clearly quite upset with me. She told me that I was a terrible boss to put her under such pressure. When she was done, she looked at me and said "You are going to fire me now, aren't you?" That idea had not even crossed my mind. I had not realized how stressful the situation had been for her.

As time goes by, this scenario is likely to be repeated many times. When employees hear "I don't know, you figure it out" often, they eventually wonder whether the managers actually have the answers to their questions or not; over time, they are likely to conclude that they don't. When that happens, they start questioning the competence of the managers: "On what basis were they promoted? They cannot answer the simplest questions."

Simultaneously, when managers are visited by their hierarchical employees every time they assign them a new task or responsibilities or every time they need to make a decision, managers start wondering "Can't they take initiative? Can't they make a decision by themselves?" When that happens, they start questioning the competence of employees: "They would not need my help if they knew what they are doing."

When both sides start to question the competence of the other, the relationship between manager and employee is likely to become unproductive. The employees' performance appraisal includes comments like "lacks initiative," which clearly stops them from advancing in the organization's hierarchy. Managers assign them routine projects in order to minimize the number of questions they have to answer;

they may also start avoiding their hierarchical employees (sometimes unconsciously, sometimes deliberately) to save themselves time.

Because loyalty to the organization tends to go hand in hand with a strong sense of hierarchy, this situation rarely ends with employees leaving the organization. When employees do not adapt their reporting style to the leadership style of the managers, the situation usually ends in the following manner:

- If employees have valuable technical skills, the managers may have them transferred into another department, move them into a technician or technical expert position, or try to provide them with some coaching to help improve the relationship.

- If employees have not demonstrated that they have valuable technical skills, they are likely to be fired. In the case of New North Americans on short-term contracts, their contracts are not renewed.

When Managers Have Significantly Less Hierarchical Employees

Let's now look at the reverse situation (i.e., the case where managers have a significantly stronger sense of hierarchy than employees). Statistically, this situation is more likely to take place when New North American professionals are promoted to managerial positions and have North American employees, or when professionals from hierarchical countries are sent on expatriate assignments in less hierarchical countries.

This situation often leads to miscommunication, extensive rework, and significant frustration on both sides. It often evolves as described in the following paragraphs.

When managers delegate tasks or responsibilities, they usually provide more information, according to employees' standards, than employees consider they need to achieve the desired objective. For example, managers may hand them a paint-by-number picture of a horse, whereas employees expect to receive only general guidelines.

They work independently from the managers. They provide updates to the managers as events warrant. They make decisions as they go along, with the idea that these are relatively minor decisions, so they can make them without getting the managers involved. They consider that they can make these decisions by themselves, without involving the managers: "Why waste their time?" In some cases, employees may discard some of the instructions the managers provide, with the idea that they will figure out what is needed by themselves as the project progresses.

After a while, hierarchical managers start wondering what employees are up to. By their standards, the updates they receive from employees are insufficient in both quantity and frequency; they receive too little information to feel that they know what is happening with the project, and this information does not come often enough. At this point, they may start questioning employees in order to get a better sense of the progress of their projects.

As hierarchical managers ask questions, they find out that employees have made some decisions without referring to them for approval—decisions that managers consider theirs to make. This may lead to rework, when managers ask employees to take a different direction. In extreme cases, this may be considered as insubordination, as in the case of the French engineer and his Iranian manager mentioned earlier.

Over time, employees tend to view the managers as micromanagers who get involved in minor decisions and expect their opinion to be followed without questioning. By contrast, managers tend to view employees as loose cannons, whose reactions and next steps are difficult to predict. In this case, managers often react by assigning less important responsibilities to these employees in order to limit the damage they can do when making decisions that do not fall in line with the managers' intentions.

This situation is characterized by extensive rework. In this case, it often (but not always) ends on the initiative of employees:

- Employees may start looking for a job outside the organization or request an internal transfer.
- When managers consider that employees' lack of respect for their authority is excessive, they will have them fired or transferred to another area.

Feedback

Giving feedback to another person is an integral part of any organization's development. Because the way feedback is given and received varies significantly from country to country, many cross-cultural misunderstandings originate from feedback misinterpretation.

Feedback in a Single Cultural Context

Feedback is a comment or set of comments provided by someone to someone else about work or behavior. Feedback can be positive or negative, so we can represent feedback as an axis, as in Exhibit 2.3.

Exhibit 2.3

Feedback in a single cultural context. Between negative and positive feedback lies the "neutral zone."

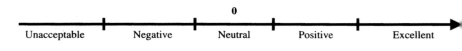

The range of possible feedback shown in Exhibit 2.3 can be described in the following manner:

- The left side of the axis, marked with "Unacceptable," corresponds to feedback of unacceptable performance. Managers commenting to employees that their performance falls in this area would be giving them notice that some fast and significant corrective action is needed ("Shape up or ship out").

- The range on the far right, marked "Excellent," corresponds to feedback for outstanding performance. This corresponds to situations where the employee will receive some form of recognition (e.g., raise, promotion, award) in the near future.

- The range between the first and second mark, in the range marked "Negative," corresponds to negative feedback. Managers commenting to employees that their performance falls in this area expect corrective action.

- The range marked "Positive" corresponds to positive feedback.

- The central range, marked "Neutral," corresponds to the "neutral zone." Feedback in this area corresponds to words that may or may not carry a value judgment. Feedback falling in this range is neither positive nor negative; additional information is needed in order to determine the true feedback. For example, comments like "It's nice" or "It's interesting," made with blank tones of voice and without gestures, do not give any indication of what the person really thinks. The feedback recipient needs to wait for the next comment to determine whether the feedback provided is positive or negative.

Note that, within a given culture, the positions of the boundaries separating the various zones vary from one individual to another. In essence, some people are more sensitive to feedback than others.

Opposite Values

Some personality attributes are viewed positively in North America and negatively in other areas of the world, or vice versa, as depicted in Exhibit 2.4. For example, assertiveness is viewed positively in North America and negatively in the Far East.

For example, many North American managers tell their Chinese employees, "You need to be more assertive. In meetings, you should speak up more often." Their Chinese employees may interpret this piece of feedback as "I am doing what I am supposed to do. Why should I be more rude?" Western assertiveness is often perceived as rudeness by Chinese people. As a result, it is difficult for them to absorb this feedback and act on it. In some cases, the feedback is ignored because employees do not believe that it is the right thing to do. When they recognize that, in North America, assertiveness is a positive attribute, they may not know how to be more assertive. For example, some Chinese employees overshoot: Their assertiveness becomes excessive by North American standards, and their behavior is now considered aggressive.

In the case of opposite values and feedback scales, the main issue consists in finding a solution rather than identifying the problem. Using a medical metaphor, diagnosis is usually not a problem, but finding the right cure is challenging because both sides see their approach as right. For example, Chinese movies often portray Westerners as overly outspoken, and Chinese comedy movies make fun of Westerners' "brash" behavior; cultural differences on this scale are generally known to both sides. Although such differences in values are often quickly identified, they usually represent significant challenges

Exhibit 2.4

When a manager from one culture gives feedback to a employee who has opposite values on the considered scale, this feedback is often misunderstood.

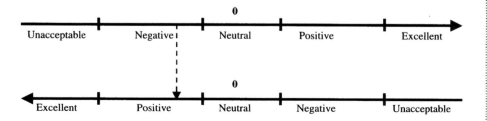

for people to overcome because doing so requires that they override their "mental programming."

Different Scales

More subtle, and therefore more difficult to diagnose, is the situation where feedback scales differ from country to country. For example, Canadian technicians may interpret comments made by some Polish engineers, which were intended to be only slightly negative, as harsh criticism. Exhibit 2.5 is a schematic description of the dynamics that lead to feedback misinterpretation. This description is oversimplified in the sense that, within any country, some people are more receptive and responsive to feedback than others; it should be considered a guideline, not a rule.

As this schematic implies, a comment intended to be neutral by a Polish manager may already be in the negative (or positive) range of his or her Canadian employee, prompting him or her to react in an unintended manner. Here is an example in the case of France and Canada (France occupies the same position on Exhibit 2.5 as Poland relative to Canada), as described by a French engineer working in Canada:

> I once wrote a report that included some potentially controversial recommendations. Before showing it to my management, I showed it to a few colleagues: Two English Canadians and one French. The comments of my two English Canadian colleagues were in essence: "Good report, I suggest you modify recommendations #4

Exhibit 2.5

(1) When a Polish manager makes a slightly negative comment to his or her Canadian employee, the feedback is often interpreted as harsh criticism. (2) A comment that is meant to be rather neutral may be received as negative.

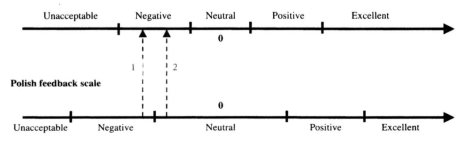

and 5 in the following manner." The comments of my French colleague was in substance: "Not bad, but some of the recommendations are totally out to lunch; you should rewrite recommendations #4 and 5 this way." The suggestions that my French colleagues recommended were the same as the recommendations provided by my English Canadian colleagues.

Similarly, negative comments made by people who have a wide neutral zone may be interpreted as far more negative than intended. Consider the situation where an Austrian engineering manager told his American employees that their presentations were "totally unacceptable." The American employees interpreted the manager's comments as if they were about to be fired, whereas he meant that they needed a lot of additional work. The relative positions of the Austrian and American feedback axes would be similar to the relative positions of the Polish and Canadian axes shown in Exhibit 2.5.

In the case of Mexico, Japan, and China versus the United States and Canada, the relative positions of the two axes are reversed, as Exhibit 2.6 demonstrates: The neutral zone of Mexicans, Japanese, and Chinese is, on average, narrower than the neutral zone of Canadians and Americans. As a result, North American managers may experience unexpected reactions from their Chinese or Mexican employees with comments that, in their minds, are either neutral or slightly negative; in the minds of the Chinese and Mexican recipients, these comments require a response or correspond to a severe warning. This is what happened in the case of the Mexican engineer resigning after he received some mildly negative feedback from his American manager.

Exhibit 2.6

Comparing the American and Mexican feedback scales.

Mexican feedback scale

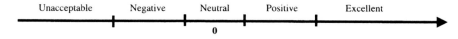

American feedback scale

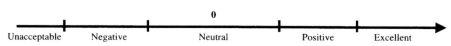

This also explains a common misunderstanding between North American expatriates in Japan and their Japanese counterparts, which is particularly common at the beginning of their assignments. A Canadian engineer working in Japan describes the situation in the following manner:

> I would make a request to my Japanese counterparts. By Canadian standards, this request is quite simple and would not raise any eyebrow. The response I would get went like this: My Japanese counterparts would take a deep breath and respond "This might be a little difficult." "A little difficult? Great! I love challenges. Why is it difficult?" I would switch to a problem-solving mode and start looking for a solution. In most cases, we would find one that seemed to work; however, in virtually all cases, nothing happened. It took me a while to realize that, when Japanese say "It might be a little difficult," they actually mean something like "Forget it. Not in a million years."

The relative positions of the feedback scales for France and Canada are similar to the relative positions for Poland and Canada. As a result, when a Canadian manager provides mildly negative feedback to his or her French employees, this feedback may appear to "fall on deaf ears." This situation is depicted in Exhibit 2.7.

The mildly negative feedback provided by the Canadian manager falls in the neutral zone of the French employee. The words are heard,

Exhibit 2.7

---

(1) When a Canadian manager makes a mildly negative comment, his or her French employee may not react because the feedback appears inconsequential. (2) The manager usually follows with a harsher criticism. (3) Only when the feedback is negative enough does the employee react.

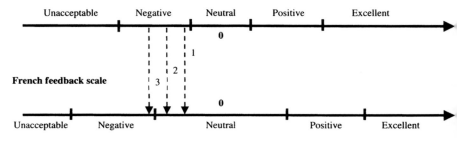

but the negative content of the feedback is not recognized. As a result, the French employee does not take any corrective action, contrary to the expectation of the Canadian manager. In many cases, the Canadian manager comes back to the issue after a little while and makes a second negative comment, which is usually more pointed. If this comment again falls in the neutral zone, the French employee will again hear the words but not take any action.

The Canadian manager usually "cranks up the volume" until he or she makes a comment that is sufficiently negative for the French employee to recognize it as negative (i.e., a comment that falls in the negative zone of the French employee). At that point, the French employee identifies that there is a problem and that he or she needs to do something about it; however, by that time, the Canadian manager has lost patience and may be ready to write off his or her French employee. By contrast, this negative feedback appears almost to have come out of nowhere to the French employee.

Note that feedback scale differences can be observed within a single culture. Some individuals are more sensitive to feedback and pick cues up faster and/or respond more rapidly than others. As one Canadian pharmaceutical marketing specialist put it, "some of my Canadian employees seem to be coming from another planet when it comes to feedback."

Positive Feedback

Similar issues can be observed with positive feedback, although their frequency and magnitude are usually significantly lower. In Exhibit 2.7, the negative feedback provided by a Canadian manager is not recognized as negative by his or her French employee. The same situation may occur on the positive side, where the French employee does not recognize the positive feedback provided by his or her Canadian manager. As a result, the French employee may feel unappreciated because he or she has not recognized the positive content of the comments made by the manager.

In extreme cases, a New North American employee may consider that his or her skills are not given the proper respect they deserve, whereas management is providing extensive recognition by North American standards. This is what happened to the Polish engineer who was looking for a job because he felt unappreciated, even though he had received all the technical and merit awards that the company had to offer. The positive feedback he was given was too mild for him to register (see Chapter 5 for more on this type of career management issue).

Approaches to Feedback

Feedback provided by culturally different managers may also be misunderstood because of differences in communication style, which are examined in more detail in Chapter 4. Managers, employees, or both may be used to different feedback delivery, leading to potential confusion:

- In Germany, negative feedback should be provided straightforwardly and should not be sandwiched between positive comments. "Germans won't understand this sort of communication; in fact, they will be made quite anxious by the ambiguity of a compliment joined with a criticism and will wonder what is really being said" (Hall, 1990). German technical professionals working in North America may have to adapt to this different approach to feedback; similarly, North American technical professionals working in German organizations may have to learn to deal with feedback that appears blunt because there is no positive comment to "soften the blow."

- The way feedback is delivered by some Italian expatriates may be considered unacceptable by North American standards, as the experience of the Canadian engineer working in Italy mentioned at the beginning of this chapter indicates.

- The timing of feedback may be an issue. In Hong Kong, employees who do not receive positive feedback (and often some financial form of recognition) shortly—within a few weeks—after they have reached important professional objectives often start looking for a job in another company. In Germany, people expect the managers to tell them, in no uncertain terms, what part of their work did not measure up to their expectations right after the event occurred (Hall, 1990).

What Can You Do?

So far, we have examined situations in which the relationship between managers and employees may not be optimal because of cultural differences. In medical terms, we have a diagnosis; we now need a range of possible cures for these issues.

In the case of cultural differences, making a correct diagnosis often represents 50 percent of the solution. In many cases, cross-cultural misunderstandings lead to significant frustration on both sides. In extreme cases, both sides consider the other as incompetent or inadequate—a strongly negative statement to be made about technical professionals who have spent many years studying in their fields of specialization and usually excelled in these studies. Knowing that the issue is not related to competence, but to different ways of accomplishing tasks and relating to people, often partly diffuses the issue. When the competence of both parties is no longer in question, they can now focus on the different ways in which competence is measured.

Adaptation

Once cultural differences have been identified, the question becomes: "What can we do about it?" Once everyone understands that people coming from different cultural backgrounds do things differently and what these differences are, the next step consists of reconciling these differences (Trompenaars, 1998).

How do we do that? There are many ways to bridge differences: We can adopt one culture as the common denominator, meet somewhere in the middle, or create new approaches that are unique to the people involved. In the case of employees and managers coming from culturally different backgrounds, three key factors need to be taken into consideration:

- *Who has the authority?* In many cases, employees adapt to a greater extent to the managers than managers do toward employees. This relationship is partly dictated by the manager's power-distance preference: Hierarchical managers are likely to expect employees to adapt to them more than participative managers; participative managers are more likely to meet employees halfway.

- *What is the corporate culture?* Corporate culture provides a standard for manager–employee relationships that can be used as a template—a starting point in a conversation between managers and employees.

- *What are the personalities involved?* Some people are more adaptable or have clearer expectations than others.

This section examines how adaptation can take place when a manager and his or her employees come from culturally different countries. We first examine the steps that each person can take individually with respect to power distance and feedback, then discuss the steps they can take together to bridge the gap between them.

Power Distance

The steps people may take individually depend on which side of the manager–employee relationship they are on and whether they are more or less hierarchical than this person.

Employees Who Report to More Hierarchical Managers

These people should consider the following steps:

- Getting back to the managers more often to ensure alignment. The managers expect more frequent reports than the employee may consider necessary.
- Checking with the managers before taking new initiatives. In particular, employees should consider running by the managers the idea of getting involved in or initiating new projects.
- Implementing decisions made by the managers without further questions. Questions aiming at understanding what the managers want to see implemented are usually more than welcome; questions aiming at making the managers reconsider their decision or data brought forward after the decision has been made are counterproductive.
- Volunteering to work on projects that are off the beaten track and not on the manager's critical path. Hierarchical managers are more likely to cut employees some slack on projects that are less important to their success than on the projects that are.
- Showing more deference to the managers than they would show other managers.

Employees Who Report to Less Hierarchical Managers

These people should consider the following steps:

- Avoiding asking open-ended questions to the managers. The managers expect them to take the initiative and make suggestions rather than ask questions. Questions like "What do you think?" or "What approach do you recommend?" are likely to irritate such managers.
- Doing their homework before asking questions of the managers. They should consider thinking of all the ways of achieving the objective they have been assigned and rating the various options according to their pros and cons. Only then should they ask the managers if they are on the right track and if there are any issues

they should consider. For example, they may ask the managers: "There are three ways of achieving the objective you have assigned me: A, B, and C. I think A is better because of X and Y. What do you think?"

- Taking initiative by getting involved in new task forces, new projects, and new initiatives. Employees should not wait for less hierarchical managers to suggest it because it may not happen.

- Requesting projects that are really important to the managers. Managers are likely to provide more direction on such projects than on less critical projects.

- Learning to accept shortcomings as learning opportunities, rather than terminal failures. In many North American organizations, the problem is not so much making a mistake, but making the same mistake twice.

Managers Who Have More Hierarchical Employees

Managers who want to work more effectively with employees who are significantly more hierarchical than they are may consider the following steps:

- Providing more information to these employees when they assign projects and tasks to them.

- Encouraging them to make decisions progressively on their own by giving them explicitly the responsibility for this decision. Statements like "I am not sure whether we need a male or a female horse in this case. I want you to weigh the pros and cons, decide which is better, then tell me what you have decided" will help hierarchical employees understand that they are expected to make the decision.

- Encouraging their hierarchical employees to take more initiative. For example, they may start with statements like "There is a new project starting in this area; your expertise may be needed. Why don't you go and ask whether your skills may benefit the team?"

- Explaining to these hierarchical employees how people from other cultural backgrounds perceive their behavior when they act in a way that shows excessive deference to them or higher-ups.

- Ensuring that the feedback they provide to employees focuses on what they have learned and how they can do better next time and avoiding blaming aspects. This approach is likely to decrease their defensiveness. Managers may consider assigning the task of analyzing past projects and summarizing learnings to highly defensive employees, in order to give them an opportunity to practice positive thinking and learn from past problems.

Managers Who Have Less Hierarchical Employees

Managers who want to work more effectively with employees who are significantly less hierarchical than they are may consider the following steps:

- Giving them more leeway when assigning tasks or projects. They may consider refraining from giving some of the hunches or directions that they would pass on to other employees.

- Delegating to these employees projects that are not on their critical path (so they can cut the employees more slack) or that require significant initiative.

- Explaining to these employees in more detail why they get involved in the employees' projects. For example, they may describe how this project interacts with other projects and other parts of the organization.

Feedback

The best approach to cross-cultural feedback issues depends on the type of misunderstandings that take place.

Opposite Values

Issues where managers and employees have opposite values are difficult to overcome, particularly when these values are important to both. In the case where manager and employee come from different cultural backgrounds and have different values in one specific area, the factor that is most likely to determine who will need to adapt to whom is the environment. For example, American managers working in China are likely to have to adapt their views of assertiveness to the Chinese point of view in order to be effective; otherwise, they may face a high turnover rate. Similarly, Chinese technical professionals often have to adapt to their surroundings and become more assertive in order to achieve their professional objectives when they work in North America.

Because changing one's values, even to a limited extent, is neither easy nor quick, getting outside help may be worthwhile in this case. Possible sources of help may include the human resources department of your company, mentoring programs, or outside consultants.

Differences in Scale or Style

Differences in feedback scales and styles are considerably easier to bridge once they have been identified, using the following approaches:

- Managers can adapt their feedback strategy to the receptivity of employees. They may "soft pedal" in the case of employees who have a narrow neutral zone or, conversely, "crank up the volume" faster in the case of employees who have a wide neutral zone.

- Employees need to ensure that they interpret the feedback given by the managers as it was meant. To ensure that they do not overreact or overlook important feedback, they need to calibrate themselves on the manager's scale. They may ask the managers to clarify the meaning of their feedback—they may say something like: "On a scale of 1 to 10, where 1 is a small inconvenience and 10 is likely to get me fired quickly, where does this issue fit?"

- An alternative approach is to find mentors, ideally from the same cultural groups as the managers. At the least, mentors should be from a different cultural group than the employees in order to avoid situations where "the blind are leading the blind" (Harris, 1999). Indeed, mentors who belong to the same cultural group as employees interpret events and give advice from the same perspective; they may unknowingly reinforce employees in repeating the same cross-cultural faux pas.

Joint Discussions

One of the most effective ways to bridge the gap between culturally different managers and employees is to have the two of them discuss the best way of working together. Such a discussion can be particularly valuable in the first few weeks of a new manager–employee relationship because it enables both parties to build a solid base for future interactions. Here are topics that should be considered during these expectation-sharing sessions:

- Who will make what kind of decisions? Using examples drawn from past experience (theirs or the experiences of others), manager and employee should classify decisions in several categories:
  - Decisions that employees make alone without informing the managers of their decisions
  - Decisions that employees make alone, then inform the managers of their decisions
  - Decisions that employees formulate first, then run by the managers for approval

- Decisions that employees and managers discuss and make together
- Decisions that managers make alone, based on information provided by employees
- Decisions that managers make alone

- When is a decision final? When is it still open for discussion? What new elements may lead to a change in direction?

- What is the best way of communicating information and decisions (e.g., face-to-face, e-mail, phone message)?

- How often should feedback be provided? In what form?

This discussion may be repeated over time (maybe every couple of months at first, less often later on) to clarify any misunderstanding. For example, manager and employee may keep a running list of the various types of decisions they need to make and the categories in which they fall (decisions made by employees alone, decisions made jointly, etc.). As new events occur, they may add them to this list. Both can then reuse this list as the starting point for a discussion with subsequent managers or employees, when the reporting structure is changed.

Such a discussion assumes that employees and managers are on somewhat equal footing. It assumes either a participative or a mildly hierarchical approach to reporting; in a hierarchical environment, the managers essentially provide most of the content of this discussion, and employees expect them to do so. Therefore, when this discussion involves very hierarchical New North American employees working in North American organizations, managers may first choose to work with these employees to help them understand what being an employee means in North America in general and to them in particular.

For best results, it is preferable to have such a conversation face-to-face, rather than through telecommunication means. Meeting face-to-face helps prevent some of the miscommunication issues described in Chapter 4 and contributes to building rapport between managers and employees. When these individuals are located in different parts of the world, the time and rework that is likely to be saved later on is often worth the corresponding travel expenses.

What Can You Gain?

Significant benefits can be derived from differences in power distance, both for managers and employees:

- For a *manager*, having a *more hierarchical employee* can be beneficial in times of urgency. A manager can then give precise instructions regarding how a specific task needs to be done, answer the employee's questions, and expect the urgent task to be completed as instructed. In "fire-fighting" situations, this relationship can be helpful.

- For a *manager*, having a *less hierarchical employee* can be beneficial in times where a clear direction is not apparent. A manager can delegate a task or project to a less hierarchical employee with fuzzy instructions and let the employee loose. When the manager does not have the time to figure out what needs to be done, this relationship can be helpful.

- For an *employee*, having a *more hierarchical manager* often provides an opportunity to learn some new technical skills. Because such a manager often welcomes questions of this nature, the employee can explore in more detail the why and how of the work, obtaining better tools for future assignments.

- For an *employee*, having a *less hierarchical manager* usually provides an opportunity to learn and think independently. By providing more latitude in how the objectives are achieved, such a manager gives the employee a greater chance to create plans and experiment with new ideas.

Summary

Relationships between managers and employees are often challenging. They usually become even more challenging when managers and employees come from different cultural backgrounds because they are likely to have different concepts of what being a manager or an employee means. Exhibit 2.8 summarizes the potential issues that may arise as a result of power-distance differences and suggests both the diagnosis and possible solutions. Exhibit 2.9 provides similar information in the case of issues related to feedback differences.

Exhibit 2.8

Common cross-cultural issues related to differences in power distance between managers and employees, their likely cause, and possible solutions.

Issue	Likely Cause	Suggested Solutions
Manager's perspective		*Manager may consider:*
• Lack of initiative • Excessive deference toward managers and higher-ups • Excessive defensiveness and negativity	Subordinate is more hierarchical (higher power distance) than manager.	• Providing more information to subordinates. • Encouraging them to make decisions on their own. • Discussing forms of greetings with them. • Encouraging them to take initiative. • Explaining their view of hierarchy and initiative to subordinates. • Encouraging them to focus on "lessons learned."
• "Loose cannon"	Subordinate is less hierarchical (lower power distance) than manager.	• Giving them more leeway. • Discussing with them who should make what decisions. • Delegating projects and tasks that are not critical or require significant initiative. • Explaining their involvement to a greater extent.
Subordinate's perspective		*Subordinates may consider:*
• Technically incompetent managers • Put on the spot	Manager is less hierarchical (lower power distance) than subordinate.	• Avoiding asking open-ended questions. • Doing their homework before meeting with their managers. • Asking managers how they want to be addressed. • Getting involved in new projects, task forces, and initiatives. • Asking to work on projects that are critical for their managers. • Taking mistakes as "learning opportunities."
• Micromanagers	Manager is more hierarchical (higher power distance) than subordinate.	• Getting back to their managers more often. • Discussing up front what decisions they can make by themselves. • Running initiatives by their managers. • Asking for projects of low importance to managers. • Showing more deference to manager.

Common cross-cultural issues related to differences in feedback interpretation between managers and employees, their likely cause, and possible solutions.

Issue	Possible Causes	Suggested Solutions
Manager's perspective		*Managers may consider:*
Subordinates overreact to their negative feedback.	Subordinates may have a narrower neutral zone than managers.	"Soft pedaling" feedback (both negative and positive).
	Difference in approach to feedback	Discussing with subordinates the best way to achieve the desired response.
Subordinates do not react to negative feedback.	Opposite values	Considering environment. Getting outside help. "Cranking up the volume"
	Subordinates may have a wider neutral zone than managers.	Discussing with subordinates the best way to achieve the desired response.
	Difference in approach to feedback	Providing more positive feedback.
Subordinates do not react to positive feedback.	Subordinates may have a wider neutral zone than manager.	Discussing with subordinates the best way to achieve the desired response.
Subordinate's perspective		*Subordinates may consider:*
Strong negative feedback strikes like lightning in a blue sky.	Subordinates may have a wider neutral zone than managers.	Taking strong corrective action, as requested by the manager.
		Discussing with manager the best way to provide and receive feedback.
Strong negative feedback seems out of proportion with problem.	Subordinates may have a narrower neutral zone than managers.	Discussing with manager the best way to provide and receive feedback.
The positive feedback does not compare with their accomplishments.	Subordinates may have a wider neutral zone than managers.	Discussing with manager the best way to provide and receive feedback.

References

Berg, M., and Magnusson, S. 2002. *Subtle differences with visible consequences*. University of Lund, Master's Thesis.

Elashmawi, F. 1998. *Multicultural management: Essential cultural insights for business success*, 2nd ed. Woburn, MA: Butterworth–Heinemann/Gulf

Hall, E.T., and Reed Hall, M. 1990. *Understanding cultural differences Germans, French and Americans*. Yarmouth, ME: Intercultural Press p. 63.

Harris, P.R. 1998. *The new work culture*, Amherst, MA: HRD Press.

Harris, P.R., and Moran, R.T. 1999. *Managing cultural differences Leadership strategies for a new world of business*, 5th ed. Woburn, MA Butterworth–Heinemann.

Hofstede, G. 1980. *Culture's consequences: International differences in work related values*. Newbury Park, CA: Sage Publications, pp. 73–84.

Hofstede, G. 1991. *Culture and organizations: Software of the mind*. New York: McGraw-Hill, p. 47.

Laroche, L.F. 2000. Negotiating abroad, *Management Magazine*, March.

Laurent, A. 1981. Matrix organizations and Latin cultures, *International Studies of Management and Organizations*, 10(4):101–104.

Tan, T. 1992. *Culture shock: Britain*. Portland, OR: Graphic Arts Center Publishing, p. 79.

Trompenaars, A., and Hampden-Turner, C. 1998. *Riding the waves of culture: Understanding diversity in global business*, 2nd ed. New York McGraw-Hill, pp. 43–47.

Wederspahn, G.M. 2000. *Intercultural services: A worldwide buyer's guide and sourcebook*. Woburn, MA: Butterworth–Heinemann/Gulf.

Multicultural Teamwork among Technical Professionals

> I had ordered some special optical elements for my laser experiment. It took several months for the order to be fulfilled; in addition, this customized equipment was expensive and fragile. When it arrived, I started unpacking it very carefully. One of my French colleagues saw me unpacking and offered to help me. I thanked him and told him that I did not need any help. He ignored my comment and started opening one of the boxes; before I had time to do anything, he broke one of the mirrors. I was just out of my mind.
>
> *—Canadian applied physicist working in France*

Within North America, the number of multicultural teams has increased significantly over the past 10 years as a result of immigration (see Appendix B) and globalization. The workforce of many research centers, IT organizations and departments, and high-tech companies is often jokingly described as the "United Nations."

In addition to these home-based multicultural teams (i.e., teams made of technical professionals born and educated in different countries who now all work in the same building), many organizations make extensive use of global teams (i.e., teams made of people located in two or more countries).

For example, in the IT sector, "follow-the-sun" support is provided, whereby users are supported from North America, then from the Far East, and finally from Europe during their respective working hours, allowing 24/7 technical support. This approach significantly increases the need for good teamwork among the various parts of the IT technical support team because they need to "pass the baton" three times every 24 hours.

In the manufacturing sector, many companies want to better amortize their development costs by spreading them over a larger number of customers, so they are trying to develop one product or one product platform for the whole world (or at least several continents). This phenomenon is particularly visible in the pharmaceutical and automotive sectors, where the costs of developing one new drug or car model are so high that there is virtually no room for error. Global teams offer many advantages:

- Assigning individuals from several countries to the same project helps avoid the "not invented here" syndrome, therefore speeding up the global roll-out of newly developed products.

- The team takes local requirements (market-specific characteristics like customer preferences and environmental regulations) into consideration at the design stage.

- The final products are interchangeable, thereby enabling companies to ship products from one part of the world to another to overcome temporary supply-and-demand imbalances.

Multicultural and global teams have one major advantage over culturally homogeneous teams: People from different cultural backgrounds bring different techniques and approaches to solving problems. This enables them to tackle the same problem in more ways and therefore have better chances at cracking it.

In order to achieve this advantage, however, multicultural teams must operate as effective, cohesive teams. Good teamwork and being a good team member are considered valuable in most countries, but these two concepts correspond to different realities in different countries. As discussed in this chapter, the different views of teamwork may conflict and generate extensive inefficiencies and tension within multicultural teams. Risks of miscommunication are increased in global teams, where team members do not have the opportunity to meet face-to-face and resolve any misunderstanding that may develop between team members.

This chapter examines the challenges and opportunities in multicultural teams that include both North American and New North American (or foreign expatriate) technical professionals. It first looks at the issues that cultural differences usually create within these teams.

It then describes where these issues come from by analyzing the dynamics of multicultural teams; in particular, it examines the evolution of such teams. The next section suggests potential solutions to cross-cultural teamwork issues. After that, potential synergies that may be obtained in multicultural teams are described, and the final section covers the additional challenges faced by global teams.

What Are the Signs of Cross-Cultural Teamwork Issues?

This section examines the most common cross-cultural issues related to teamwork. Within the range of cross-cultural issues presented in this book, they are among the most difficult to identify. Many New North Americans who have lived and worked in the United States and/or Canada for many years have not recognized the cultural differences that exist in this area. As members of North American teams, they interact with their colleagues in ways that are characteristic of good team players in their home countries. In many cases, the conflicts and issues that these interactions create are misdiagnosed as personality issues. Using the framework of the cultural iceberg presented in Chapter 1, the concept of teamwork lurks far below the surface, and differences are not readily visible for two reasons:

- Overwhelmingly, this concept of teamwork is learned informally rather than formally. Few technical education programs include a course on teamwork; technical professionals learn teamwork when practicing sports, doing projects, and so on.

- By definition, teamwork involves many people. In order to identify that other cultures have different concepts of teamwork, you need to work with several people from the same cultural background in similar situations (e.g., an American working with several Chinese people over a period) and observe trends. These conditions are not often met, in the sense that teams are rarely stable for long periods. North American technical professionals may not work with people from the same cultural backgrounds often enough to identify behavioral trends.

As in the case of manager–employee relationships examined in Chapter 2, cross-cultural teamwork issues are usually experienced by many team members simultaneously, but in different manners.

Interference

Interference is a common (and often devastating) issue in multicultural teams. It is more commonly experienced by North Americans working with people of other cultural backgrounds. Interference usually elicits strong, negative reactions from the North American technical professionals whose areas of responsibility are encroached upon. By North American standards, this behavior is totally unacceptable. Here are some of the behaviors associated with this problem:

- Some team members are taking over part of another team member's responsibilities. They may offer help when none has been requested. They may start doing a task that falls into someone else's area of responsibility without being asked. In extreme cases, they start helping even when help has been explicitly declined, as the experience of the Canadian applied physicist working in a France, mentioned at the beginning of this chapter, demonstrates.

- In meetings, they may answer questions about points that fall under someone else's jurisdiction. For example, during a project review by high-level managers, they may answer questions that pertain to parts of the project for which they are not personally responsible.

Are We Really a Team?

This issue is more likely to be experienced by people from cultures other than North Americans when working with North Americans. It occurs more often in global teams. In essence, some team members wonder whether the team is really a team because their North American counterparts appear to be members of the team only as far as it furthers their own professional goals. Here are some of the behaviors that lead them to this conclusion:

- North American team members do not provide enough information to their New North American teammates (or team members located outside North America). New North American team members often learn about the activities and progress of their North American teammates during review meetings with management.

- In meetings, North American team members do not come to the rescue of their teammates when they experience difficulties. For example, during a project review, when high-level managers ask questions that put a New North American team member on the spot by probing into areas that this person has not examined in detail, North American team members do not suggest answers based on their own experience. They may, however, provide suggestions to their New North American teammate after the meeting, on a one-on-one basis, leaving this teammate with the feeling that he or she was let down during the meeting.

"Shooting from the Hip" Versus "Analysis Paralysis"

Some multicultural teams become polarized between team members who want the team to move forward quickly and team members who want to make sure that the team moves in the right direction. Simply put, some team members consider that others are constantly jumping to conclusions, whereas others are prone to "analysis paralysis" (i.e., they need so much data and information before making any decision that nothing ever gets done).

"Let's Make Sure We Know What We Are Doing"

For some team members, the motto is: "If you are in St. Louis and you want to go to San Francisco, driving as fast as you can on the interstate eastbound gets you farther and farther away from your goal." These team members see teammates who want to move quickly in the following manner:

- They keep "shooting from the hip." With two data points, they draw a straight line, extrapolate to other situations, and start acting on this extrapolation. For example, after a couple of experiments that are part of a larger designed experiment, they may start altering the remainder of the experimental plan.

- They confuse activity and progress. They emphasize action and movement; they seem to place little value on thinking about possible obstacles and planning for them. They tend to schedule discussions on these topics at the end of meetings, often adjourning or cutting the meeting short when the team reaches these topics.

- They want to solve technical problems by throwing experiments at them. Rather than thinking about what impact a change in a given variable is likely to yield, they would rather run the experiment. They appear to solve problems (technical or otherwise) through trial and error, with limited analysis of the errors.

- When they try a new possible solution, they allow little time to determine whether this new solution is working. They seem to jump from one potential solution to the next.

- Understanding what is actually happening in the physical system they are dealing with is not nearly as important to them as getting the result they seek. As a Canadian engineering manager told a French engineer:

> The company needs test product tomorrow morning. You are in charge of this experiment. I do not care how you do it, as long as the test product is in the warehouse tomorrow morning. If little fairies make it during the night shift, that's fine with me.

- With this somewhat random approach to solving problems, these team members may be able to achieve a particular result on a good day without being able to duplicate it the next. They may also be able to solve a specific problem on a particular system without knowing how to adapt it to a similar situation that is likely to appear on a nearby system later.

"Come On! We Have Talked about This Long Enough. It's Time to Move On!"

For some team members, the motto is: "If we stand still, competition will pass us by. Trying something will enable us to learn, even if it does not give us what we want." These team members see teammates who want to ensure that the team is moving in the right direction as overly conservative:

- They keep asking for more data and information. When one team member obtains unusual experimental results, they usually come up with a range of effects that may explain these results and their conclusion is invariably: "We need to run some more experiments to make sure we understand what's going on."

- They seem to place little value on action. They seem to be caught in an endless thinking limbo. They want so much to ensure that they have the right framework and that they have considered all possibilities that they appear to never get anything done.

- They spend much of their time thinking about problems rather than attempting to solve them. Here is the experience of a Canadian engineer working in Italy:

> At one point, two of my Italian colleagues got into an argument about whether the fact that our product did not meet specifica-

tions was due to a lack of heat or excessive humidity. They talked about it for a good half-hour during one of the team meetings and neither of them would let go. During all that time, I kept thinking to myself: "The only thing we can change on the line to improve the product is the temperature. Increasing it will take care of both anyway. So it really does not matter whether the problem is temperature or humidity. Thinking and planning are fine and dandy, but at some point, the rubber has to hit the road.

- They put far too much emphasis on theory. They spend all their energy trying to understand why the system operates the way it does, rather than focusing on how they can get it to do what they want it to do. Why and how it functions is not nearly as important as getting it to work.

- When they think they have a solution because of some theoretical argument, they keep trying and trying to get it to work, even though it is clearly not working. They get stuck in a rut and do not move on easily.

Outcome

Because the mandate of most technical teams consists of collecting technical data and information, drawing conclusions, and making recommendations based on this data, this issue can really create havoc. The team may split between those who want the team to move forward quickly and those who want to ensure that the team is going in the right direction. At the same time, as discussed later, this is one of the areas where multicultural teams can benefit extensively from the diversity of thought and experience of their members.

Team Breakdown

When these problems (interference, selfishness, differences in the ways decisions are made and problems are analyzed) persist and become too severe, multicultural teams may break down into sub-teams. The breakdown process depends on whether there is only one culturally different team member (e.g., a team made of several Americans and one Mexican) or more.

Teams with More Than One Culturally Different Team Member

When the team includes more than one culturally different team member, breakdown often takes place as described in the following paragraphs.

At first, team members work more and more closely with other team members of similar cultural backgrounds, forming a subteam. For example, a French–American IT team splits into a French subteam and an American subteam.

As time goes by, collaboration between the various subteams decreases quickly. In particular, information exchange between members of different subteams is almost nonexistent. It only takes place during formal meetings. At this point, the subteams work side-by-side and ignore one another.

Subteams are likely to start identifying themselves as such by giving themselves a name. For example, in one team made of British and Latin American technical professionals, the British form a group known as the "Brit pack." Members of subteams socialize together, but do not socialize with members of other subteams. As one British member of the "Brit pack" put it: "Yes, we are all going to the pub this evening to watch the soccer game. And guess what? Only Brits are invited."

Mistrust between the various subteams increases over time. Information provided by the members of one subteam to the members of another is double-checked. For example, members of one subteam may duplicate the experiments run by members of another subteam.

In extreme cases, the different subteams start to compete with one another. This situation is more likely in the case of global teams, where interactions between team members and management are less frequent, making duplication and lack of progress less immediately apparent than in situations where everyone is in the same building.

Teams with a Single Culturally Different Team Member

The breakdown process takes a different form when there are not enough members of different cultural groups to create subteams. When the team is made of culturally similar people with a single exception, team breakdown occurs when culturally similar team members ostracize the culturally different team member. For example, in the case of a team of technical professionals that includes several Americans and one Mexican, team breakdown leads to the exclusion of the Mexican from the team by the American team members. The Mexican team member no longer receives any information from other team members, he or she may not be notified or invited to some team meetings, nobody picks up on what he or she suggests during meetings, and so on.

Although most people involved in such situations agree that a problem exists, they often diagnose this problem differently. American team members clearly see a personality conflict: The Mexican member of the team is ostracized because he or she is a poor team player. Depending on his or her past experience and values, the Mexican team member may see a cross-cultural problem ("I don't understand what's wrong with Americans. I can't work with them; they are so selfish.") or a discrimination problem ("Americans discriminate against me because I am Mexican.").

In this situation, a more accurate diagnosis is that the Mexican is acting within the team according to *Mexican standards* and that these standards go against *American team standards*, making the actions and words of the Mexican team member unacceptable to his or her teammates.

Outcome

Obviously, team breakdowns lead to ineffective teams. As time goes by, everyone involved in the project recognizes the lack of progress, and the organization eventually determines that pursuing the project does not make much sense because it amounts to throwing good money after bad. The project is cancelled and the team is disbanded, with limited learning from this failed experience; generally, team members have different interpretations of why they did not achieve their objectives.

Making Decisions

Many misunderstandings arise in multicultural teams (and even more in global teams) around making decisions. Has a decision been made or is it still open for discussion? Consider the experience of an Italian engineer working in a multicultural team made of Americans, Canadians, Italians, and Germans:

> All team members flew to Germany for a three-day meeting. We had a series of presentations and discussions. At the end of the three days, when we were all shaking hands, the Americans congratulated one another, saying how good this meeting had been. They kept saying "We made a lot of good decisions in this meeting." I turned to my Italian colleagues and asked in Italian: "We made decisions?" They shook their heads in disbelief.

Who is responsible for making the decision? The split of responsibilities between several positions may not be the same in different parts of the world, even within the same company. Consider the experience of a Canadian engineer working on the same U.S.– Canadian–Italian–German team:

I went to Germany to run an experiment there. We had a six-week window to run this experiment. Since I thought we would need eight weeks to run it properly, I expected the German process engineer to set up the experimental apparatus right away so that I, as product development engineer, could run it—this was normal operating procedure in our Canadian plant. After two weeks of him doing nothing, I could not take it any more and asked him what was going on and why he was not setting up the equipment. He looked at me like I fell from Mars and replied, "But I thought *you* were responsible for setting up this equipment." In that discussion, I found out that, in our German plant, the product development engineer sets up the equipment and the process engineer runs it.

Starting Off on the Wrong Foot

You only get one chance to make a good first impression. This is also true in the case of multicultural teams, but what you need to do to make a good first impression varies from country to country. The way people in one culture attempt to build teams can be irritating and counterproductive in other cultures, as the following situations illustrate.

A French IT specialist working in a joint American–French team described the first meeting with his American counterparts:

It was awful. They bused us to some field. There, a guy showed us a pile of parts and told us that, together, these parts make a go-kart and we could race it around the field once we built it. So the Americans jumped on it and started building it, while I, like many of my French colleagues, just watched. When they were finished, we each had a turn at driving the thing around the field. When that was finished, we had hamburgers and hot dogs on a barbecue; everyone was standing there, with a plate in their hands, talking about how much fun driving the go-kart had been. Then we drove back. That was it. I did not learn anything about my American colleagues in this event.

An American scientist described his first encounter with his Argentinean colleagues:

It was awful. They told me to show up at noon in their offices, but they did not arrive until 12:30 p.m. The meeting started by people introducing themselves extensively; they told me what universities they graduated from, what companies they had worked for, what positions they had held up to now, how many times they had been to the United States, where, when, what for, etc. Everything but the project itself. By the time we went for lunch, I was starving. Lunch was no more productive; we talked about the economic and political situation in Argentina, they gave me suggestions for places I should visit that evening, including the names and addresses of places where I could see some good tango dancing, etc. The wine did not help. Every time I started talking about the project, they would dodge the issue and talk about something else.

What Is Going On?

As the previous section describes, the dynamics of multicultural teams can be both complex and dramatically different from the dynamics of culturally homogeneous teams. This section examines these dynamics (the special case of global teams is covered later). It starts with a description of three factors that play a significant role in team dynamics: individualism, risk tolerance, and context. Then it examines how a multicultural team evolves over time and explains where the issues just described originate.

What Makes a Team?

A team is a group of people working together to achieve a common objective. This definition is essentially universal; however, the way a team is expected to function depends significantly on how individualistic its members are. Let's first look at the concept of individualism and its impact on multicultural teams.

Individualism

Individualism measures the extent to which people view themselves as individuals, as self-contained entities (individualistic), or as members of a group, as elements of a larger entity (collectivistic). It is a measure of the importance people assign to their individual interests relative to the interests of the group to which they belong.

In an individualistic society, the interests of the individual are considered more important than the interests of the group. People define themselves through individual characteristics rather than by group characteristics. Adult members of such societies are expected to be independent and are not encouraged to rely on others.

In a collectivistic society, the interests of the group are considered more important than the interests of individuals. The group to which people belong and their position within this group are a vital part of their identity. Loyalty to the group is strong, and group members receive protection and extensive financial, emotional, and practical advice and support from the group. In turn, they contribute financially, practically, and psychologically to other group members. This exchange takes place over time; for example, younger members of the group may receive advice and support from their elders while elders may receive assistance with physical tasks and respect from younger group members.

The group to which people identify often depends on the country:

- Mexicans identify with their family (which North Americans call extended family) and friends. Mexicans take vacation all together, as a family. Typically, several siblings, their spouses, their children, and their common parents will all go on vacation together. Such vacation plans cannot be changed easily because so many people are involved. As a result, last-minute business needs that may take precedence over such plans in North America (like the visit of an executive or client coming from overseas) are unlikely to do so in Mexico.

- Japanese, particularly those who work for one of the large corporations (e.g., Sony, Honda, Toyota), identify with their company—they are "Honda people," for example. Japanese hardly ever criticize the decisions made by their company and are often shocked when North Americans do so. If the company requires them to go overseas, the need of the company is likely to take precedence over family needs, and they will likely go where the company wants to send them.

- Somalis identify with their clan. In Toronto, Somalis want to live near other members of their clan. They would rather live in the apartment buildings located in the part of the city where other Somalis live and commute extensive distances than live in a house in the suburbs near their place of work.

Individualism is a key component of many cross-cultural management studies (Hofstede, 1980; Trompenaars, 1998). In his study of IBM subsidiaries around the world, Hofstede (1980) created a measure of individualism, thereby enabling a comparison of 40 national cultures on this scale. Exhibit 3.1 represents graphically the individualism scores of the 40 countries covered by Hofstede's study.

Exhibit 3.1 shows that individuals and groups around the world have a wide range of attitudes. As in the case of power distance, there is no absolute right or wrong on this scale: A country with a score of 80 is not better or worse than a country with a score of 20; it is

Exhibit 3.1

Individualism scores of 40 countries. High scores correspond to individualistic countries. Conversely, collectivistic countries have low scores on this chart. Adapted from Hofstede (1980).

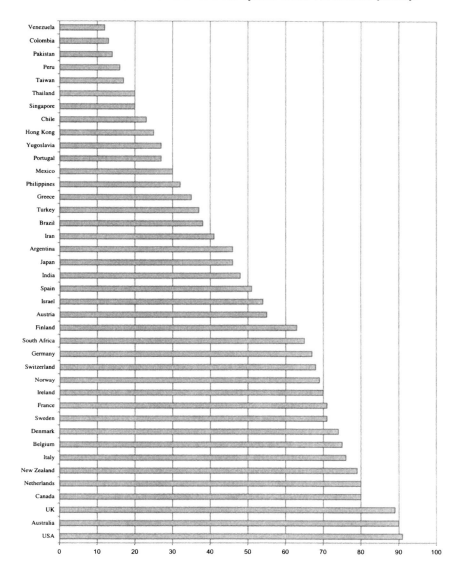

simply different. There is, however, a relative right and wrong: Using an individualistic style of management (like the American management style) in a collectivistic country (like Japan) will usually not yield much result, and vice versa.

On this scale, a difference of 20 can be considered meaningful: For example, most Americans who go on expatriate assignments in countries that have scores lower than 70 (e.g., France, Japan, China) will notice a significant difference in this area. In most cases, they will need to modify their managerial style to some extent to achieve their professional objectives in these countries.

The United States is the most individualistic country in the world and Canada is not far behind it. As Appendix A shows, most recent immigrants come from countries that are significantly more collectivistic than Canada and the United States. Exhibit 3.2 illustrates some

Exhibit 3.2

Language, achievement, decision making, and friendships as a function of individualism.

	Individualistic	Collectivistic
Language	• Extensive use of "I" • Frequent reference to person and personal accomplishments	• Extensive use of "We" • Frequent reference to the group and group accomplishments • Often alludes to or explains his or her position within the group
Achievement	• People succeed of their own initiative ("self-made man").	• People succeed or fail as a group.
Decisions	• Based on own area of responsibility. This area of responsibility may be a whole project, in which case the responsibilities will span several areas. • People responsible for other areas need to speak up if a decision affects them aversely. • Decisions tend to be made by specific individuals.	• Based on whole group • Everyone is expected to consider the impact of decisions on everyone else. • Within a group, decisions tend to be made by the group through consensus (hierarchy may distort this rule).
Friendships	• Friendships are often short-lived.	• Friendships tend to last longer.

of the differences that may be observed in the workplace related to individualism.

Individualism can be seen at play in the following situation: Two people enter a restaurant where only one table is occupied; where will the maitre d'hotel sit them? In the United States, the maitre d'hotel is likely to sit them away from the occupied table (the assumption being that people want to be alone). In France and other collectivistic countries, the maitre d'hotel is likely to sit them near the occupied table (the assumption is that people want to be together).

Individualism also has a major impact in many professional arenas, including the response to inequities and the sense of responsibility. In collectivistic countries, responsibilities belong to the group. For example, a Canadian engineer managing an automotive parts plant in Mexico said that, when he asked who is responsible for a given task, the response was invariably the name of a department, like "The maintenance department," rather than the name of a person, like "Carlos" or "Maria."

By contrast, responsibilities in individualistic countries are individual. More important, as far as individualistic people are concerned, responsibilities cannot be shared. In individualistic countries, a responsibility that belongs to everyone belongs to nobody—and nobody will take care of it.

When an organization acts against the interests of its members unfairly, individualistic and collectivistic employees are likely to respond in different ways. Individualistic employees are more likely to initiate a lawsuit against the organization, whereas collectivistic employees are more likely to initiate a strike.

Individualism can also be observed in the layout of offices: Individualistic people tend to prefer having their own space (even if it is small), whereas collectivistic people prefer sharing offices with other people. Japanese offices, with one floor containing up to 100 desks without any separation, offers a stark contrast to the cubicle or individual office environment commonly used in North American organizations.

Because teamwork is about work performed by a group of people, teams made of individualistic people and teams made of collectivistic people operate according to different principles.

Individualistic Teams

In individualistic countries, team members are expected to be experts in their own technical areas and to take care of their own tasks and responsibilities. Roles are clearly defined, and the boundaries between the responsibilities of individual team members are sharp.

The motto of such teams can be summarized by "If we each take good care of our own area of responsibility and follow the plan, we will all achieve our objectives." Exhibit 3.3 shows a schematic representation of a team composed of individualistic members.

In such a team, one of the first questions that individualistic team members ask during their "kick-off" meeting is: "Who is responsible for what?" Work cannot start without team members having a precise answer to this question. In essence, the first step of an individualistic team consists in breaking down something collectivistic (like a project) into individual roles and responsibilities.

Throughout the life of the team, information is exchanged, both within the team and between the team and the outside world. Individualistic team members typically share more information with their teammates than with outsiders; however, because they see themselves as individuals first and as team members second, these information flows are of comparable magnitude. For example, if the information flow between team members has a magnitude of 5, the information flow between team members and the outside may have a magnitude of 3.

In an individualistic team, team members are expected to take care of their own responsibilities and not interfere with others' areas of

Exhibit 3.3

Schematic representation of a team composed of individualistic members. Each letter represents a team member. Arrows represent the quantity of information exchanged between team members and between team members and the outside.

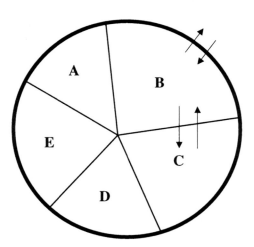

responsibilities. In particular, they are expected to refrain from commenting on other team members' tasks and progress, particularly if this team member is present. If someone outside the team asks a difficult question to one team member, other team members do not volunteer a response unless they are asked.

One of the key differences between individualistic teams and collectivistic teams lies in the actions expected of team members when they consider that one of the tasks under the jurisdiction of one of their teammates is not done as they think it should be. For example, let's consider an American team and let's assume that Charlie (represented by C in Exhibit 3.4) is responsible for collecting data. Let's also assume

Exhibit 3.4

(a) B is concerned that C will miss the deadline. First, B talks to C; this discussion will likely take place one-on-one. (b) If talking to C does not alleviate his or her concerns, B talks to the team leader.

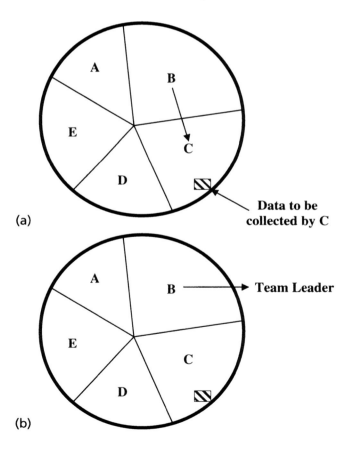

that Bob (represented by B in Exhibit 3.4) will use this data in his report, to be delivered to the final client. Finally, let's assume that Bob believes that Charlie will not complete his experiments on time.

In this case, as in real life, it does not matter whether Charlie has things under control or not: As far as Bob is concerned, Charlie will not have the results by the scheduled date; this perception is his reality. What will Bob do?

The most likely first reaction of Bob will be to talk to Charlie one-on-one (see Exhibit 3.4a). During this conversation, Bob will ask Charlie how the data collection is going, whether it is on schedule, and whether Bob can expect to receive the results by the scheduled date. If Charlie answers that everything is under control, Bob cannot do much more in this case (because any further questions would likely become an interference in Charlie's responsibilities) and will likely stop the conversation. At most, Bob will stress the importance of these results for his report.

If, after this conversation, Bob still has concerns about Charlie's task completion date, Bob's next step will consist of talking to Sally, the team leader (see Exhibit 3.4b). In this conversation, Bob will update Sally on his progress and mention the fact that the data Charlie is collecting are critical to Bob's report. Bob will likely say something like: "If I do not receive this data by the due date, I will not be able to complete my report by the end of the month, so the team will be late in delivering to the client."

To an individualistic team leader, the message is clear: "I have concern about this. I cannot do anything because it is outside my jurisdiction. Because you have overall responsibility for the output of the team, I suggest you look into this—you and I know that the client will blame you if the report is late." Depending on Sally's assessment of Charlie's progress, she may go talk to Charlie to find out how things are going and ensure that he really has everything under control.

Gender does not play a major role here. The dynamics of this team would be essentially the same if Beverly, Carol, and Sam replaced Bob, Charlie, and Sally.

Collectivistic Teams

In collectivistic countries, the motto of teams is "One for all, and all for one." Team members have general areas of expertise; however, the boundaries between these areas are not as clearly delineated as they are in individualistic countries. Tasks are not considered the responsibility

Exhibit 3.5

Schematic representation of a team composed of collectivistic members. In this figure, each letter represents a team member. *Arrows* represent the quantity of information exchanged between team members and between team members and the outside.

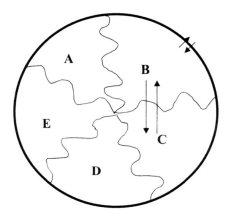

of an individual, but of the team. Exhibit 3.5 shows a schematic representation of a team composed of collectivistic members.

In a collectivistic team, team members are expected to provide support and to cover for one another. Being part of a team implies a significant amount of involvement and commitment to one's teammates. Therefore, one of the first questions that members of a newly formed collectivistic team ask during their "kick-off" meeting is: "Who is part of the team? Who is not?" In essence, team members want to determine how far their commitment stretches.

As in the case of individualistic teams, collectivistic team members exchange information both with other team members and with the outside. Because a collectivistic team is "One for all, and all for one," members of collectivistic teams tend to share a large amount of information with their team members; in order to provide effective support to one another, team members need to know what is going on at all times.

By contrast, a collectivistic team provides less information to the outside than an individualistic team; the goal here is to keep the team from airing its dirty laundry in public. As a result, the flow of information within a collectivistic team is often of a much higher magnitude than the flow of information from the team to the outside. The difference between collectivistic teams and individualistic teams in this area is often striking to both sides:

- In an individualistic team, the flow of information within the team may be rated at 5 and the flow between the team and the outside may be rated at 3.
- In a collectivistic team, the flow of information within the team may be rated at 10 and the flow between the team and the outside may be rated at 1.

In a collectivistic team, team members are expected to take care of one another. For example, if someone outside the team asks a difficult question to a team member, other members of the team are expected to help find a suitable answer. Whether the person answering the question is responsible for the area in question is not important; the important point is that the team as a whole has provided a satisfactory answer.

Let's look now at a collectivistic team (e.g., a Mexican team) where Carlos (represented by C in Exhibit 3.6a) is responsible for collecting data. Let's assume that Juan (represented by B in Exhibit 3.6a) needs the results of Carlos's experiments for his report. Finally, let's assume that Juan believes that Carlos will miss the scheduled completion date. What will Juan do?

The most likely first reaction of Juan will also be to talk to Carlos. During one of the team meetings, Juan will ask Carlos how his experiments are going and mention the importance of this data for his report. He will likely offer to help Carlos, either by working with him on the experiments or by taking over some other tasks that Carlos needs to do so that Carlos can concentrate on these experiments. If these experimental results are really important to Juan and he needs this information urgently, Juan is likely to start helping Carlos immediately, whether Carlos has requested help or not (Exhibit 3.6b). This help matches Carlos's expectation that team members need to support one another in all circumstances—all for one, and one for all.

Mixed Individualistic–Collectivistic Teams

When a team contains both collectivistic and individualistic members (see Exhibit 3.7), the behaviors of individualistic team members are often misinterpreted by collectivistic team members, and vice versa.

As far as individualistic team members are concerned, the information flow between collectivistic team members is excessively high. They

Exhibit 3.6

(a) B is concerned that C will miss the deadline. First, B talks to C during one of the team meetings. (b) If talking to C does not alleviate his or her concerns, B offers help or jumps in and starts helping immediately.

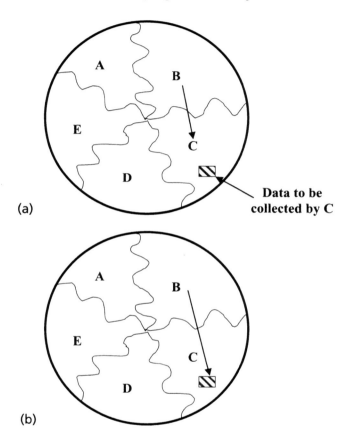

(a)

Data to be collected by C

(b)

receive far more information than they consider necessary from their collectivistic teammates. For example, they are copied on numerous e-mail messages that they consider irrelevant to their work. As a result, individualistic team members often consider their collectivistic teammates to be inconsiderate of their time. In some cases, they "tune out" their collectivistic teammates by ignoring their e-mail or voice-mail messages.

Collectivistic team members consider that they do not receive enough information from their individualistic colleagues. They would like to know more about what these people are working on, what

Exhibit 3.7

Schematic representation of a team made of individualistic (B and C) and collectivistic (A, D, and E) members. *Arrows* represent the quantity of information exchanged between team members and between team members and the outside.

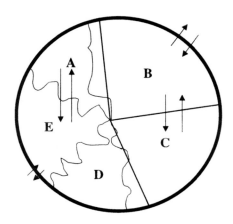

progress they have made, what new information they have gathered, and so on. The insufficient amount of information they receive often leads collectivistic team members to conclude that their individualistic teammates are in it for themselves, but not for the team. They are not *sharing* enough information.

Many North American organizations have an information-sharing policy that is structured on a "need-to-know" basis. Such a policy does not provide enough information for team members to determine what information they should share. Both collectivistic and individualistic team members are sharing information that they think others need to know, but their standards for "need to know" are different.

In some organizations, teams are expected to determine who is *Responsible* for making a specific decision, who needs to *Agree* with this decision, who needs to be *Consulted*, and who needs to be *Informed* (RACI). In teams that include both collectivistic and individualistic members, this process is likely to yield an extensive discussion. Relative to their individualistic teammates, collectivistic team members are likely to expect that decisions are made by the team rather than one person and that more people need to be involved and to a greater extent. For example, individualistic team members may think that someone only needs to be informed of the decision, whereas collectivistic team members believe that the same person needs to be consulted.

Exhibit 3.8

Schematic representation of an American–French team, in which Bernard considers that Charlie's experiments are not progressing fast enough. Bernard first talks to Charlie during a team meeting, then Bernard jumps in and helps.

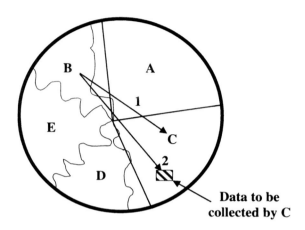

Data to be
collected by C

The frustration experienced by team members with respect to information flow acts, in many cases, as background for the team breakdown when the situation examined earlier (where one team member considers that another team member is not performing a task as it should be performed) takes place across cultural boundaries. As the following scenarios illustrate, the original misunderstanding does not really matter; in the end, the team breaks into two or more subteams along cultural fault lines. Here is how this happens in the case of a French–American team.

First, let's start with the situation where Bernard, a French—collectivistic—team member, considers that Charlie, an American—individualistic—team member, will be late in completing his experiments (Exhibit 3.8). Bernard needs Charlie's experimental results for his report. As any good French team member would do, Bernard talks to Charlie during the team meeting, asking how the experiments are progressing and offering Charlie his help. If Charlie's experimental results are critical to Bernard, Bernard is likely to start helping Charlie right away; for example, Bernard might start collecting some of the data or doing some of the literature search himself.

From Charlie's perspective, this behavior is totally unacceptable. Bernard's questions during the team meeting are likely to put him on the spot and make him feel defensive. Bernard's offer to help or, worse, his jumping in and helping when help was declined are tantamount to publicly questioning Charlie's ability to do his job and his professionalism. This action is a major offense for Charlie, who is likely to react negatively to this interference in his area of responsibility. As far as Charlie is concerned, Bernard is a poor team player who cannot be trusted. From this incident forward, Charlie will restrict the flow of information to Bernard in order to avoid giving Bernard another chance to meddle in his work.

As the experience of the Canadian engineer working in a French research laboratory demonstrates, the desire to help other team members is strong in collectivistic team members. For them, the fact that one of their teammates does not want any help is difficult to comprehend.

In a team that includes several Americans, Charlie is likely to go out for a beer with his American teammates and tell them about the difficulties he recently encountered with Bernard. During this conversation, his American colleagues are likely to talk about their own challenges in working with their French teammates. As a result, slowly but surely, the Americans agree that working with French technical professionals is really difficult and not worth the effort. People start making comments like, "The team would make progress much faster if we did not have to deal with these crazy French!" American team members will try to push the important tasks toward themselves to make sure that these tasks are "done right." The American team members are creating their own subteam; information is readily shared within this subteam, but is not shared readily with the French teammates.

The reverse situation yields essentially the same outcome (Exhibit 3.9). In this case, Bob (American) considers that Christian (French) will be late in completing his experiments. Bob needs Christian's experimental results for his report. As any good American team member would do, Bob talks to Christian one-on-one, asking how the experiments are progressing and whether he will receive the results by the scheduled completion date.

If Bob finds the response unsatisfactory, his next step will be to talk to the team leader. When the team leader talks to Christian about his progress, Christian will quickly connect that event with the conversation he and Bob had earlier and realize that Bob talked to the team leader about his progress. From Christian's perspective, this behavior is totally unacceptable, as unacceptable to him as Bernard's behavior is to Charlie. Christian considers that Bob reported him to the team leader and stabbed him in the back. The reaction is strong. As far as Christian is concerned, Bob is a poor team player who cannot be

Exhibit 3.9

Schematic representation of an American–French team, where Bob considers that Christian is not progressing on his report fast enough. Bob first talks to Christian, then talks to the team leader.

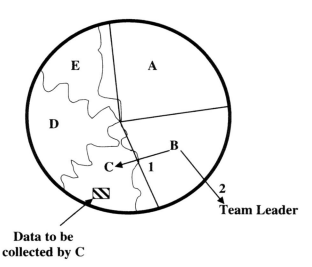

Data to be
collected by C

trusted. From this incident forward, Christian will restrict the flow of information to Bob in order to avoid giving Bob another opportunity to talk to the team leader about his lack of progress.

In a team that includes several French teammates, Christian is likely to go out for lunch with his French teammates and tell them about the difficulties he has recently encountered with Bob. During this conversation, his French colleagues are likely to talk about their own challenges in working with their American teammates. The reactions and comments will be the mirror image of the comments made by their American teammates over a beer: "The team would progress much faster if we did not have to deal with these crazy Americans!" The French team members will try to push the important tasks toward themselves, to make sure that these tasks are "done right." As a result, slowly but surely, the French are creating their own subteam; information is readily shared within the subteam, but is not shared easily with the American teammates.

Whether the starting point comes from a French offending an American or an American offending a French person, the result is the same: In the end, the team has split into two subteams, one American and one French. The two subteams communicate as little as possible and may actually compete with one another. At that point, outside intervention is urgently needed to avoid further loss of time and resources and prevent the team from breaking down altogether.

In situations where the team is made of people coming from the same cultural background with a single exception, the team break-down initially proceeds along the same path. For example, if the team is made of several American and one Mexican technical professionals, the team breakdown starts when the Mexican team member starts "interfering" with one of his or her American teammates' area of responsibility. At this point, the American team members will start forming a subteam; in this case, the subteam is the team minus the Mexican team member. The Mexican team member is slowly ostra-cized. Team breakdown is final when the activities and ideas of the Mexican team member are completely ignored and considered irrele-vant by his or her American colleagues.

Moving Quickly in the Right Direction

Multicultural technical teams have one important function: They need to collect data and information in order to make or help man-agement make decisions. But how much data and what kind of data are needed? There are huge variations on this theme around the world; these variations are one of the leading causes of tension within multi-cultural technical teams. At the same time, they are one of the leading areas for potential synergies.

Risk Tolerance

The future is unknown; this is a fundamental fact of human life. However, the way people deal with this fact depends on their cultural backgrounds: In risk-tolerant countries, people cope well with risky situations where the outcome is unknown and difficult to predict. They are used to unstructured situations and like it that way. By contrast, people from risk-averse countries do not enjoy and are usually uncom-fortable in risky situations. Risk-averse cultures react to the uncer-tainty of the future by creating rules and structures that make (or at least attempt to make) life more predictable. Risk-averse people are used to rules and regulations and like it that way.

Hofstede (1980) identified this cultural dimension, which he called "uncertainty avoidance," in his study of IBM subsidiaries around the world. He created a measure of uncertainty avoidance that enables a comparison of countries around the world on this scale. In order to show graphically how much risk people can tolerate, the scale used in Exhibit 3.10 shows the risk tolerance score of a country, which is 100 minus the uncertainty avoidance score of that country.

Exhibit 3.10

Risk tolerance scores of 40 countries. High scores correspond to risk-tolerant countries. Conversely, risk-averse countries have low scores. Adapted from Hofstede (1980).

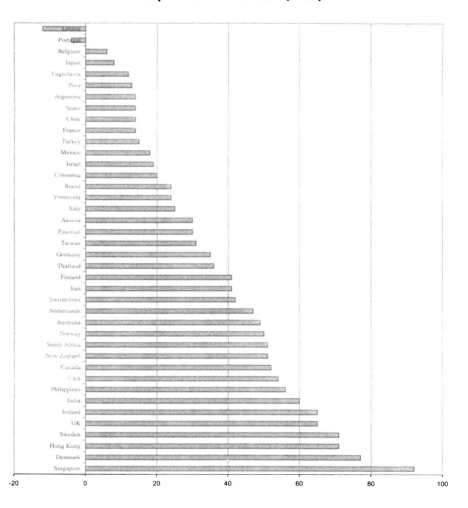

Exhibit 3.10 shows that people around the world have a wide range of attitudes toward risk. As in the case of power distance and individualism, there is no absolute right or wrong on this scale: A country with a score of 80 is not better or worse than a country with a score of 20; it is simply different.

There is, however, a relative right and wrong: In the workplace, at the individual level, risk tolerance translates into the following question: "How much information do I (we) need in order to ensure that I am (we are) making the right decision?" Making decisions the North American way in Hong Kong will usually seem conservative, whereas it will likely be considered reckless in Japan. As on the individualism and power-distance scales, a difference of 20 can be considered meaningful.

As Exhibit 3.11 suggests, risk tolerance has a major impact on the financial sector of a country: In countries where people do not tolerate risk easily, insurance companies tend to flourish; Germany, France, and Japan, for example, have developed larger insurance companies relative to their economic sizes than the United States and the UK. By contrast, selling insurance is more difficult in countries where people have a much higher risk tolerance.

Risk-tolerant people tend to invest more in the stock market and similar forms of investments that carry the prospect of higher returns at the expense of higher risks, whereas risk-averse people tend to invest in more secure places. In risk-averse countries such as Mexico, the most common form of investment is real estate because "no matter what happens to the stock market, real estate will always be there."

Exhibit 3.11

Planning, vacations, finances, and stress as a function of risk tolerance.

	Risk Averse	Risk Tolerant
Planning	• Plans over a longer horizon. • Includes more contingencies in plans.	• Plans over a shorter horizon. • Includes fewer contingencies in plans.
Vacations	• Plans vacations well in advance.	• Prefers spur-of-the-moment vacation plans.
Finances	• Avoids incurring debt. • Buys more insurance products. • Invests in more secure products, even if the return is lower. • Sets aside a higher percentage of income for savings. • Venture capital is less developed.	• Debt is not a major issue. • Buys fewer insurance products. • Invests in higher-return products, even if the return is not guaranteed. • Sets aside a lower percentage of income for savings. • Venture capital is extensively developed.
Stress	• Background stress level is generally higher.	• Background stress level is generally lower.

Conversely, venture capitalism is more developed in risk-tolerant countries.

Risk tolerance also has a significant impact on organizational structure: Institutions and organizations in risk-averse societies have clear structures, strong codes of behavior, and standardized management practices. They tolerate less deviation from these structures, but in return they tend to support their employees extensively. For example, French employees have a strong need to know where they fit in the organization. French labor law mandates that organizations keep their organizational charts up to date. When an American expatriate in France overlooked this fact and published an incomplete organizational chart, the French employees who did not find their names concluded that they were about to be fired or laid off. They talked to their union representatives, who started to work toward a strike.

Organizations in risk-tolerant societies encourage individual employees to take initiative and risks. Employees have the freedom to do their own thing, but are given little support if things go wrong. An extreme example of this situation was the robotic company that Isaac Asimov imagined in his science fiction novels, where "an employee never made the same mistake twice—he [or she] was fired the first time."

How Much Information Do We Need?

In the workplace, tolerance to risk translates directly into the amount of information needed to ensure that one is making a good decision. People educated in risk-tolerant countries are used to making decisions with less information than people educated in risk-averse countries. The following paragraphs show some examples of these differences as they apply to technical professionals.

Japan is a country where risk tolerance is fairly low relative to North America. As a result, becoming an approved supplier of a large Japanese company usually takes significantly longer than becoming an approved supplier of one of its North American counterparts. It often takes automotive part suppliers two to three years of formal and informal meetings, during which they provide extensive data, information, and samples and create a network of trusting relationships between the Japanese organization and theirs. Some of the technical information requested by Japanese prospects seems completely irrelevant to their North American counterparts (Gercik, 1996).

By contrast, Hong Kong has a much higher tolerance for risk than North America. In Hong Kong, two businesspeople may meet for the first time and sign a contract worth several million dollars over lunch, based primarily on a good recommendation by a joint business friend and good chemistry. For example, a Mexican businessperson who had built a good reputation for himself in Hong Kong obtained large orders for instant chicken bouillon after presenting appropriate samples to Hong Kong prospects.

Exhibit 3.12 represents graphically the amount of information that people from two different cultures (such as Japanese and Americans) usually need to make a given decision. For example, let's assume that an American company and a Japanese company are considering forming a joint venture. Japanese managers involved in such transactions are likely to gather significantly more information about their U.S. counterparts, their technology, their reputation, and so on compared with the American managers involved in the same transactions, as represented by the different sizes of the two circles. This does not apply to all areas: American managers usually need significantly more information than their Japanese counterparts when it comes to legal matters.

In addition to collecting information on a wider range of topics, risk-averse people tend to insist on higher precision and accuracy on the data they collect. By contrast, risk-tolerant people often work with more approximate numbers. For example, where a risk-tolerant

Exhibit 3.12

Comparing graphically the amount of information needed (on average) by American and Japanese managers before making a decision.

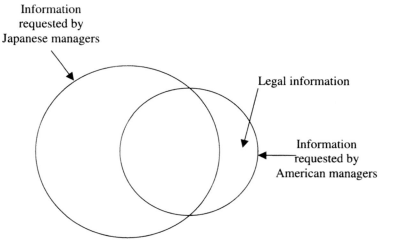

engineer might say that the material goes through approximately 1,200 degrees of turn on either side while traveling on an assembly line, a risk-averse engineer might say that it goes through 1,140 degrees of rotation on the top side and 1,230 degrees on the bottom side.

Many misunderstandings arise when people from different cultural backgrounds ask for information in an area that is not important in one's culture. In that situation, people may react by dismissing the request, in which case no information is provided, or by answering it summarily, sending only part of the information or sending it inappropriately (e.g., handwritten note on a quick fax, when the requester expects a formal letter). This response usually generates a negative reaction; because the request is not taken seriously, the requester may read into the response that he or she is not considered seriously. When this phenomenon is repeated, team members start wondering whether other team members are serious about reaching the team objective. "How can we achieve our objectives if they will not give us the data we need? Are we really part of the same team?"

Solving Problems

Hofstede (1997) points out that "grand theories are more likely to be conceived within strong uncertainty avoidance cultures than in weak ones." As Appendix C shows, the courses that students need to take in order to become technical professionals vary significantly from country to country.

In risk-tolerant countries, technical studies tend to emphasize the practical aspects of their professions. Education is hands-on and includes a greater amount of internships and on-the-job training. Students learn to focus on getting things to work, even if they do not have a complete understanding of why and how they do.

In risk-averse countries, technical studies tend to emphasize the theoretical aspects of their professions. Technical education generally includes a large amount of mathematics and limited on-the-job training. Students learn to focus on getting a solid understanding of the fundamentals of technical problems.

There is a strong affinity in risk-averse countries for "unifying theories" (i.e., theories that encompass all aspects of a particular field). Obviously, this requires a fair amount of theoretical work that may or may not be worthwhile depending on the circumstances (it may be more valued in an academic setting than in a product development center). In this search for unifying theories, risk-averse people tend to look for underlying trends and patterns; as such, they may have developed this skill to a greater extent than risk-tolerant people and may identify patterns in the data or system that do not exist for their risk-tolerant counterparts. At the same time, looking for overall patterns and general trends may lead them to overlook important pieces of information and data that may not fit patterns and trends.

This difference in approach to technical studies is reflected in the approach to solving technical problems. In risk-tolerant countries, technical professionals faced with a complex problem will usually start with trying things out on the system itself, using their previous experience with similar systems as a guide. If this does not yield satisfactory results quickly or if it is impractical, the next step often consists of creating a "quick-and-dirty" numerical model, or building a small-scale version of the system (bench scale or pilot unit). If this does not work, more complex tools (e.g., differential equations, Pareto analysis, fishbone diagrams) are employed to help determine what is going on inside the system in detail.

In risk-averse countries, problem solving often starts with a complete problem analysis, from a theoretical standpoint. What variables may affect the system? The next step may consist of writing the differential equations that govern the system in order to solve them analytically (when possible) or numerically (when no analytical solution can be found). Experimentation on the actual system or a small-scale version may be used; in that case, this is usually done through designed experiments with many variables.

A good example of the difference in approach to solving technical problems is the proficiency that Japanese engineers and scientists have in using statistical data analysis and designed experiments, which is generally much higher than their North American counterparts. When they are faced with a specific technical problem, Japanese technical people make a list of all the variables that may influence the outcome and study these variables at the same time. They often end up using designed experiments with anywhere from 7 to 12 variables. By contrast, North American technical people faced with the same list of variables will generally eliminate some of them based on experience and reduce the list down to a few (three or four at most) variables, thereby eliminating the need for extensive designed experiments and statistical analysis.

Mixed Risk-Tolerant–Risk-Averse Teams

In multicultural teams that include people with significantly different levels of risk tolerance, tension and misunderstandings often occur when a significant decision needs to be made. The more risk-averse team members will push the rest of the team toward making sure that the team is making the right decision. They often ask for more data and further studies before a conclusion can be reached. They see their more risk-tolerant teammates as "shooting from the hip" and making risky decisions.

By contrast, the more risk-tolerant team members will push the rest of the team toward making decisions faster. They consider that their risk-averse teammates are "gathering data for the sake of gathering data" and see them as overly conservative; in extreme cases, they will go as far as calling them "anal retentive" (Gercik, 1996).

Misunderstandings may also arise when risk-tolerant and risk-averse technical professionals are trying to solve a given problem together. The theoretical/comprehensive approach that risk-averse team members take appears to be a complete waste of time to their risk-tolerant colleagues ("We will never get there by writing differential equations or by performing a 12-variable designed experiment. It will take years!"). Meanwhile, the risk-averse team members consider that the practical approach of their risk-tolerant teammates is akin to a "walk in the dark, where people may stumble on the right solution but will not be able to reapply it tomorrow on another similar system."

In addition, the desire for a high level of precision and accuracy displayed by risk-averse technical professionals is perceived as "splitting hairs" and wasting time by their risk-tolerant colleagues. Conversely, risk-tolerant technical professionals are perceived by their risk-averse colleagues as unprofessional because they are not trying to provide accurate and precise information (e.g., slightly different numbers may be provided for the same parameter).

The tension and misunderstandings resulting from differences in risk tolerance can lead to the breakdown of multicultural teams through the following process:

- Because convincing their risk-averse teammates to move forward takes a lot of time and usually involves additional collection of data that they consider unnecessary, risk-tolerant team members start making decisions without involving the whole team.

- Because convincing their risk-tolerant members to collect more information is challenging, risk-averse members go ahead and collect the data they think is necessary, without discussing it with their risk-tolerant teammates. This way, they will have all the data they consider necessary when it's time for the team to make a decision.

Obviously, neither behavior contributes to building trust within the team, which may split over time into different subteams, as in the case of individualism.

Context

Context is "the information that surrounds an event; it is inextricably bound up with the meaning of that event" (Hall, 1990). Context includes the collection of social and cultural conditions that surround and influence that event. As discussed in the next chapter, context has a major impact on communication. It also has a major impact on how people read a given event.

In high-context cultures, a higher proportion of the attention is placed on the surrounding circumstances of an event. In the case of a team in its initial stages, high-context team members will consider who is part of the team, where and when they meet for the first time, and who introduces the team members and gives them their mandate. These pieces of information will be read as cues to the importance of the project assigned to the team and its probability of success. In low-context cultures, circumstances surrounding the event itself are given significantly less weight. The primary message of the event is in the words that were spoken. Low-context cultures tend to focus on the message to be delivered to the other person.

Countries around the world can be placed on a relative scale ranging from high context to low context, with Japan and many Far Eastern countries at the high end of the scale and Switzerland and Germany occupying the other end (Exhibit 3.13). Note that the words "high" and "low" do not imply any value judgment here: A high-context culture is neither better nor worse than a low-context culture; it is simply different.

When a team gets started, low-context people tend to get down to business quickly. Low-context introductions generally consist of a name, company or department, and position. This information is usually sufficient for low-context people to get started. Although relationships and more detailed knowledge of one another may develop over time, they are likely to be considered byproducts of the project; they are by no means a requirement for the team to do its work.

By contrast, high-context people tend to provide (and require) far more information about their counterparts before they can place them in their proper context. High-context introductions during team "kick-off" meetings usually include degrees, alma mater, work history, number of direct and indirect reports, travel(s) to the countries of their counterparts, and so on. Introductory meetings often include discus-

Exhibit 3.13

Comparison of various cultures around the world on the context scale.

High context

Far East (Japan, China, etc.)

Indian subcontinent

Arab countries

Latin America

Eastern Europe

Latin Europe, UK, Quebec

English Canada

US

Scandinavia

Germany

Switzerland

Low context

sions of topics such as the economic, political, and social situation or the arts, history, and culture of the team members' countries. High-context people will also often ask whether their teammates are married, have children, have siblings, and so on. All of this information is useful to high-context people in order to get a sense of their counterparts and place them in their proper context. Here is the experience of a Canadian engineer working in Corsica (the French island where Napoleon was born):

> Corsican introductions are always a source of amazement for me. When two Corsicans meet for the first time, they start the conversation by determining how closely related they are. They both go through their genealogical tree (every Corsican knows his or her ancestors and parents, going back several generations, both upwards and sideways), the cities they grew up in, their friends, their connections, etc. Sometimes, it feels to me that they are going back all the way to Moses. This animated discussion will last anywhere from 30 seconds to 10 minutes; it usually ends when they have found a common point (a common friend, a common distant

relative, etc.). Then they turn their attention to the transaction that brought them together in the first place. Sometimes, they spend more time on finding this common point than on doing the transaction. One day, I asked a Corsican why they go through these preliminary discussions. Her answer was immediate: "I need to know how closely related we are in order to know what quality of information I should provide. If the person I talk to is closely related, I will make more of an effort than if the person is a complete stranger."

In a high-context team, establishing some relationship among team members is an essential part of teamwork, particularly at the beginning. Rather than a byproduct, it is a necessary step for the team to take, almost a prerequisite. This is one of the purposes of the extensive introductions and getting to know one another: High-context people test one another to determine the potential for relationships, the breadth of one's knowledge, one's ability to explain oneself, and so on. In essence, they are determining how much of an effort they will make for these people.

When a team includes both high- and low-context members, misunderstandings are likely: Low-context people want to get going before high-context people have had a chance to gather the information they need about one another. This misunderstanding can start the whole team on the wrong foot, as the anecdotes mentioned earlier indicate.

Evolution of Multicultural Teams

So far, we have examined how cultural differences impact the dynamics of technical teams. In the remainder of this section, we examine how this impact is felt at different stages in the life of a team. We first look at how a team evolves over time, then examine how differences in individualism, context, risk tolerance, and power distance may affect the evolution of a multicultural team.

Life of a Team

Drexler and Sibbett (1999) have created a model that describes the seven stages that most teams go through as they move from the first encounters to the end of the project. In order to move from one stage to the next, teams need to answer the critical question that pertains to this stage.

In the case of multicultural teams, an additional step needs to be included upfront, namely the selection of team members, resulting in the following eight-stage model (Exhibit 3.14):

Exhibit 3.14

The critical questions that need to be addressed at each stage in a team's life. Answering the question to the satisfaction of team members enables the team to move on to the next stage; not finding a suitable answer often sends the team back one or more stages, as in the "chutes and ladders" (or "snakes and ladders") game. Adapted from Drexler and Sibbet (1999).

Stage	Critical Question	Resolved	Unresolved
Selection	Who is needed?	Team composition, membership	Void, incomplete team
Orientation	Why am I here?	Purpose, personal fit	Disorientation, uncertainty
Trust Building	Who are you?	Mutual regard and respect, forthrightness, spontaneous interaction	Caution, mistrust, facade
Goal and Role Clarification	What are we doing?	Explicit assumptions, clear and integrated goals, identified roles	Apathy, skepticism, irrelevant competition
Commitment	How will we do it?	Shared vision, allocation, organizational decisions	Dependence, resistance
Implementation	Who does what, when, and where?	Clear processes, alignment, disciplined execution	Conflict, confusion, nonalignment, missed deadlines
High Performance	Just do it!	Flexibility, intuitive communication, synergy	Overload, disharmony
Renewal	Why continue?	Recognition, change mastery, staying power	Boredom, burnout

1. *Selection.* This stage takes place before the first team meeting, when the idea of having a team is still going through people's minds. Who will attend the first team meeting? Who is expected to be part of the team? Who makes the decision about the team composition? These are critical questions to answer at this stage.

2. *Orientation.* During the first encounters, all team members want to know why they are part of this new team. They wonder what the team objectives are, who is part of the team, and what each member will be expected to contribute.

3. *Trust Building.* Team members need to learn about their teammates and determine their strengths, their limitations, and the extent to which they can be trusted.

4. *Goal and Role Clarification.* As the more detailed work starts, team members start working out the roles and responsibilities of everyone.

5. *Commitment.* At this crucial point, team members commit resources (their own time as well as money and staff from their departments) to the team project.

6. *Implementation.* This is the action stage. Team members implement what they have planned and adjust plans as they progress.

7. *High Performance.* When the team has reached a high level of cohesion and maturity, it can respond flexibly to new challenges and constraints.

8. *Renewal.* When the team has achieved its objective(s), the sense of purpose may be lost. Team members need to revamp the team and redefine its objectives, thereby starting the whole cycle again.

Cultural differences sometimes have a major impact on the progress of teams as they move through these eight stages.

Individualism

Individualism has a major impact throughout the life of the team because people with different views of individualism have different views of what a team is. In particular, individualism has a major impact in the early stages of the team's life.

In individualistic countries, people tend to move quickly through stage 3. Because a team is a collection of individuals all responsible for their own areas, interactions among various team members and their responsibilities are minimized. Creating a team does not require a large amount of trust among team members.

Collectivistic people are expected and expect themselves to make a much larger investment in the team and other members. As a result, the trust building stage (stage 3) usually lasts longer in collectivistic teams than in individualistic teams.

Teams that include both North Americans and more collectivistic people often face a challenge in stage 3. At that point, collectivistic team members often see their individualistic teammates as self-centered, whereas individualistic team members see their collectivistic teammates as sticking their noses in areas where they should not.

North Americans working in more collectivistic countries may be put to the test by their collectivistic colleagues who want to see to what extent they can subordinate their own needs to the group's needs. For example, this test is fairly common in the case of Americans working in Japan (Gercik, 1996).

The degree of individualism of team members also has a significant impact on stages 4, 5, and 6: In individualistic cultures, team members tend to separate roles and responsibilities and compartmentalize their work. They tend to get started before they have fully considered all the interactions among the various tasks that team members will need to accomplish. They tend to move through stages 4 and 5 faster than collectivistic people. In stage 6, the progress of an individualistic team requires many meetings during which team members examine their relative progress and adjust plans when necessary. They use these meetings to synchronize their work, which may be thrown out of sequence by interactions that they had not previously considered. In collectivistic cultures, team members examine the interactions among their tasks extensively during stages 4 and 5. As a result, they tend to move through these stages much slower than individualistic team members. The investment that collectivistic people make during stages 4 and 5 provides return in stage 6: They are usually able to move through the implementation stage faster and with fewer meetings than individualistic people.

Throughout stages 4 and 5, individualistic team members tend to view the extensive discussions related to the interactions among team members' activities as preventing them from moving on, whereas collectivistic team members see these discussions as essential to good team progress. During stage 6, the numerous meetings needed by individualistic team members become a source of frustration for their collectivistic teammates, who see them as preventing real work.

Context

As mentioned earlier, high-context people tend to provide more information about themselves during the orientation phase (stage 2), usually more than low-context people would want to receive. The impact of context extends far beyond the first stage because high- and low-context people follow different tempos throughout the life of their teams.

High-context people tend to make a significant investment of time and energy in their teammates: They want to get to know them to a significant extent before the work can begin in earnest. As a result, the trust-building stage (stage 3) tends to last significantly longer in high-context teams than in low-context teams. High-context teams tend to recover that investment at later stages, when the extensive knowledge each team member has about the others can be used to speed up communication considerably.

Low-context people, by contrast, tend to make a limited investment in time and energy in their teammates. As a result, they move more quickly through stage 3. This higher speed comes at a price, however: Communication within the team requires extensive communication of background information in later stages (see Chapter 4 for more on the differences in communication styles between high- and low-context people).

In a team that includes both high- and low-context members, this difference in tempo and communication style can create significant tension. High-context people are moving more slowly in the early stages of the team's life than their low-context teammates consider reasonable, whereas high-context people believe they do not receive enough information to build trust and create the team cohesion they consider necessary.

Risk Tolerance

Differences in risk tolerance usually become apparent in stages 5 and 6 of the team's life. In risk-averse countries, stage 5 is not about commitment; it is about planning the upcoming implementation. In that stage, team members are visiting and revisiting the overall project and planning extensively for contingencies. They continuously ask "What if?" questions until they believe they have enough information and a solid enough plan to move forward. In risk-tolerant countries, stage 5 is about commitment. Team members are expected to commit to the objectives of the team; how the team gets there is examined during the implementation phase (stage 6).

When a team contains both risk-averse and risk-tolerant members, tension is likely to rise during stage 5, which requires extensive planning for risk-averse team members. In many cases, they consider that their risk-tolerant teammates are rushing them to make commitments about delivering something to the team or the organization before they have a chance to determine how they are going to do it and what their probability of success is. They may experience considerable stress as a result of being caught between a rock and a hard place.

Stage 5 only requires commitment from risk-tolerant team members. In many cases, they consider that their risk-averse teammates are constantly putting the brakes on the team's progress by continuously asking about contingency plans. As far as risk-tolerant team members are concerned, the answer is simple: "We will cross that bridge when we come to it." A commitment to deliver an objective may be made even when the plan to deliver this objective has a low probability of success.

Power Distance

Power distance makes a major difference in stages 1 and 2 (selection and orientation). Indeed, the way teams are formed depends on how hierarchical the organization is: In highly hierarchical countries, team members are selected and assigned by the managers. A highly hierarchical manager may select the team objective, its members, and its leader, then gather everyone in a room and tell them, "Here is the objective; here is the team leader; here are the team members." The team sponsor is usually the person who created the team and the project.

In highly hierarchical countries, teams tend to consist of people at the same level in the organization. Teams that include people at different levels are inherently unstable because the lower-ranking people will have difficulties expressing their opinions to the higher-ranking people, and the higher-ranking people will often overlook the comments made by the lower-ranking people. One of the first questions that hierarchical people will ask during the first meeting is "Who is in charge?" From their perspective, no work can be done until this question has been answered to their satisfaction.

In mildly hierarchical countries, people have more of a chance to volunteer and select their teams and projects. In North America, selection of team members is often done through discussions among individuals, namely the managers and the team leader; how much weight is given to the opinions of these people and who initiates the discussion may vary. In mildly hierarchical countries, there is usually a team leader; however, this may not be explicitly stated during the first few meetings.

In participative countries, team members tend to co-opt one another. The project may have been initiated by someone at a low level in the organization. The team may not have a sponsor and may include members at different levels in the organization; everyone is expected to bring something to the table based on his or her perspective. A small participative team may operate without a leader.

Power distance also plays a critical role in stages 4, 5, and 6, when team members are making decisions regarding the direction the team will take and the way it will follow to get there: In highly hierarchical countries, decisions are often made at high levels in the organization. Technical teams often gather information that is then passed on to the next level for decision making; the team is expected to make a recommendation, but not the final decision. As power distance decreases, teams make more decisions by themselves. When they have made decisions, they usually communicate their decisions to people at higher levels in the organization.

In a team that includes people with different power distances (e.g., Swedes and Canadians, or Americans and Mexicans), team members often perceive one another in the following manner: Less hierarchical team members consider that their hierarchical teammates tend to defer to management and to experts too often. They appear to be kowtowing to higher-ups and never make a decision alone. The insistence that hierarchical people place on knowing upfront who is the team leader often ruffles their feathers—why is this point so important?

Hierarchical team members consider that their less hierarchical teammates are not showing enough respect for management and authority figures. They seem to be questioning management's decisions and to make decisions that are not theirs to make. Hierarchical people often do not understand why their less hierarchical teammates take so much time in answering the question "Who is in charge?"—for them, this is a simple and yet essential question that requires a clear-cut answer.

This difference becomes particularly acute during stage 5 (commitment) because hierarchical people believe they cannot commit resources to the project without referring to the managers, whereas less hierarchical people consider that they can make these commitments on their own. The situation within the team can become quite tense at that point.

At a meeting in stage 5, team members discuss the resources to be allocated to the team. At the end of this discussion, the less hierarchical team members consider that everyone has made a commitment with respect to resources. As far as hierarchical team members are concerned, they have not made a commitment because only the managers can do so. They have a proposal that they submit to the managers.

If the managers of hierarchical team members disagree with the proposal and reduce the resources that are available to the team, the following team meeting yields extensive tension within the team. Less hierarchical team members consider that hierarchical team members have broken their commitments. Trust within the team usually takes a major hit at that point. Combined with other misunderstandings, this situation can lead to a team breakdown.

Finally, situations in which outcomes do not meet expectations are more often handled through blame in hierarchical countries than in participative and mildly hierarchical countries. As a result, hierarchical team members may react to such situations in ways that their less hierarchical teammates consider counterproductive (as in the case of manager–employee relationships, see Chapter 2), and vice versa: Hierarchical team members may produce evidence (in the form of saved e-mail messages, documents, and meeting minutes) that shows that another team member is to blame for the team's shortcomings.

Conversely, less hierarchical teammates appear not to try and learn from their own mistakes; they appear to brush them off and chalk them up to experience, whereas paying a bit more attention could have prevented them (as far as their hierarchical teammates are concerned).

Multicultural teams that include members who are at different levels in the organization need to pay particular attention to power distance. For example, in many jurisdictions throughout North America, health and safety regulations mandate that a Health and Safety Committee be formed, with representatives of both employees and management. In such teams, power distance may create major issues because the intent of these committees is to give everyone a say on how health and safety are managed in the organization. Hierarchical managers may not appreciate the way some less hierarchical employees express their concerns (it may appear to them as disrespectful), whereas hierarchical employees may be afraid of voicing their concerns if doing so leads them to disagree with management.

Multicultural Team Progress

With all of these potential pitfalls at each stage of the way, multicultural teams often struggle through a significant part of their existence. When a team includes only people from similar cultural backgrounds, it is relatively easy for team members to know where the team stands, whether it is making progress, and what remains to be done. Progress is comparatively predictable.

By contrast, the progress of multicultural teams is usually much harder to gauge. The initial stages usually involve a fair amount of rework resulting from misinterpretation of the information provided by team members, their actions, their intentions, and their objectives.

As a result, progress often appears slow initially compared with the progress of culturally homogeneous teams.

When cultural differences are not understood and resolved, the team may continue to function at a low level of effectiveness. Progress is likely not to meet management expectations, and the project is terminated. Team breakdowns often lead to this situation; at that point team members spend so much time disagreeing with one another that the team is not producing much, if anything.

Over time, when the team identifies, understands, and resolves the cultural differences among its members, the effectiveness of the team may take off, as in Exhibit 3.15. At that point, team members start creating new ways of solving problems, and their approach to teamwork positively combines the strengths of each one of them. Such multicultural teams can accomplish a great deal.

Clearly, creating a cohesive multicultural team is easier said than done because so many aspects must be considered. There are, however

---

Exhibit 3.15

Dashed line: **A culturally homogeneous team progresses at a predictable pace.** *Solid line*: **The progress of a multicultural team is often slow and unpredictable at the beginning. (a) It may accelerate as team members learn to work effectively together, or (b) management decides to terminate the project if it does not come together.**

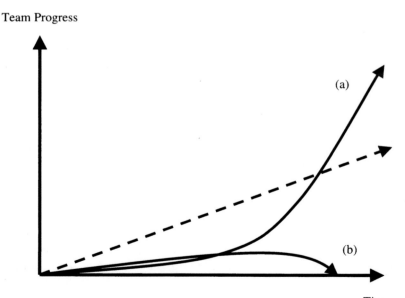

ways to improve the odds of success and to reap the benefits of cultural diversity within a team, as described in the next section.

What Can You Do?

As in the case of power distance and manager–employee relationships, awareness of the potential issues represents half the solution. Once team members are aware of the impact that cultural differences may have on their teams, they can work on identifying the kind of issues their team is facing and on addressing this particular issue (or issues) in the manner described as follows.

The impact of cultural differences on multicultural teams can be examined at two levels: the individual level and the team level. First, we look at the steps the team can take as a whole. We then focus on what team members can do individually when they realize that teammates have significantly different preferences on one of the four scales (i.e., individualism, context, power distance, and risk tolerance) examined so far.

Team Action Steps

This process corresponds to situations where team members recognize that cultural differences are affecting the team's progress; they may then decide to address this issue explicitly. Identification of cultural differences as a potential issue may result from different events: (1) team results may not meet expectations (in terms of deadlines, quality, quantity, or resources needed); (2) the team leader may identify cross-cultural issues and decide to work on them; or (3) team members may identify issues themselves. In any case, the team as a whole may take steps to improve its effectiveness and employ its diversity of thought and experience. Some of these steps apply to all four dimensions, whereas others apply only to specific dimensions.

Finding the Right Balance

At the team level, the key is to balance the needs of different team members. For example, in the early stages of the team's life, the team needs to find a balance between the need for speed and the need for getting to know one another. Where the optimal balance can be reached depends on several factors, such as the following:

- *Team demographics.* Are there more collectivistic team members than individualistic team members?

- *Team leader.* Is the leader a true leader or a coach? Is he or she high or low on the context scale?

- *Personalities and positions of team members.* Some members may be more flexible, more adaptable, more persuasive, or more powerful than others.

- *Organizational culture.* Is the organization as a whole more or less risk tolerant? Is the team part of a joint venture or the result of a merger or an acquisition?

In order to find its center of gravity, the team needs to discuss how it will operate at the same time as it discusses its actual project work. For example, people have implicit expectations of how long the trust-building step (step 2) should take. In North America, the length of this step is often measured in hours; it may take a few days in the case of executive teams resulting from mergers and acquisitions, but no longer. In collectivistic countries, this step may take weeks, months, even years. As a result, there is a need for a mixed collectivistic–individualistic team to discuss upfront how long the team should spend on building trust, how much trust is needed to move forward, and specifically how it will build that trust. Such a discussion is tricky because it ends up taking place before they have had a chance to build trust—facilitation by someone outside the team can make a major difference in this case.

Consider the situation where French and American IT specialists built a go-kart and then had a barbecue, as described earlier in this chapter. This event met the needs of American team members but did not provide any opportunity for French team members to get to know their American colleagues in a way that met their needs. Both needs could have been accommodated by having the go-kart building and driving event followed by an extended sit-down dinner in a fancy restaurant, with no business agenda.

Such discussions, which are the team equivalent of expectation-sharing sessions between managers and employees (see Chapter 2), are usually more productive when they are facilitated by someone who has experienced both kinds of teams and can therefore anticipate the specific types of issues that may arise in this team. Such a person may be an employee who is familiar with these differences because of personal experience or an outside facilitator.

As in the case of manager–employee expectations, team expectations need to be revisited on a regular basis (frequently at first, less frequently as team members get to know one another). This process ensures that new developments are considered by everyone and evaluated consistently by all team members.

An important step that organizations as a whole can take to increase the probability of success of their multicultural teams is to keep the composition of these teams stable over time. Because it takes a while to introduce new members and achieve a working level of team cohesion, changing team members too often can prevent the team from ever getting off the ground.

Power Distance

In the case of multicultural teams that include people at different levels in the organization and different views of hierarchy, it is critical for the team as a whole to establish ground rules regarding participation. Team members may consider the following action steps:

- They may establish the extent to which employees can express their concerns without being disrespectful (or being seen as disrespectful) toward management.

- It can be helpful for team members who have higher positions in the organization to voice their opinions after other team members in lower positions have expressed theirs, so that hierarchical employees are less influenced by the opinions of higher-ups.

- They may also establish as a team what kinds of decisions the team can make on its own, what decisions require making a recommendation to management, and what decisions will be forwarded to the next level in the organization.

To be most effective, these discussions need to examine real-life scenarios, rather than abstract principles, because it is often easy to agree on the guiding principles while disagreeing on how these principles are put into practice. Again, facilitation by someone who has the corresponding experience and who is not a team member can greatly increase the effectiveness of such discussions.

Individual Action Steps

One team member may see that his or her teammates are significantly higher or lower than him or her on the individualism, context, risk tolerance, or power distance scales. In that case, this person may decide to modify his or her approach to teamwork in order to increase the overall team effectiveness. The steps that individual team members can take to bridge the gap between themselves and their teammates are described as follows for each of the scales.

Individualism

If your teammates are more individualistic than you are, you may:

- Focus on your own role and responsibilities and let your teammates take care of their own. Any attempt to influence or help them is likely to be perceived as an intrusion. Wait until you are asked for help to provide it.

- If progress is not what you expect, talk to the team leader focusing on how the lack of progress affects your area of responsibilities. Do not comment on other people's work; defer to them for comments.

- Talk about your personal accomplishments. Learn to separate what the team did from what you did personally. This becomes particularly important if the team leader and/or your manager are also more individualistic than you are.

- Check whether you are providing too much information to your teammates. Ask yourself whether they really need to know what you are going to tell them. How will it help them do their job better?

- Offer your objections to your counterparts' decisions; do not expect them to know how their decisions affect your work.

- You are likely to see interactions among the work of your team mates that they do not see. Determine whether it is worth pointing out these connections to them before acting on this knowledge. When you decide that you should point it out, lead them to the answer through questions. Telling them that they are overlooking something will not work; as far as they are concerned, they are not overlooking anything because this interaction does not exist.

- Expect pressure in the early stages of the team's life for moving on and getting to the next stage faster than you might consider optimal. Later, expect more meetings than you might think necessary. Be patient with your teammates; at the same time, do not hesitate to express your point of view if the pace of the team seems excessively fast.

Conversely, if your teammates are more collectivistic than you are you may:

- Spend more time considering the influence of your actions and decisions on your teammates and their areas of responsibilities. They expect that when you make a decision or suggest a course of action, you balance the needs of the whole team.

- Talk about the team's accomplishments. Learn to put forward what the team did rather than what you did. Beware of taking credit (or being seen as taking credit) for the work of the whole team. Avoid singling out individual accomplishments in public.

- Check whether you are providing enough information to your teammates. Ask yourself whether they would like to have more information on what you do. What additional information might they want to have? Use the information that you receive from them as a guideline for the type of information they would likely want to receive from you.

- Ask your teammates how your decisions affect them; they may not volunteer this information.

- When your teammates make decisions, they are likely to have considered the impact of their decisions on your work. Phrase your questions and concerns carefully to avoid raising their defense mechanisms.

- Your teammates may see interactions among activities that are minor or can be minimized. This may lead them into discussions that are not particularly productive. You can contribute significantly to the team in this area by helping the team move past such hurdles and keeping it going.

- Expect longer discussions during the early stages of the team's life than you might consider optimal. Conversely, expect resistance to frequent update meetings when the team is implementing its plan. Be patient with your teammates; at the same time, do not hesitate to express your point of view if the pace of the team seems excessively slow.

Context

If your teammates have higher-context traits, you may:

- Provide additional background information when you introduce yourself. Your introduction to high-context teammates may require your formal education and your personal history (e.g., where you lived and worked, for how long, what you did).

- As the team progresses, decrease the amount of background information you provide about the project and your work to your high-context teammates. Repeating information that they already have may be considered as an insult to their intelligence.

If your teammates are lower context than you are, you may:

- Reduce the amount of background information that you provide to your teammates during the team formation stages. In particular, practice introducing yourself in a low-context manner, stating only the minimal amount of information about yourself (e.g., name, company, position, responsibility). A typical introduction in North America takes fewer than 30 words.
- Throughout the life of the team, continue providing background information to your low-context teammates about the project and your work. Without it, your low-context teammates will not be able to interpret properly the information you are giving them. Over time, you may provide them with the same piece of information on several occasions. Keep your goal in mind: They need to understand what you mean.

Risk Tolerance

If your teammates are more risk averse than you are, you may:

- *Collect more data.* The team as a whole may decide that more data and information is needed than you think, so you might start collecting this data right away.
- *Demonstrate the value of moving ahead.* If your teammates think that more data are needed, they are unlikely to accept the idea of moving along, so you will need to build a case for that. How much will the project gain by moving along? How much time and money will the collection of additional data cost? How can we gather data as we go, rather than wait until the data are collected?
- *Give them time to get used to changes in direction.* Your risk-averse teammates are likely to take more time than you do to adjust to a sudden change, such as a new project direction or a new manager.

If your teammates are more risk tolerant than you are, you may:

- *Forego some data collection.* The team as a whole may decide to move along, even though you believe that a large area of uncertainty and risk remains.

- *Demonstrate the value and necessity of the additional data you want to collect.* If your teammates want to move ahead, they are unlikely to accept the idea of stopping and waiting for the collection of some additional information unless you build a case and demonstrate the need for this information. How much uncertainty is there without additional data? How much does this uncertainty affect the possible direction and outcome of the project?

- *Stay the course.* Your risk-tolerant teammates may change directions quickly. On some occasions, this may lead them to change course several times before coming back to the original course. Waiting for the high-frequency noise to die down may limit the amount of confusion you experience. This can be important in the case of extensive experimental plans, where your risk-tolerant co-workers may decide to change the plan after a few experiments.

Power Distance

If your teammates tend to be higher on the power-distance scale, you may:

- Pay more attention to people's position in the organization and consider that factor as you offer your ideas. For example, you may consider focusing your attention more on the higher-ranking team members.

- Use more authority arguments when you present your ideas to the team. Ideas that come from people at high levels of the organization or from recognized experts have more weight in the minds of hierarchical people than ideas put forward by people at lower organizational levels.

If your teammates tend to be lower on the power-distance scale, you may:

- Pay less attention to people's position in the organization and ignore that factor as you offer your ideas. For example, you may consider focusing your attention more equally on all team members.

- Avoid using authority arguments when you present your ideas to your teammates. In their minds, the fact that someone at a high level in the organization or some recognized expert thinks the same way as you do does not make your idea correct. This approach is likely to ruffle the feathers of your less hierarchical teammates.

What Can You Gain?

Cultural diversity within a team can lead to tremendous synergies once the initial challenges of understanding how other team members think and how to best communicate with them are overcome. This section examines these benefits in detail.

Individualism

Synergy between collectivistic and individualistic team members can create a team that is more than the sum of its parts: Collectivistic team members can learn to reduce interactions among various parts of the project, to decrease the amount of information they need about one another in order to get started, and to think more of their own contribution to the project. They can then reapply these skills in other teams and increase the initial pace of these projects. In multicultural teams, collectivistic team members can provide new team members with extensive support and information about the various team members, their responsibilities, and the interactions among their tasks to these new members and bring them into the fold more quickly. Individualistic team members can learn to anticipate interactions among various parts of the project, to get to know their teammates more, and to think more of the team as a whole. Again, they can then reapply these skills in other teams to speed up their progress. Individualistic team members can help new team members more quickly define their roles and responsibilities when they are added to the team.

Together, they can find the right balance in the team—one that leads to the best solutions to the problems the team encounters. They can move quickly through the initial stages of the team's life while building a significant level of trust among themselves and consider the interactions among their activities without getting bogged down by such discussions.

When solving problems, collectivistic team members are likely to make parallels with situations that, to them, appear similar to the problem at hand (to their individualistic team members, this parallel may not exist). By applying principles from other areas of science or engineering, collectivistic team members may come up with innovative solutions. Conversely, individualistic team members may contribute their extensive experience in their field to solving the problem.

Context

The biggest gains to be made in teams that include both high- and low-context people are in the area of communication. They are described in Chapter 4.

Risk Tolerance

In technical teams, differences on this scale can be challenging. At the same time, they offer some of the biggest opportunities for synergy: In stages 5 and 6, the team usually benefits greatly from discussions that aim at balancing the benefits and costs of gathering additional data. Such analysis may reveal that collecting a little additional data at a low cost may significantly increase the probability of team success. A cost–benefit analysis of data enables the team to reach the optimum in the balance between speed and risk minimization.

Synergy may also occur when team members blend their approaches to solving technical problems. In that case, they can use both experience and theory to determine which variables should be examined first. They may also blend the systematic approach of extensive designed experiments with more direct experiments by designing small experiments that collect information and data that fits within a larger designed experiment. This way, the first experiments can be reused as part of a large designed experiment if they are not sufficient to yield the desired results.

They may also combine various techniques in order to increase the effectiveness of their processes. For example, a Somali technician contributed significantly to the progress of a team of chemists and chemical engineers who needed to decrease the amount of de-ionized water used by a particular process. Indeed, because Somalia has neither water nor energy in large quantities, Somalis have developed extensive knowledge regarding how to minimize the amount of distilled water used to accomplish specific operations.

At the individual level, risk-averse team members may learn to take a bit more risk, to try a few things out before jumping on a full-fledged mathematic or designed experiment approach. Conversely, risk-tolerant team members may learn to be a bit more systematic in their approaches. The following situation, which is described by a French engineer working in the United States, illustrates both the challenges and benefits of differences on the risk-tolerance scale:

> When I first started here, I remember a time where an American engineer and I were assigned to work on the control problem of a complex distillation column. It simply was not working; it did not

do what it was expected to do. My American colleague and I went to have a look at the column; it was part of the Distillation Department of the plant. We noticed that there was another column right next to the one we were working on, which was used as backup. When we came back from our visit, we each started thinking about how we would solve this problem. I started immediately writing differential equations and transfer functions— the works. My American colleague decided that he would run an experiment on the column and spike the feed to see how the column would respond.

After a few days of working side-by-side in completely different directions, we had a major debate. What was the best way to solve the problem? His tinkering approach seemed futile to me. How would we reapply what we learned on the first column to the other? What would happen if the column needed to be modified in the future? The plant would have to redo our study from scratch. Clearly, my general approach made much more sense. Once we had a solution, we could reapply it to a wide range of cases.

My American colleague argued in essence: "Maybe, but how long will it take you to solve all these differential equations? Since there are probably no analytical solutions, how are you going to solve them? I can redo my experiments many times in the time it will take you to understand what is going on, and in the meantime the column will be running and making money." After much discussion, we agreed on a simulation-based approach that would focus on both columns of the same type. We identified the parameters of both columns so that we could simulate them both; the minor differences between the two columns helped us increase the robustness of the solution we eventually found.

Power Distance

At the individual level, the biggest gain you can make by working with people who are significantly lower or higher on the power-distance scale is to learn a new management style. You may or may not like what it yields, but it gives you an opportunity to learn new approaches to management. This is often the case for expatriates coming back from countries that are significantly higher or lower on the power-distance scale.

Special Case of Global Teams

In addition to the challenges mentioned so far, global teams need to contend with issues specific to their situations:

- The *geographic distance* among the various team members makes face-to-face meetings and informal discussions by the water cooler much more difficult.

- In many cases, *time difference* between team members is such that little overlap exists between working hours. For example, there is no overlap between East Coast and Japanese working hours.

- *Differences in the level of development* of the countries involved can make collaboration difficult.

The biggest challenges associated with geographic distance and time difference are related to communication; these are covered in the next chapter. Here, we examine how to create team spirit despite geographic distance and time difference and how to handle differences in technology levels.

Creating Team Spirit

One consequence of geographic distance and time difference is that it is often much easier for global team members to relate with teammates who are in the same location as they are than to relate with teammates who are located several thousand miles and several hours away. As a result, the chances of global teams splitting into an "us versus them" pattern that leads to a team breakdown are significantly increased.

It is therefore critical for global team members and global team leaders to ensure that their actions reflect an inclusive approach to the team (i.e., they underlie a "We are all in this together" approach to teamwork). The team needs to create a team spirit. To achieve this objective, team members may consider action steps such as the following:

- Provide new information to all team members at approximately the same time. This avoids situations where team members get information generated by other team members located in another part of the world through a third party.

- Be sensitive to their cultures. For example, the team should refrain from scheduling events on days that are special to some team members. When a French group of engineers attempted to schedule a telephone conference call on Thanksgiving, they certainly did not score points with their American counterparts. Similarly, when the Dean of the Faculty of Engineering in a French university asked his Canadian counterpart whether "they had any Indians on campus, with the feathers," it did not go over too well.

- Ensure that all team members have a chance to provide input and to participate in making team decisions and recommendations to their satisfaction.

- Show respect for other team members' opinions by taking them into consideration. Here is an example where this did not take place:

> The American CEO of an IT company operating with two headquarters (one in the United States, one in France) wanted to increase the effectiveness of the organization by creating a common set of corporate values. He created a Corporate Value Team that reported to him and included Western European and North American members. During one of their videoconferences, the team had an extensive discussion (over an hour and a half) about one word, which really did not appeal to the Western European team members. The team agreed on a different word. When the team presented its recommendation to the CEO, he removed the new word and put back the old one. From that point on, the Western European team members stopped attending team videoconferences.

- Search for solutions that balance the needs of various geographies. Here is the experience of a German product development engineer working with North American counterparts:

> The product development team had extensive discussions with respect to what environmental standards the product should meet. We agreed on the principle that our products needed to meet the toughest environmental standards in the world, so that they would be seen as first-class everywhere. During the discussion, it became quickly apparent that my American colleagues considered the U.S. standards as the toughest in the world and were designing to these specifications. I was not able to convince them that pending German environmental standards would be more stringent than current U.S. standards. When our products came out, they did not meet the German environmental requirements.

- Update team members regularly so that everyone is kept informed of everyone else's progress. The best approach to update may vary from team to team, but having a mechanism for regular updates is usually helpful.

- Make an effort to visit team members in other countries when one travels to that country for business. Any face-to-face contact helps build trust in the team. Otherwise, when team members in another country find out that one of their teammates went to their office but did not meet with them, they are usually unimpressed.

- Shift work hours to increase the overlap in their working days. For example, in the case of a team split between the East Coast and Western Europe, North American team members may consider starting their day earlier, while Western European team members may shift their working hours toward the afternoon to increase overlap. This makes telephone communication and quick questions much easier to handle.

- Socialize as a team whenever possible.

- Ensure that the goals of individual team members are aligned with the team objectives, so that team members put their full effort and commitment into the team.

- Find the right balance for the team on the individualism, context, risk tolerance, and power-distance scales.

- Have a face-to-face kick-off meeting at the beginning of the project, so that everyone has a chance to shake hands and get to know the other team members.

Because of their complex nature, global teams are the focus of extensive research these days. Additional information on this topic can be found in other publications within the Managing Cultural Differences Series, which are listed at the front of this book.

Differences in Development Level and Technology Transfer

When a global team includes members in both developed and developing countries, team members often need to contend with another important difference in problem-solving approach. Machinery and equipment are comparatively more expensive in developing countries than in developed countries, whereas labor is more affordable in developing countries than in developed countries. As a result, the tradeoff between equipment and labor is different in developing and developed countries. Here is the experience of one Canadian meteorologist:

> I was working on a joint proposal with some Indian scientists to build a meteorological tower there. We kept going back and forth, not making much progress, until I realized that, every time they revised the proposal, they would do anything they could to replace equipment by people, whereas I was doing the opposite. Since the

tower was going to be operated in India, I figured we should do it their way—as long as we would get the same quality of data.

This difference in approach became particularly noticeable when it came to insurance. I thought that insuring expensive equipment overseas would cost an absolute fortune. My Indian colleagues told me not to worry and allocated a very small amount of money in the proposal for insurance. Their solution consisted of hiring an unemployed worker, building a house for him and his family at the foot of the tower, and paying him to make sure that nobody would touch it.

This difference is especially visible on construction sites: North American construction sites usually involve a few people with several large pieces of machinery, whereas construction sites in developing countries involve many people with simpler tools.

This difference in development difference also affects the familiarity that workers have with tools and technical equipment. One French engineer working in Central Africa remarked that:

One of the biggest issues faced by French engineers in that part of the world is that, when they hire local workers to install equipment, these people have little to no training in using tools, particularly power tools. As a result, many workers would break parts during the installation or maintenance of the equipment; they would not know when to stop tightening screws, for example.

These differences in technical development may lead to significant problems during technology transfer projects. At the same time, North American technical professionals need to be careful when they go overseas on such projects. Many foreign technical professionals, particularly at high levels, have received a technical education comparable to the education provided in North American universities; some have studied in North American, Western European, or Japanese universities. As a result, questions that may be interpreted as doubting their technical expertise and the level of development of their country (like "Do you guys have computers?") are usually not well received.

In such projects, it is important to ensure that the technology to be transferred can be effectively received by the recipients. Creating long-term dependency on technology transfer—because people have purchased complex equipment that requires complex tools, extensive training, and expensive parts for proper maintenance—may not be the best route for developing countries. Adapting the technology to the needs and technical abilities of the people who will operate it is critical for long-term success. One way to achieve this objective is to partner with people (such as local institutions) who can translate the needs and abilities of locals in terms and specifications that technical professionals in developed countries can work with (Harris, 1999).

Summary

Multicultural teams face many challenges above and beyond the challenges faced by culturally homogeneous teams. Specifically, team members often have different ideas of what being a team implies and what they should do to make the team more effective:

- The "everyone takes care of his or her own responsibilities" approach of individualistic team members often goes against the "one for all, and all for one" approach of collectivistic team members.

- Tension often exists in teams that include both risk-averse and risk-tolerant members because the latter want to make decisions and move the team forward, whereas the former are concerned that the team does not fully understand the issues it faces and needs to collect more information.

- High-context and low-context people have difficulties getting to know one another satisfactorily and establishing the trust they need to have in order to work together effectively.

- Expectations relative to the pace of the team and what needs to be done at various stages in the team's life are likely to be different.

- Culturally different people often have different approaches to making decisions. As a result, team members may have different ideas of what decisions the team can make versus what decisions it needs to refer to people at higher levels of the organization.

- Differences in problem-solving approaches can lead to serious misunderstandings among team members.

When these challenges are suitably overcome, cultural differences can become major competitive advantages for technical teams. They can find the right balance between:

- Collecting data and moving quickly—in essence, multicultural teams can learn to move quickly in the right direction.

- Planning extensively for contingencies and making rapid progress
- Considering in too much detail the interactions among team members and their areas of responsibilities and possibly overlooking them, thereby learning to focus on the main interactions within the team

Because of the geographic distance and time difference among team members, global teams are more prone to team breakdown than are multicultural teams. It is important for global team members (particularly global team leaders) to work on creating team spirit and focus on cohesion at the same time as they focus on delivering results.

References

Drexler, A., and Sibbet, D. 1999. Drexler/Sibbet team performance™ model. http://www.grove.com/services/tool_modeltp.html; accessed on August 12, 2002.

Gercik, P. 1996. *On track with the Japanese.* New York: Kodansha America, pp. 184–198.

Hall, E.T., and Reed Hall, M. 1990. *Understanding cultural differences: Germans, French and Americans.* Yarmouth, ME: Intercultural Press, pp. 6–10.

Harris, P.R., and Moran, R.T. 1999. *Managing cultural differences: Leadership strategies for a new world of business,* 5th ed. Woburn, MA: Butterworth–Heinemann, pp. 140–141.

Harris, P.R. 1994. *High performance leadership,* Amherst, MA: HRD Press.

Hofstede, G. 1980. *Culture's consequences: International differences in work-related values.* Newbury Park, CA: Sage Publications, pp. 73–84.

Hofstede, G. 1997. *Cultures and organizations: software of the mind,* New York: McGraw-Hill, p. 133.

Trompenaars, A., and Hampden-Turner, C. 1998. *Riding the waves of culture: Understanding diversity in global business,* 2nd ed. New York: McGraw-Hill, pp. 51–69.

Communicating Technical Information

We were having dinner all together in a restaurant. There were several Canadians, male and female, and one Tunisian female engineer. At one point, I made a joke about my Tunisian counterpart. I cannot remember what I said, but I remember clearly that she threw an ashtray directly at my face; I had to duck to avoid it. Her intent was clearly to hit me. Afterwards, I asked my female Canadian colleagues if they found my joke offensive—they did not think so, they could not understand her reaction either.

—*Canadian engineer working in a multicultural team*

A critical part of technical people's activities consists of communicating the results they obtained to their colleagues and managers. Cultural differences often represent a challenge in the communication process because what makes a good presentation, report, or meeting varies from country to country. This chapter examines communication among technical professionals from different cultural backgrounds, where some are North Americans and others are New North Americans (or foreign expatriates working in North America).

What Are the Signs of Cross-Cultural Communication Issues?

Cross-cultural misunderstandings related to communication are usually readily identified. Going back to the iceberg analogy of

Chapter 1, cultural differences related to communication are generally either above the surface (e.g., differences in languages, alphabets) or just below it. The difficulty in dealing with such differences is not so much their complexity (as in the case of teamwork) as their frequency. There are so many instances of communication in an average business day that even a small percentage of error on each event may generate several misunderstandings every day. Over time, these misunderstandings may accumulate and add to other, more complex misunderstandings.

Communicating information and ideas from one person to another involves three steps:

1. *The sender creates a message.* This may be in the form of a written document (e.g., e-mail message, report) or an oral message (e.g., plain speech, presentation).
2. *The message is transmitted to the receiver.* In the case of face-to-face communication, this transmission is instantaneous. Transmission becomes more apparent in the case of reports (particularly when they are distributed as hard copies) or e-mail messages; because transmission-related issues are more common in global teams, this particular point is examined in the "Special Case of Global Teams" section at the end of this chapter.
3. *The receiver receives the message and interprets it.* This step involves either reading or listening, depending on the message format.

When communicating, we use four skills: listening, speaking, reading, and writing. Cross-cultural issues may arise with every one of these skills. Issues related to the transmission of messages, particularly over distance, tend to be more common in the case of global teams; again, they are covered in the latter part of this chapter.

Speaking

Some of the most common cross-cultural issues related to presentations include the following:

- Presenter receives far more or far fewer questions than anticipated.
- Audience is visibly confused by the presentation.
- Audience is asking for more details in an area that is not important to the presenter or seems uninterested by some of the information presented.

- Audience asks questions about topics that come much later in the presentation.
- Audience asks questions that the presentation answered much earlier or planned to answer much later in the presentation.
- Presentation includes humor that is not appreciated by the audience.
- Presentation may contain sweeping conclusions unsupported by data or a lot of data with limited analysis and conclusions.
- Presenters use jargon, acronyms, and abbreviations that are unknown to the audience, creating confusion.

Some of the most common cross-cultural issues related to direct face-to-face speaking include the following:

- People speak when others do not expect them to, either while someone else is speaking or after a long silence.
- People use much stronger language than others expect.
- People make their points through allusions and indirect comments that are hard to interpret.
- People make their points bluntly, without any regard for the impact their statements will make on others.
- People stand or sit too close or too far for comfortable conversations.
- People use analogies that are impossible to decipher.
- Non-native English speakers make sentences where the words sound right, but the sentences as a whole do not mean anything.
- People feel uneasy around non-native English speakers when they use their language to communicate.
- People make jokes that are not understood or that offend others.
- People may misinterpret the position and status of others based on their physical appearance or language ability.
- Some people start discussing the emotions of another person during a meeting, thereby making this person uncomfortable. Others may try to change the topic at that point, making the first set of people uncomfortable.

Writing

Some of the most common cross-cultural issues related to reports include the following:

- The report provides either too much or not enough background information or details.
- The information is presented in an order that does not make sense to readers.
- The report presents conclusions that are not substantiated by data or presents a lot of data with limited analysis and conclusions.
- Documents are difficult to understand.

Some of the most common cross-cultural issues related to e-mail include the following:

- The message contains too much or not enough background information.
- The message contains unwanted personal information.
- The message is cold and impersonal.
- Poor grammar and/or spelling make the message difficult to read and understand; for example, "U R" instead of "you are."

Reading

Some of the most common cross-cultural issues related to reading include the following:

- Readers misread or are confused by diagrams.
- Readers are offended by an e-mail message and respond with a message that expresses the offense they read.

Listening

Some of the most common cross-cultural issues related to listening include the following:

- People do not seem to be listening. They may have their eyes closed, keep looking continuously at the ceiling, or avoid eye contact.
- Listeners feel overwhelmed by the emotions expressed by the speaker.
- Listeners cannot "read" the speaker.

- Listeners laugh or are offended at times when the speaker did not try to use humor or make people react.

Meetings

Some of the most common cross-cultural issues related to meetings include the following:

- Some people participate a lot, but others do not.
- Some people digress frequently, whereas others insist on sticking to the agenda.
- Some make a long speech when they present a point, but others go straight to the point.
- People are overdressed or underdressed.
- People are overly formal or informal.
- Participants show up for the meeting at different times.
- Some participants start side conversations.
- Some participants make their points in an overly aggressive manner, whereas others do not make their points clear.
- Some meetings have an agenda and meeting material provided ahead of time, whereas others have agendas created just before the meeting starts and some have no agenda at all.
- At the end of the meeting, participants go back to their respective offices. Days go by without any real progress on the agenda items arising from the meeting.

What Is Going On?

Compared with manager–employee relationships and team dynamics, cultural differences related to communication do not run as deep, but they do run wide. Many aspects must be considered in order for effective communication to occur between people from different cultural backgrounds, thereby generating many opportunities for misunderstandings.

In this section, we examine the main factors that need to be taken into account, namely language, context, expressiveness (which corresponds to the extent to which emotions can be displayed in the workplace), power distance, risk tolerance, and individualism. As this long list indicates, identifying why communication among people of different cultural backgrounds is ineffective can be challenging.

Language

In most North American organizations, the working language is English. English is not the first language of many New North Americans: Less than 10 percent of the world's population speaks English (Harris, 1999), and most recent immigrants come from countries where English is not an official language (see Appendix B). As a result, New North Americans are constantly working in and communicating with a language that they learned as a second language. This point has many consequences, which are described here.

Fluency

Within the New North American population, there is a wide range of fluency levels, from beginner to fully fluent. When someone asks a question in English of someone closer to the beginner end of the spectrum, that person usually mentally translates the question in his or her language, formulates the answer, then translates the answer back into English. When people translate back and forth mentally, the sentences they verbalize are likely to be close to the sentences they made mentally in their own language: They "speak their own language with English words." This can create confusion for native English speakers because the answer may not make sense in English—the order of the words and the grammar of the sentence may not work in English.

This mental gymnastics takes time and much concentration. When this process takes place in a meeting, it results in a silence or a slow response. Some North Americans are uncomfortable with this situation and start speaking before they have received a complete answer. This can make the non-native English speaker uncomfortable and self-conscious about his or her language skills.

Such slow answers are sometimes interpreted as a lack of knowledge. For example, a New North American technical professional may know why the equipment does not do what it is supposed to do, but if he or she explains it very slowly, in broken sentences, North American counterparts may not understand what he or she is trying to say. At that point, the contribution of the New North American to the discussion is considered negatively. If this is repeated over time, his or her North American colleagues may get into the habit of "tuning out" the New North American in meetings.

As non-native English speakers' level of fluency improves, the translation–back translation step becomes less frequent; however, the need for additional concentration tends to remain for a while. Therefore, people who are fairly fluent in English end up being more tired at the end of a day of meetings in English than at the end of a day of meetings in their native language. This can create difficulties for them in the following situations:

- Conferences (e.g., if they are presenting at the end of the day)
- All-day training sessions
- All-day meetings, particularly if decisions and action steps are discussed after a day of presentations
- All-day interviews—Candidates for many technical positions, particularly in research environments, make a presentation and are interviewed by several people; the process takes the whole day. This can be quite taxing for them, making them perform below their potential toward the end of the day. Here is the description of a French engineer interviewing for a position in the Netherlands:

> This was the first time I was going through all-day interviews in English. I had done this in French before, so I did not think twice about it. By the end of the day, I was exhausted and I could not think any more. I was tempted to tell the last interviewer: "Look, I cannot do this any more. Let's just drop it. I will not get the position, just let me go back to the hotel and sleep."

Accents create much difficulty. They often lead people to ask others to repeat themselves several times, until they either get it or give up. Being asked to repeat several times also creates self-consciousness in people.

Operating in a second language can create significant difficulties when New North Americans work with a restricted vocabulary. Indeed, they have to focus their communication on the most essential features of what they are trying to say because they do not have the ability to express fully what they have in mind. When New North Americans lack the ability to express feelings such as sympathy, sorrow, apology, and regret or to disagree with people in a way that does not offend them, this may lead to communication breakdown.

Another issue that non-native English speakers face to a greater extent than native English speakers is background noise. Everyone has experienced the difficulty of communicating with others in a noisy environment (like a party or a rock concert). Background noise tends to affect the ability of non-native English speakers to distinguish words and understand sentences much more than native English speakers. As a result, a somewhat noisy environment may be fine for native English speakers but not suitable for conversations with non-native English speakers. The signal-to-noise ratio matters more to non-native English speakers than to native English speakers.

Confusion may also result when non-native English speakers use a word that does not mean what they are trying to say. This situation is more common with people who speak languages that are relatively close to English (e.g., German, Danish, French, Italian). These languages include words that are similar to English words but have different meanings. For example, the French word "figure" means "face" in English (the English word "figure" means "silhouette" in French).

With respect to written documents, translations performed by people who are not qualified to do them (like translators who are not familiar with the topic covered in the document) may result in complete reader confusion. Automatic translation software still has a long way to go before it can replace human translators. Poor translations of operator manuals can lead to serious difficulties, while poor translations of labels and marketing material can have an adverse effect on sales (Ricks, 1999). For example, the magazine *Protégez-Vous* runs a monthly column on poor label translations (into French); having products showcased in that column does not make a favorable impression to French-speaking consumers.

Humor

Humor is a double-edged sword in multicultural settings. A good joke that everyone understands may help reduce tension, create a friendly atmosphere, and help build rapport and trust among people. At the same time, a joke may be misinterpreted. People from different cultural backgrounds may be offended by a joke that is perfectly acceptable in another culture, as the example of the Canadian engineer working with a Tunisian counterpart (mentioned at the beginning of this chapter) demonstrates.

Another situation in which humor may create misunderstandings is presentations. North American presenters often use humor (in the form of jokes or cartoons) at the beginning of their presentations to lighten up the situation. This may backfire in multicultural situations, particularly in global teams, because audiences in many countries may interpret this action as belittling them; using humor means to them that the presenter does not take them seriously. In addition, cartoons may be reserved for children in their cultures.

Humor needs to be treated with the utmost care. Many jokes do not translate well and are therefore lost on non-native English speakers who are not fluent. Puns, for example, are based on the fact that one word has two meanings; when each of the two meanings is translated by a different word, the pun disappears. Many jokes require that the audience have knowledge of current affairs in the area where the person making the joke lives; in global teams, this may be a tall order. As a result, the chances of jokes falling flat are high in multicultural settings.

Some translators deal with this issue in a way that illustrates the extent of the problem; here is the experience of an Italian translating during joint-venture negotiations between Chinese and Italians:

> At one point, the negotiations were quite tense. One Italian guy tried to ease the tension by making a joke. Unfortunately, the joke would not translate at all in Chinese. I turned to the Chinese participants and said: "He made a joke." They all laughed and I was relieved.

There Is More to Language than Meets the Ear

The view that people have of language itself varies from country to country. In North America, language tends to be viewed as a communication tool: "As long as others understand what I mean, everything is all right." By contrast, people in many other countries use language to convey indirectly other important pieces of information about themselves, such as social class and country or region of origin. For example, in the UK, people can tell from which part of the country and to which social class others belong from their accent and the quality of their English (measured in terms of vocabulary, syntax, and grammar). This is also true in other parts of the world, such as Latin America, Latin Europe, and in German- and Arabic-speaking countries.

People coming from cultures where language also conveys social class tend to project this view of language onto English, therefore putting pressure on themselves when they are in North America. They often feel that they need to speak English as properly as they speak their own language in order to regain the social status that they enjoyed in their home country. This approach usually leads to extensive self-consciousness, which actually impairs their ability to communicate: They avoid speaking in order to avoid making mistakes. Because practicing at speaking English is the best way to improve, this attitude may actually slow down their progress.

In countries where the way people speak is a reflection of their social class, complex grammatical sentence structures and unusual words are viewed positively. For example, in French, the more words containing three syllables or more that people use, the better the document and the higher the social class of the writer (this correlation is not 100 percent, but it is common). A good case in point is the writings of Marcel Proust, which includes sentences that run as long as two printed pages. Contrast this approach with the "Keep it simple, stupid" (KISS) approach to communication used in North America and the index provided by word-processing programs to determine whether the text you write is too complicated for its intended audience.

Language is also used in some countries, such as Germany, to indicate technical expertise. In these countries, using the wrong technical word is quickly interpreted as a lack of expertise. For example, the English phrase "to rent" translates into *mieten* or *vermieten* depending on whether you are on the renter's side or the owner's side, and using one for the other will confuse many German real estate agents. This can create significant challenges when technical professionals from different countries participate in a meeting, as the experience of a Canadian consulting engineer working in Germany illustrates:

> I almost lost a contract because of the German requirement for precise language. During the negotiations, I kept using the terms "water purification" and "water treatment" interchangeably—to them, these were two very different things. The fact that I kept using one for the other could mean only one thing to them: I did not know what I was talking about. How could I solve their problem?

Conversely, people who insist on using the right word when others see little difference may be perceived as "nitpickers," creating tension in a meeting when they appear to be correcting someone else.

Silence

The presence or absence of silence can also generate misunderstandings (Trompenaars, 1998). In North America, pauses are rare during conversations; North American conversations can be compared to jazz music, where one person stands up, plays or says his or her piece, sits down, and someone else immediately stands up to play or say his or her piece. People alternate and pay attention so that they do not overlap or leave any gap. People demonstrate respect for the speaker by waiting for him or her to finish his or her piece.

Silence is rare in Latin cultures. Latin conversations are compared to symphonies, where people play at the same time. People often start speaking before others are finished. This is a sign of interest and attention. A good Latin listener who wants to show that he or she has well understood the point that the speaker is trying to make does so by finishing his or her sentence, saying the same words at the same pace and in the same tone as the speaker. Note that both speaker and listener are actually speaking at the same time. Both speaker and listener interpret this as "We are completely in sync; we really understand one another."

In Far Eastern cultures, silence is common. People do not speak at the same time, and they do not speak back to back. People use silence to process information and think about what they are about to say. They may also use silence as a way to disagree implicitly. Silence may become even longer and more frequent in meetings and conversations held in English—people may be translating back and forth mentally between English and their own language.

The contrast is striking when comparing televised baseball games and cricket test matches. During baseball games, North American sportscasters fill in gaps in the games with statistics and anecdotes; there is no silence in the broadcast. During cricket games, BBC commentators do not attempt to "fill in"—if nothing is happening, they do not say anything; all viewers hear is the wind in the microphone.

In meetings that involve people from different cultural backgrounds, these differences in communication patterns can create significant problems. North American participants consider the interruptions of Latin participants rude, while Latin participants consider that their North American counterparts do not pay enough attention to what they say. North American participants consider that Far Easterners do not contribute sufficiently to the meeting, whereas Far Eastern participants consider that they are not given the opportunity to do so.

Using Different Versions of English

Difficulties may also arise when communicating in English when people have learned and use different versions of English: English as it is spoken in the United States is not the same as in Canada, the UK, Australia, South Africa, India, or other parts of the Commonwealth. Some words may have different meanings, resulting in misunderstandings that can be embarrassing both in and out of the workplace:

- To "table an issue" means putting this issue up for discussion in the United States and delaying the discussion about this issue in the UK.

- To "strike out" means to go after an opportunity in the UK and to fail in the United States.

- A "bomb" is a failure in the United States and a success in th UK.
- To "root" means to be a supporter (of a sports team) in th United States and to have sexual intercourse in Australia Australians usually get a good laugh when someone says "I roo for the Yankees" down under.

Similar misunderstandings may result from the different connota tions that the same word has: A word may be considered positive i one part of the world and negative in another, which can create havo in advertising. For example, a dragon is viewed positively in Chin and negatively in the West. Assertiveness is a positive characteristi about people in the United States but a negative characteristic in th Far East.

Misunderstandings may also result from the use of words, acro nyms, or idioms that are not shared. On the North American side, th use of three-letter acronyms (TLAs) and "sports English" can b confusing for non-native English speakers (see Appendix E for a lis of expressions that often confuse New North Americans). On th New North American side, the use of idioms that mean something t them but not to their North American counterparts can be equall confusing.

Using a Language Other than English

Differences in language can create unease when people who speak language other than English use this language to communicate in th workplace. People who do not understand what is said may becom nervous and defensive, particularly if the exchange in a foreign lan guage ends in laughter: "Are they talking about me? Are they makin fun of what I said?" Several points need to be taken into consideratio in these situations.

Because humor is cultural, New North Americans may make joke that simply would not translate at all. New North American may be aware of that fact, in which case they may not even try t translate. In most cases, this joke is not about the remainder of th audience.

Because participating in a long meeting in English can be tiring fo New North Americans, they may be "blowing off some steam" b using their own language and their own sense of humor.

Communication among non-native English speakers is usually muc faster and more comprehensive in their native language than i English. As a result, when people from the same cultural backgroun meet in the cafeteria, they are likely to use their own language rather than English, particularly if everyone involved speaks the language they use. When native English speakers come and sit down next to them, they may switch to English in order to create a single conversation. If that does not happen, it is much easier for them to switch back to their native language.

In some cases (often in the case of negotiations), non-native English speakers may switch to their own language in order to discuss what was said "in private." They do so in the presence of native English speakers, assuming that they cannot be understood (Trompenaars, 1998).

Gestures and Body Language

Gestures are another form of communication that is affected by cultural differences (Axtell, 1998; Morrison, 1995). Each culture has evolved its own set of gestures, which are sometimes conflicting, as the following examples demonstrate:

- The gesture that means OK in North America means "money" in Japan, "zero" in France, and is vulgar in Brazil and Russia. When North Americans travel to France and have dinner in a restaurant, a common misunderstanding takes place when they are asked if everything is to their liking: If they respond by a gesture, the French maitre d'hotel is often confused.

- The "V" sign (for victory) is the same in the United States and in Australia; however, the same sign with the hand reversed (i.e., with the palm facing the person making the sign instead of the back of the hand) is the equivalent in Australia of giving someone "the finger" in the United States. When George Bush arrived in Australia for an official visit there, he came out of the plane unintentionally giving the finger to everyone in the audience. Australian newspapers had a field day printing his picture on their front pages.

- Showing the soles of your shoes to people in many Muslim countries is a major insult.

- Chinese people count from one to ten on one hand. Westerners can follow up to five, but the combination of fingers used by the Chinese to indicate numbers from six to ten eludes most Westerners. For example, the gesture indicating "eight" (thumb and forefinger extended, other fingers folded) is used to imply "pointing a gun" in North America and "two" in France (French count on their fingers starting from their thumb rather than their forefingers).

Misunderstandings related to gestures are more common in global teams than in multicultural teams. As New North Americans work and live in North America, they quickly learn the gestures that North Americans use and their meanings. Members of global teams do not benefit from such exposure and are therefore more likely to run into such issues.

Differences in eye contact are felt in many multicultural organizations. Eye contact means different things in different cultures. In North America, making eye contact is a sign of trustworthiness. In some cultures, making eye contact demonstrates respect; in others, avoiding eye contact shows respect (Trompenaars, 1998). People from cultures where making eye contact with people in higher social positions is considered disrespectful often have difficulties during interviews in the North American workplace. Interviewers often interpret (usually subconsciously) this lack of eye contact as a sign that "this candidate cannot be trusted."

Another form of body language that leads to misunderstandings is smiles. Because the situations in which people are expected to smile depend on their cultural backgrounds, make sure you are not reading in their smiles something that is not there. Consider the function of the smile in these countries:

- In the United States, and to a somewhat lesser extent in Canada, people smile in order to be friendly to strangers.

- In Germany and Switzerland, people smile only "when there is something to smile about," meaning that the business relationship is moving in the right direction. Germans and Swiss do not smile to people they do not know (Clauss, 2001).

- In France, people who smile to strangers are either simple-minded or trying to take advantage of them. Therefore, most French people react defensively to strangers who smile to them.

- In the Far East, people often smile to hide their embarrassment. For example, Filipinos may smile when someone brings up a topic that they would rather not discuss, like the death of a loved one. This can lead to serious confusion when North Americans bring up such topics because they may not understand how someone might smile about such a topic.

Communicating through Other Senses

People communicate—and therefore may misinterpret—using other forms of communication besides gestures and words. Some colors have special meanings in certain countries; this may lead to embarrassment, like someone showing up at a funeral in North America in bright-colored clothes. For example, yellow is reserved for the Imperial family in Japan. Red is the color for weddings in Vietnam. The choice of color can be particularly difficult in advertising because colors are used to communicate a specific message, which may not correlate in other cultures. Colors may have an impact that people from other cultures may not anticipate, as the following anecdote illustrates:

> In several African countries, a significant fraction of the voters are illiterate, so people vote by choosing papers of different colors (each color represents a party). One African government manipulated elections by choosing a color for the opposition party that many voters considered as bringing bad luck.

There is also a language of flowers. In Germany, France, and several other European nations, red roses represent a declaration of love, and only that. This has lead to misunderstandings when North American guests bring red roses to their hosts and hostesses when they are invited over for dinner. Chrysanthemums represent mourning in several European countries, whereas lilies represent mourning in China.

Smells and perfumes are another source of unspoken misunderstandings. In North America, the increasing number of allergic reactions people have to various scents has led to "perfume-free workplaces" or "perfume-free conference" policies. People in other countries may have difficulties understanding such policies. For example, the French use perfume as a form of communication (each perfume is associated with a specific emotion).

People in some parts of the world use large amounts of spices in their food, and the odor of these spices can be noticed on their clothes. This may create issues for people who are not used to such smells. This effect has a particularly negative impact during job interviews, if it makes the interviewer uncomfortable.

The choice of clothes also communicates a message that may be misread. North Americans in general, and Californians in particular, tend to be less formal in dress code. As a result, visitors from other countries are often overdressed and appear that they are trying to impress people with their suits. Conversely, North American visitors going overseas may be underdressed and appear that they are not taking people seriously.

Latin Americans and Latin Europeans often communicate their social status through their clothes; this is done by wearing fashionable clothes of good fabric and cut with carefully matched colors and accessories, particularly in the case of women. This behavior can lead to significant misunderstandings, as described by a female French Canadian engineer:

> I was part of a Canadian delegation on an official visit to Peru. This delegation was lead by an older woman who dressed quite conservatively—dark-colored suits, nothing feminine. Like many Quebec women, I dressed more femininely, used brighter colors, make-up and accessories (jewelry, scarf, etc.). When we met our Peruvian counterparts, they thought I was the leader of the group and started paying me the corresponding respect. I had to redirect them to the actual delegation leader, who was not pleased.

Communicating through Pictures and Diagrams

A picture is worth a thousand words, but the words people use to describe a figure or diagram may not be the same in all cultures. In North America, the triangle is commonly used in diagrams and presentations. North Americans like the fact that this shape defines a clear direction. By contrast, Far Easterners tend to have more affinity for circles, which provide a sense of harmony.

In Western societies, people read from left to right, whereas Arabs read from right to left. This difference has led to confusion for a laundry detergent manufacturer: The box contained a drawing showing dirty clothes, then a washing machine with the detergent, then clean clothes, from left to right. In Arabic markets, consumers interpreted the drawing as showing clean clothes, a washing machine with the detergent, then dirty clothes. Sales did not meet expectations until the diagram was suitably modified.

Context

As described in Chapter 3, context has a major impact on teamwork through the way people introduce themselves and get to know one another. Context also has a major impact on communication, as shown in Exhibit 4.1.

In high-context cultures, more information is communicated through body language, tone of voice, facial expression, and other nonverbal communication rather than explicitly in the spoken message

Exhibit 4.1

High- and low-context communication. The full rectangle represents the total message to be communicated; the rectangle labeled "Verbal" represents the part communicated through words, and the rectangle labeled "Nonverbal" represents the part communicated nonverbally (e.g., gestures, body language, facial expressions, tone of voice).

| Verbal |
| Non-verbal |

Low context message

| Verbal |
| Non-verbal |

High context message

sage. Low-context communication is the opposite, where the primary message is in the spoken word. Low-context cultures tend to focus on the message to be delivered to the other person.

Context is made of several elements: space, information flow, time, and relationships. Differences in each of these areas can create communication issues, as described in the following sections.

Space

We all carry around ourselves a bubble of space that we consider our own personal space—our "comfort zone." We usually allow only people who are close to us emotionally (e.g., children, parents, spouse, boyfriend or girlfriend, close friends) to come close physically (Hall, 1990). When strangers enter this bubble, their presence within our personal space generates a strong emotional reaction that can be summarized by "flight or fight." We become tense and defensive or step back.

This feeling is strong and tends to override any logical thought. As a result, it is difficult to have a conversation with someone who is physically too close relative to the relationship we have with this person. The "flight-or-fight" feeling prevents us from listening properly to this person.

In the workplace, people are rarely emotionally close enough to enter someone else's personal space. The usual distance between two people having a conversation corresponds to the size of their personal space, each person standing at the edge of the personal space of the other.

In multicultural situations, misunderstandings may arise because the size of this invisible bubble varies from culture to culture. As the context of a culture increases, the size of this bubble of personal space decreases. For example, when two Germans have a discussion in the workplace, they usually stand at arm's length. People in Italy or Latin America usually stand closer to one another (they may be less than 1 foot [30 cm] apart) in the same circumstances. As a result, a misunderstanding can arise before people from different cultural backgrounds even start their conversation, as the following example indicates:

> I worked in a team that included both Italian and German engineers. During the first meeting of the whole team, one of the Italian engineers walked up to one of the German engineers to introduce himself. He came too close and the German guy took a step back. The Italian was visibly puzzled by this reaction.

When high- and low-context people have a conversation, two things can happen:

- If they stand at the distance that feels "right" for the high-context person, this distance is too small for the low-context person. The low-context person has this "flight-or-fight" feeling that tends to prevent him or her from following the conversation. Subconsciously, the low-context person may be annoyed because the high-context person "does not have the right to come this close"; the high-context person is not emotionally close to the low-context person.

- If they stand at the distance that feels "right" for the low-context person, this distance is too large for the high-context person. The high-context person is likely to feel (again subconsciously) "snubbed," perceiving the low-context person as behaving in a standoffish manner. The high-context person may read a put-down that is not intended by the low-context person.

The sense that people have of the right distance can be strong, as the experience of an English Canadian scientist in the UK demonstrates:

> I went for an interview there. I was brought into a room where two gentlemen were sitting side-by-side behind their desks. There was a chair in front of them, about six feet away from their desks.

As I walked into the room, they showed me the chair, inviting me to sit down. I walked up to the chair. It was too far from their desks for my liking, so I picked it up and moved it forward by about three feet. Their faces showed that they were both unpleasantly surprised. I did not get the job—I was told I would not fit in the organization.

Personal space is small in some parts of the world, as the experience of a Canadian engineer working in Tanzania indicates:

I went to villages to install water pumps. The first thing I would do was to talk to the head of the village. He and I were standing at the right distance—no problem there. Except that, between him and me, there were three rows of children packed shoulder to shoulder, all trying to touch me. I was probably the first white man to enter the village in their lifetime. Initially, I had a very hard time concentrating on what the village chief was saying. It took some work.

Who we allow to enter our personal space also varies: The sense of closeness varies with the sense of individualism that people have. Collectivistic people tend to consider more people close to them than individualistic people; as a result, they let more people enter their personal space and they enter the personal space of more people. This can create serious misunderstandings when high-context people demonstrate this sense of closeness to low-context people through gestures and physical contact.

Chinese female friends and Arab male friends often hold hands when walking down the street. When they extend their friendships to Westerners, serious misunderstandings may result. In Latin countries, male and female professionals working side-by-side often greet one another with a small peck on the cheek. After a few business encounters, Latin American men are likely to greet you with *abrazos* (embraces).

For low-context people, who apologize after any accidental physical contact, these behaviors can be threatening. In some cases, these demonstrations of friendship have been mistaken for sexual harassment, as in the case of a Quebec sales representative working for an American company. His sales record in Montreal was excellent, so his company promoted and transferred him to the Boston headquarters. He had to be transferred back to Montreal because his female colleagues interpreted his physical closeness, the pats on the back he would give them, and the compliments he paid them on their clothes as sexual harassment. Back in Montreal, this behavior was received positively by his female sales assistants.

Information Flow

The way information is handled depends on the cultural context. In high-context cultures, information is expected to flow freely from person to person—it has a life of its own. High-context people have created and keep nurturing throughout their life networks of people who provide them with information that may be useful to them at one point or another. In many high-context cultures, people take pride in being the first to have a new piece of information and to communicate it to others. High-context people tend to rely on other people as information sources: When they need information on a specific topic, they know or look for the person who is best informed and talk to that person.

In low-context cultures, information flow is compartmentalized. Low-context people do not provide information "just in case"; they provide information "as needed." The information-gathering networks they form are less extensive. Low-context people rely on documents as information sources. When low-context people need information, they look for a document (either in printed or electronic form) that covers what they need.

As discussed in Chapter 4, high-context people need to create common understanding and share information in many areas in order to create a shared context. From that point forward, their communication is fast because they do not need to repeat background information that everyone has. By contrast, low-context people move faster through the "getting to know one another" stage by sharing less information at that point. Later on, this information is provided in the form of background information that is repeated at the beginning of every discussion.

This difference in the way information is handled creates misunderstandings in multicultural technical organizations, particularly in research and development centers. In presentations, low-context people tend to bring people up to speed at the beginning and to make their points explicit. High-context people tend to consider this as both a waste of time, since they already have the information, and an insult to their intellectual abilities, since they could figure these points out themselves. For example, when an American cook says on a cooking show something like "Take a clean towel and pat the meat dry," high context people tend to think: "What did he or she think? That I was going to use a dirty towel?"

Contrast this situation with high-context presentations. High-context people tend to make indirect references to facts that everyone in the audience is expected to know already. These allusions tend to make low-context people feel left out because they may not have that information or may not understand the connection between the two. High-context presentations may not contain explicit conclusions—participants are expected to reach these conclusions by themselves (e.g., this is often the case with Japanese presentations). This leaves low-context participants wondering what the point of the presentation was.

When they need information about a specific topic, high-context people look for the person who knows that topic best in order to get information from him or her. If this person is a high-context person, he or she is likely to receive this request for information positively; it implies that he or she is the expert on the topic. If this person is a low-context person, he or she is likely to receive this request negatively; it represents an interruption in their work. Their most likely response is to provide the information seeker with a book or reference—not at all what that person expected.

When they seek information about a specific topic, low-context people look for a written source of information. If the high-context person who is considered the expert on that topic finds out that their expertise was not sought, they may interpret this as a challenge to their expertise.

This difference of approach to the flow of information also has an impact on office layouts. The best positions in high-context offices are usually in the center; senior managers want to be continuously updated by everyone in their department. In low-context offices, the best positions are on the sides (the corner office), where the flow of information can be more readily controlled.

Approaches to Time

Differences in the sense of time are generally well known. Some have even made their way into the English language: When North Americans say that something will happen *mañana*, they imply that the probability of this event happening is lower than when they say "tomorrow." This refers to the different sense of time that Latin Americans and North Americans have (Hall, 1990; Trompenaars, 1998).

In his studies of cultural differences, Hall (1977, 1983, 1987, 1990) differentiated between monochronic and polychronic cultures. In monochronic cultures, people tend to do one thing at a time. They tend to concentrate on the task at hand and try to avoid interruptions. Monochronic people take schedules and deadlines seriously. Because schedules are important to them, they value promptness. They also tend to put significant emphasis on privacy and private property.

In polychronic cultures, people tend to do many things at once. They tend to concentrate on the relationships at hand and welcome interruptions. Polychronic people take people and information seriously; schedules become objectives to be achieved, if possible (i.e., if there are no interruptions). They tend to change plans according to the needs of the people who are closely related to them. They put less emphasis on privacy and private property—objects and information are more readily shared in polychronic cultures.

North Americans tend to be on the monochronic end of the spectrum, although Quebecers and Hispanics tend to be polychronic. Communication between monochronic and polychronic people is often challenging in many areas, such as the following:

- *When does a meeting start?* In monochronic cultures, a meeting starts at the scheduled time, regardless of who is in the room. In polychronic cultures, a meeting starts when the key participants are ready, regardless of whether this takes place on time or 30 minutes later. When monochronic people start on time, polychronic people showing up late often require that what was said at the beginning of the meeting be repeated. When polychronic people wait for key participants, monochronic people consider that their time is wasted.

- *"Let's meet tomorrow, Insh'Allah (God willing)."* In monochronic cultures, a meeting scheduled at a specified time tomorrow has a high probability of taking place; it takes a major event for monochronic people to change their schedules on short notice. In polychronic cultures, a business meeting may be rescheduled at the last minute if people who have close ties with one participant happen to visit him or her. Monochronic people have difficulties juggling their schedules on such short notice and feel that their time is wasted (a major issue for them), whereas polychronic people feel that the relationships they hold dear are devalued by adhering rigidly to schedules.

- *Who is responsible for keeping information private?* In monochronic cultures, the sense of privacy is strong—people are not supposed to look at documents that are not addressed to them. In polychronic cultures, the sense of privacy is much weaker and information is expected to flow freely between people: if you do not want others to read a document, you are responsible for hiding it. This creates problems with faxes or photocopy machines. Polychronic people will read documents that are left unattended, whether they are addressed to them or not, thereby infringing on the privacy of monochronic people.

- *"Time is up."* Monochronic people tend to end a meeting or conversation at the scheduled end time. Polychronic people tend to end when the meeting or conversation runs out of steam—they rarely specify an end time for a meeting. When they work together, polychronic people may think that the meeting ends abruptly, before they have had a chance to say their whole piece. By contrast, monochronic people may consider that polychronic meetings go on past the point of effectiveness.

- *"What are we discussing now?"* Monochronic people like to create an agenda for meeting and discuss one topic at a time. Polychronic people rarely use agendas for meetings and jump from one topic to the next whenever a connection is made. Polychronic meetings confuse monochronic people—"Can we please stick to the topic at hand?"—while monochronic meetings constrain polychronic people—"If another topic is more important than or is connected to the topic at hand, why not move on to that one?"

In low-context societies, schedules take precedence over people; in high-context societies, the reverse applies. This leads to many misunderstandings: High-context people expect to be able to simply show up in people's office or call people and get the answer to their questions right there and then. The idea that they need to schedule a meeting with that person may not cross their mind, particularly if they have only a few simple questions to ask. Here is the experience of a French engineer in Canada:

> I had scheduled a meeting with one English Canadian engineer from 10 to 11 a.m., then another meeting with a second English Canadian engineer from 11 to 11:30 a.m. The meetings went fine and ended on time. At 11:30 a.m., I realized that I had not asked the first one for his business card, so I asked the second person I met to take me to his office. When I showed up at the door of his office at 11:30 a.m., the first engineer clearly had no idea what to do with me—I was not on his schedule at this point, so what was I doing there?

In high-context societies, relationships among people are importan and are constantly nurtured through small talk, gifts from time to tim (on average, Japanese families make 30 gifts per month), and frequer communication. By contrast, low-context people tend to communicat with others only when there is something to communicate; small tal is much more limited (in many German meetings, people say "Hi" an start right away).

As a result, high-context people may perceive low-context people a being interested in others only when they need something from then the absence of communication when there is nothing to communicat slowly unravels the relationships they have with high-context peopl Conversely, low-context people may perceive high-context people a wasting their time with chit-chat and communication that has n apparent purpose; the only purpose of this communication is to nu ture the relationship, something that is not necessary in low-contex cultures.

Approaches to Conflict Resolution

When a misunderstanding arises in a multicultural work group, th question becomes how to resolve it. Unfortunately, conflict resolutio approaches are not standard around the world. Actually, the best wa to resolve conflicts in low-context cultures tends to make the confli worse in high-context cultures, and vice versa.

In low-context cultures, conflicts between two people are expecte to remain between the two people. They are expected to step aside an discuss their differences of opinion separately and directly. People wh are not initially involved in the conflict tend to either "stay out of it or take sides. In low-context cultures, "triangulation" or mediatio (i.e., looking for a third party who can intervene in the dispute) is on of the worst things someone can do to resolve a conflict.

In high-context cultures, serious conflicts between two people ar rarely dealt with directly. In most cases, a third party who has the trus of both sides will be sought by one or both sides. This third party wi act as a *neutral* go-between, trying to present to each side the othe side's position in terms that they may find acceptable, looking for po: sible compromises and ways to smooth out differences until both side are close to an agreement. At that point, the two conflicting parties ca be brought back together.

When a high-context person and a low-context person have a mi: understanding, they often run into a second conflict immediately: Hov are they going to resolve the first one? When the low-context perso attempts to discuss the issue directly, in a frank and open manner, th approach only compounds the issue as far as the high-context person is concerned. Simultaneously, the attempts that the high-context person makes to discuss the issue through third parties are strongly opposed by the low-context person. There are now two conflicts, the first one and a conflict on how to resolve a conflict.

Time Orientation and Horizon

Some cultures are oriented toward the past, whereas others are oriented toward the future (Hall, 1990; Trompenaars, 1998). This orientation is coupled with different time horizons: When planning for the future, people in some cultures tend to plan over a longer time horizon than in others (the difference between Japanese and North Americans is striking in this respect). The same applies to the past: When considering events that have shaped the current situation, people in some cultures tend to go farther back in time than in others.

North America as a whole tends to be oriented toward the immediate future. Most corporations are concerned with their next quarterly results, and many people plan their career over the next two to three years. In this area, like any other discussed in this book, there are important variations among people. Within the same culture, some people may be much more past-oriented than others or plan over a longer time horizon than others. There are, however, discernable trends that often need to be taken into consideration. The following differences have a major impact in professional interactions.

People who are oriented toward the past often make allusion to the heydays of their cultures. For example, Chinese refer to their 4,000 years of continuous history; French refer to the 18th century (the "siècle des Lumières"); British talk about the time when the "sun never set on the Empire"; Danes mention the Viking era; Greeks and Italians refer to Ancient Athens and Rome; and so on.

For people who are future-oriented, these references may be considered irrelevant, amusing, or annoying (the latter is more likely when these references become too frequent for their liking). As far as they are concerned, this is all "water under the bridge" and has no bearing on the current situation. When they ignore or diminish these cultural accomplishments, future-oriented people may unwittingly offend these people. For past-oriented people, this past is very present, and it is a part of them. Ignoring this past is like ignoring them.

The time horizon considered as relevant within a culture will have a strong impact on people's presentations because the presenter will likely refer to events that took place throughout the period considered as relevant. Many German presenters start their presentations at the beginning of the project, even if that took place several years ago, and take the audience through all the developments since then. For most North American audiences, this is more information than they wanted; only the most recent developments are considered relevant. The experience of a French engineer working in Canada illustrates this point:

> I had arranged a meeting between the Dean of the Faculty of Engineering in a Canadian university and the person in charge of Student Exchange Programs in a French Grande Ecole. When the Canadian Dean said: "Tell me about your university," the French guy gave him a five-minute lecture on its history, starting from its creation in the late 18th century and taking him through all the famous alumni. After a few seconds, the Canadian Dean started composing a letter. He perked up when the French guy started talking about what happened in the last five years.

Issues also arise in business or technical discussions when people discuss planning for the future if they consider different time horizons. Because the short term is generally more predictable than the long term, people who plan for the short term do not need to take as many events and contingencies into consideration. When people who plan for the long term inquire, "What about this issue?", people planning for the short term often answer in essence, "This is not important, we will cross that bridge when we come to it." This approach is often perceived as short-sighted by people who plan for the long term; in their minds, paying attention to this issue now would require only a little bit of effort, whereas ignoring it now and addressing it later will require much work and investment. Their approach is more like "one ounce of prevention is worth a pound of cure."

Feedback

The difference in feedback scales (see Chapter 2 for more details) can create major issues when communicating with people from different cultural backgrounds, particularly in meetings. When someone offers an idea, the response of other meeting participants may be misinterpreted. For example, let's consider the situation where a North American technical professional suggests an idea during a team meeting.

A team member may attempt to make a comment that is slightly negative, trying to say something like "Have you considered X? It may play a role here" with the idea that handling X may require some adjustment to the idea just suggested. If this person comes from a cultural background where feedback is given more forcefully (e.g., Poland or France), the comment may be received by the North American idea generator as "How can you think of such a crazy idea? It will never work because of X."

The opposite situation does not generate nearly as many issues: When someone from a different cultural background makes a positive comment that sounds more positive than it actually is meant to be, the idea generator rarely objects. Conversely, a team member may attempt to make a negative comment but is ignored because the comment is not made in words that indicate that it warrants consideration. The idea generator may understand something like "You may want to take X into consideration," whereas the person providing feedback meant "I have tried something like this before; honestly, it is unlikely to work because of X."

Expressiveness

The role that emotions can play in the workplace varies significantly from country to country and can create havoc in multicultural teams (Trompenaars, 1998). In this respect, two aspects need to be considered: (1) the range of emotions that can be displayed in a professional setting and (2) the speed at which people can change their emotional state.

Acceptable Range of Emotions

Different cultures allow different ranges of emotions to be displayed in a professional setting, as demonstrated by Exhibit 4.2. Variations do occur from person to person: Within a given culture, some people are more extroverted than others. At the same time, the range of emotions that is acceptable in an Italian workplace is wider than the range of emotions that can be displayed in North America, which is itself wider than the range of emotions that can be displayed in a Japanese or Chinese office.

This point is often clearly illustrated during the Academy Awards Ceremony. When the Best Foreign Movie Award goes to an Italian movie (like *Life is Beautiful*) or a Spanish movie (like *All about My Mother*), the recipient of the award usually displays significantly more emotions than his or her American counterparts. The Italian director accepting the award for *Life is Beautiful* stood up, climbed on his chair, and raised his arms in victory. When the Latin American actress announcing the award saw the name of the winner, she screamed happily "Pedro!"

Exhibit 4.2

The range of emotions that can be displayed in the workplace varies from country to country.

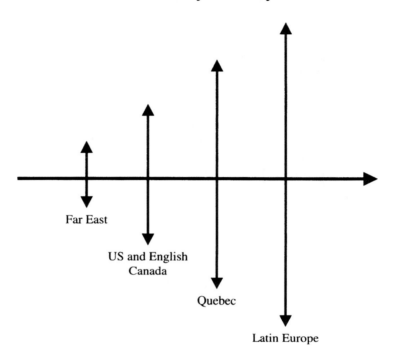

Far East

US and English
Canada

Quebec

Latin Europe

By contrast, many North Americans mention the challenge of reading people from Far Eastern countries when doing business with them. To many Americans and Canadians, the face of an unhappy Japanese person does not look very different from the face of a happy Japanese person. The Japanese show their pleasure or displeasure nonverbally, but the nonverbal cues they use are more subtle and may be easily overlooked or misread by people who are used to a wider range of displayed emotions.

Using a measurement analogy, the issue here is the same as trying to measure a physical variable (like voltage) with an instrument that is not designed for the range of measurements that you are trying to make. If your instrument is designed to measure smaller voltages, the needle goes to the maximum position; the instrument is saturated and you cannot do much with the measurement. If your instrument is designed for much larger voltages, the needle hardly moves from zero and the uncertainty on the measurement is huge; again you cannot do much with the measurement.

In multicultural teams, when people from one cultural background display strong *positive* emotions by the standards of colleagues from different cultural backgrounds, this does not create much of an issue. In the best situations, team members who tend not to express their emotions may join their more demonstrative colleagues and express their joy or happiness as well. In other situations, they may see this display of strong positive emotions as childish (in most countries, children tend to show more emotions than adults until they learn how to keep their emotions in check and express them in a way that is culturally suitable).

On this scale, there is a significant difference between Quebec and the rest of Canada: Quebecers tend to express their emotions more than their English Canadian counterparts. On the positive side, English Canadians refer to this as the *joie de vivre* of French Canadians. On the negative side, they refer to the emotional and irrational aspects of French Canadians.

Serious problems are likely to occur when people from one cultural background express a negative emotion that goes beyond the range of negative emotions of other meeting participants. In that case, the less expressive or neutral participants are saturated by these strong negative emotions, like the voltmeter that reaches its maximum value and no longer moves from that position. The statements made by the more expressive participants are interpreted by the neutral participants as "This is the end of the world, we will never make it." Because the less expressive people are overwhelmed by this strong negative emotion, they cannot absorb the ideas and suggestions made by the more expressive participants.

Conversely, neutral participants at that point are likely to make statements that sound too mild to expressive participants. To them, it sounds as if neutral participants do not understand the gravity of the situation or are not taking it seriously. In that situation, they may try to increase the emphasis in their statements in order to make neutral participants understand how serious the situation is, leading to a runaway situation.

This often ends in communication breakdown. When expressive participants show excessively negative emotions about the chances of success of a project, neutral participants are likely to "write them off," thinking something like: "How can we do business with such lunatics and doom-sayers? They are totally out of control!" At that point, neutral participants may let expressive participants say whatever they have to say without making any comment, end the meeting as quickly as possible, then reconvene without the expressive participants in order to do business with "reasonable people."

In a meeting that includes both expressive and neutral participants, expressive participants may disagree among themselves and show emotions that exceed the range of emotions that neutral participants consider acceptable in the workplace. At that point, the expressive participants look like they are "about to kill each other" to the neutral people involved, whereas they consider that they are having a "frank and open discussion." Conversely, expressive participants are likely to miss the cues that indicate that someone "has lost it," as the experience of a French engineer working with Canadians indicates:

> We were in a meeting with our manager, our manager's manager, and his manager, Jack. At one point, Jack started making jokes about treating the product by dipping it in a vat of toxic material and using that as a way of avoiding the current design problems. When we left the room, my colleagues were commenting on how Jack had "lost it" in the meeting. I thought to myself: "He did? If this is what a Canadian who has lost it sounds like, what do they say when a French guy loses it?"

Meetings among people from different cultural backgrounds may also run into difficulties when neutral participants express discomfort, unease, or disagreement with an idea or the situation. Expressive participants may either miss or misinterpret their cues. Over time, the situation may deteriorate. Like misinterpreted negative feedback, it may lead to "lightning in a blue sky," when neutral participants walk out of the room, or confusion, when neutral participants never follow up on the meeting and expressive participants have no idea why (Gercik, 1996).

Another issue arises when expressive people attempt to discuss emotions with neutral people in the workplace. Neutral people tend to view emotions as something that prevents people from thinking clearly. They usually avoid discussing emotions in professional settings because emotions are not supposed to be there. By contrast, expressive people tend to view emotions as a fact of life that can be discussed objectively.

Expressive people consider that progress and setbacks in a project lead legitimately to positive or negative emotions and will discuss these emotions, why they have them, where they come from, and what will happen next. Every time they meet someone, expressive people (in particular, Latin Americans) will look that person over from head to toe and back in order to judge his or her current state of emotions (Malinowicz, 2001). They will then use that piece of information to decide how to bring up specific topics or whether they should bring up these topics at all.

In a meeting that involves both neutral and expressive participants, misunderstandings arise when expressive participants bring up the topic of emotions ("How do you feel about this issue?"). As far as neutral participants are concerned, this is a nontopic: Emotions are not there, or at least they should not be. When these neutral people attempt to change the topic, they irritate their expressive colleagues for whom this information is important to the decision-making process.

Rate of Change in Emotions

In addition to displaying a wider or narrower range of emotions, people in expressive or neutral cultures have different rates of change in emotions, as described in Exhibit 4.3. Using an analogy with spring and weight systems, the less expressive people are, the more damped their emotional response is. Very expressive people (like Latin Europeans and Latin Americans) tend to move much more quickly from a positive emotion to a negative emotion and back. Less expressive people tend to move more slowly between the two.

Exhibit 4.3

The rate of emotion change varies from country to country. *Dashed line*: Expressive cultures. *Solid line*: Neutral cultures.

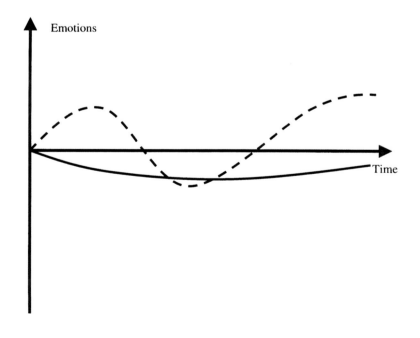

This difference in rate of change is such that people can become quickly "out of sync" during meetings or negotiations. For example consider a meeting involving both neutral and expressive people where things start on the wrong foot and the discussion turns into a dis agreement, as in Exhibit 4.4. Expressive people are likely to move into negative territory faster and more significantly than their neutral coun terparts. At that point, neutral participants may not understand the strong negative statements made by expressive participants.

When things are clarified and the disagreement starts to disappear expressive participants move back into positive territory quickly whereas neutral participants move more slowly in that direction. In this case, the meeting may end with expressive participants thinking that the meeting went well, whereas neutral participants are left with a negative impression.

Emotions in Written Documents

References to emotions in written documents tend to be rare in neu tral cultures and more common in expressive cultures. Expressive peo

Exhibit 4.4

A difficult meeting between expressive and neutral people. Solid line: The reaction of expressive participants. Dashed line: The reaction of neutral participants.

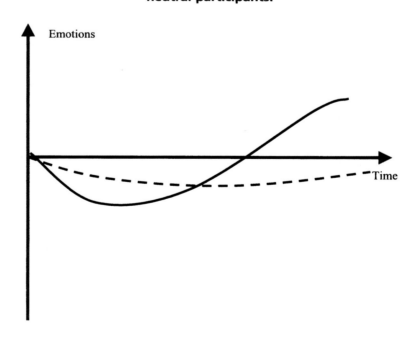

ple make references to hunches, feelings, and guesses that are considered inappropriate in written documents by neutral people. Statements like "I feel we are on the right track" may be acceptable in documents for expressive readers and unacceptable for neutral readers.

E-mail messages are particularly prone to this type of misunderstanding: An expressive sender may write a quick e-mail that includes some emotionally charged comments that neutral receivers find out of place and difficult to interpret. Conversely, the messages that neutral people send to expressive receivers are perceived as cold and void of the emotions that expressive readers want to see—it enables them to gauge how relationships and projects are moving along.

Power Distance

Power distance has a significant impact on communication. In hierarchical societies, people who have power are expected to show this power, and those who do not are expected to show respect and deference to those who have power. Here are ways in which this respect and deference are shown:

- People use titles, formal greetings, and formal forms of address (e.g., last names, formal version of you in French, German, Spanish) extensively.
- Presenters usually direct their attention to the highest-ranked person in the room. Reports and documents are addressed to the highest-ranked person who made the request.
- The opinion of the highest-ranked person in the room carries much weight for hierarchical people. When this person has spoken in one direction, this usually ends the discussion on this specific topic.
- Seating arrangements during meetings and business meals reflect the hierarchy. For example, during one visit of Canadian engineers and scientists in Japan, the Japanese hosts assumed that the female member of the Canadian delegation was a secretary and placed her at the corresponding table. When they found out that she was in fact one of the highest-ranking members, they apologized profusely and gave her a beautiful gift.
- People seek the opinion and approval of those who are in high-ranking positions and may bypass others at lower levels in the organization.

By contrast, in participative societies, those who have power are expected not to show this power. In meetings and presentations, all participants are assumed to be relatively equal; they are expected to have an equal opportunity to contribute to the discussion, and presenters often share their attention more or less equally among everyone in the audience. Most participative people consider titles as something that applies only to their business card; using titles as a form of address may make them uncomfortable.

When hierarchical and participative people communicate with one another, some participative people consider the special attention that hierarchical people pay to powerful people unpleasant. Conversely, some hierarchical people consider that the lack of special attention demonstrates a lack of respect.

Risk Tolerance

As discussed in Chapter 3, risk tolerance translates directly in the workplace in the amount of information people need in order to know that they have made the right decision. In meetings, presentations, and documents, this translates into the following:

- Risk-averse people tend to make presentations that contain a large amount of information. They also tend to discuss what may go wrong and how it can be avoided. They emphasize structure in the presentation—going through the right process, both in experiments and in the presentation.

- Risk-tolerant people tend to make presentations that contain less information. The focus tends to be on what can be gained. They emphasize the outcome—how this outcome is achieved tends to be more secondary.

A good illustration of this difference is the contrast between Japanese and North American technical presentations: Japanese presenters tend to show transparency after transparency of data—10 rows across, 20 rows down, full of numbers. A good Japanese presentation is designed to convince the audience that the presenter's group has turned absolutely every stone and that there is only one possible conclusion that can be drawn from their data. This conclusion, however, is often not stated explicitly, as is often the case in high-context presentations—the audience is expected to infer it.

By contrast, North American technical presentations state their conclusions right up front, provide more background and significantly less data than Japanese presentations, and repeat their conclusions explicitly at the end.

When risk-tolerant people communicate with or present to risk-averse people, the main obstacle is the number of detailed questions that risk-averse people ask. Some of these questions may appear totally irrelevant to risk-tolerant people, but they are clearly important and need to be answered for risk-averse people to accept the conclusions or decisions.

Risk-tolerant presenters may also confuse risk-averse audiences when "the numbers do not match." In a presentation that contains similar information (e.g., a control sample) on different slides, risk-averse audiences will be constantly checking that the same value is used for the same variable throughout the presentation. If there is a discrepancy, they will immediately flag it to the presenter and ask why. If the answer does not satisfy them, they are likely to write off the presentation as inconsistent. Comments that include "things do not add up" or "the units do not match" often result in the same outcome.

When risk-averse people communicate or present to risk-tolerant people, the former often lose the latter when they go through the extensive data and detailed information they have collected. By the end of the meeting or presentation, risk-tolerant people are asking: "What should I remember out of all this?" To risk-averse people, many points in the presentation are important, more than to risk-tolerant people.

This point is particularly striking in written documents. Risk-tolerant people ask for executive summaries and "one-pagers" that get to the point. This is a continuous challenge for risk-averse people, for whom many more details are important. In particular, calculations, which are usually relegated to the appendices of technical reports in risk-tolerant countries, are included in the body of the report in risk-averse countries.

In general, risk-averse people tend to check that the information presenters or authors are putting forward is correct and will usually go through it with a fine-toothed comb before accepting their interpretation. When they are satisfied that the assumptions, definitions, methodology, sources, logic, data, and experiments are solid, then they accept the conclusions and the recommendations that come with them.

By contrast, risk-tolerant people assume that presenters or authors have done their homework and have already verified that the assumptions, definitions, methodology, sources, logic, data, and experiments are solid beforehand. In essence, risk-tolerant people accept the information provided at face value and turn their attention to its implications. Recommendations are discussed to a much greater extent in risk-tolerant countries.

Individualism

People communicate differently in individualistic and collectivistic societies. For example, "it is often said that in groups, Japanese people tend to talk about each other while Westerners talk about themselves—imagine the imbalance when you combine people from both cultures in one setting!" (Boyle, 2001).

As a general rule, individualistic people use the pronoun "I" extensively. They tend to talk about their own accomplishments, their work, and their responsibilities. People in individualistic countries are encouraged and taught to identify and express their needs; after all, "the squeaky wheel gets the grease."

It is often considered inappropriate for an individualistic person to talk about what they would do if they were in your shoes; this would assume that they can think the way you do, which is not possible because you are two different individuals.

When individualistic people want to give someone advice, they often surround that advice with extensive qualifiers, such as "This is only my opinion, you need to determine what is best for yourself." They may also talk about what they did personally: "Here is how I handled this situation; you may consider doing some of the same things, or not. It's up to you."

As a general rule, collectivistic people talk about "you" or "we." They focus on the group's accomplishments, responsibilities, and work. It is often considered inappropriate for collectivistic people to talk about their own personal accomplishments. Collectivistic people also learn to think of the needs of the group to which they belong before their own needs; as such, they may not be able to distinguish between their own needs and the needs of the group (Japanese say that "the nail that sticks out gets hammered down").

In collectivistic cultures, people are brought up to put themselves in other people's shoes—this creates a stronger group. When collectivistic people want to give advice to someone, they often give this advice from that person's point of view: "If I were you, I would . . ."

When collectivistic and individualistic people work together, situations where one provides advice to the other often result in misunderstandings. The advice provided by collectivistic people to individualistic people is received as an interference in their own lives, while advice provided by individualistic people to collectivistic people is often not recognized: "You did X, that's fine, but that does not tell me what I should do now."

The difference between collectivistic and individualistic people also plays a role when giving gifts. In collectivistic societies, providing one gift for the group is common; it is much more rare in individualistic societies. This difference becomes striking when giving out documents (like promotional brochures or printouts of a presentation); individualistic people all expect to receive their own copy, whereas collectivistic people may expect one copy for two people to share or one copy for the whole group. Here is the experience of a Canadian engineer in Brazil.

> Three of my Canadian colleagues and I were visiting a plant in Brazil. At lunchtime, the four of us went out by ourselves. We found a restaurant we liked and sat down. A waitress brought us a single menu. I asked, "Could we have three more?" The waitress answered, "Why? They are all the same"!

Finally, the distance that individualistic people keep between themselves and the organization is such that they can and will, at times, make critical statements about its management, direction, or policies. Such statements are much more rare in collectivistic organizations; because collectivistic people *are* the organization, making critical statements about the organization is equivalent to making critical statements about themselves. Collectivistic people are often surprised when they hear individualistic people comment negatively about their organizations—they see it as lacking respect for oneself. At the same time, the continuous absence of negative statements makes individualistic people wonder whether collectivistic people have a mind of their own.

What Can You Do?

Usually, cross-cultural communication issues are relatively easy to identify; either you do not understand what others have in mind or they do not understand what you mean. Identifying which specific issues are at play in a complex communication event (like a meeting, presentation, or negotiation) becomes challenging because there are many possible sources of miscommunication.

For each potential issue, several small steps can be taken. Some apply to a range of multicultural situations, whereas others apply to cultural differences in specific areas (e.g., context, risk tolerance, power distance). This section first suggests some steps people can take individually in order to improve communication with others. As in the case of manager–employee relationships, groups of culturally different people who communicate with one another regularly are encouraged to examine as a group how they can best communicate together. Suggestions for group guidelines are provided at the end of this section.

Language

With respect to language, the steps that people can take depend on whether they are native English speakers or not. The following steps apply to both:

- Define the meaning of key technical words and acronyms at the beginning.

- Avoid nonstandard abbreviations, such as "U R" instead of "you are."

- Make sure that you explain the meaning of idiomatic expressions (e.g., sports English in the case of North Americans).

- Try to remain cool and composed, even when you have made a mistake that results in embarrassment for others or for you (in most cases, they did not mean to embarrass you).

- Ensure that translations are performed by translators who are familiar with the topic covered in the document.

- Avoid chewing gum or smoking as you speak; anything that distorts your enunciation is likely to be an impediment to communication.

Native English Speakers

When native English speakers communicate in English with people who have learned English as a second language, they may consider the following:

- Simplify your message by using less complex sentence structure and vocabulary (this applies to an even greater extent to the British).

- Never shout to be understood.

- Avoid humor until you know your audience well. You may want to get to know what is likely to make them laugh (e.g., by watching comedy movies coming from their cultures) before you attempt to use humor.

- Avoid "isn't it?" questions. Because this way of formulating questions does not exist in many other languages, it can be confusing for non-native English speakers. To the question "You are coming, aren't you?" they may answer "Yes (I am coming)" or "No (I am coming)" depending on how they interpret the question.

- Learn to understand and adapt to the conversation pace. When dealing with Far Easterners, do not rush to fill in silence, thereby providing them with some time to process information. When dealing with Latin Americans or Latin Europeans who are fluent in English, recognize that their interruptions are not meant as a lack of respect. Prepare yourself for interruptions, and do not hesitate to interrupt people as well.

- If you do not understand a word used by a non-native English speaker, you may:

  ○ Ask the person to spell the word.
  ○ Ask him or her to write it down (during a face-to-face meeting or videoconference).
  ○ Ask him or her to use a synonym.
  ○ Ask him or her to say this word in his or her native language and have someone else translate.

- Avoid places that have background noise (e.g., airports, train stations, bars) or echoes. Whenever possible, look for a quiet place for your meetings. When using telecommunications, try to avoid static; for example, hanging up and trying to call once again to get a clear line may be well worth the time.

- If you get a voice-mail message from a non-native English speaker that you do not understand, you may consider having another non-native English speaker from the same linguistic background listen to it and "translate" for you. This person has a better chance of figuring out what the message means because he or she is familiar with the accent and the typical mistakes that people from that linguistic background make when speaking English.

- In continuous meetings, provide some rest time so that non-native speakers can take a break from the concentration required to follow the conversation.

- Consider providing English as a Second Language (ESL) courses to the New North American members of your staff or team. Courses designed to help participants modify their accents can be particularly beneficial.

- Offer to proofread their documents or presentations.

- Try to slow down your delivery and articulate each word more. Avoid contractions ("gonna," "wanna," etc.) that are difficult for non-native English speakers to grasp.

- In face-to-face meetings, face the people to whom you speak and do not cover your mouth with your hand or a handkerchief. Non-native English speakers often use lip-reading in combination with the sounds they hear to determine what was said.

- Be patient when New North Americans are trying to explain new ideas using broken English. Make sure you understand their point, rather than dismissing their idea because you do not understand what they are trying to say. Only then will you be able to determine the value of their ideas.

Non-Native English Speakers

When non-native English speakers communicate in English with native English speakers, they may consider the following:

- When you are asked to repeat a word or a sentence a third time, try using a synonym or rephrasing your idea rather than repeating the same words.

- If your organization offers ESL courses, take them, even if your English is already functional. Courses designed to help you modify your accent to make it more understandable by native English speakers can be particularly beneficial. Keep in mind that, if people do not understand what you are trying to say, they cannot judge whether you have good ideas or not and they cannot make use of your suggestions—so your career opportunities will be limited.

- Keep a dictionary handy and ensure that the words you use mean what you think they mean.

- Ask for and get help with your documents and presentations from a native English speaker. This approach may also be used in the case of sensitive e-mail messages or phone calls—running your approach or message by a native English speaker is likely to help remove some sources of potential misunderstandings. As a non-native English speaker, I often run sensitive e-mail responses by my wife before sending them.

- Before calling a native English speaker on the phone, think of what you want to say. This way, you have a chance to look up the words you are missing ahead of time rather than on the phone. If you are leaving a voice-mail message, you can compose this message on paper, then read it aloud to the answering machine. This decreases considerably the chances of misunderstandings.

- If you come from a country where language conveys social class, you can take some of the pressure off yourself because this is not the case in North America. As long as people understand what you say, you are communicating well. Keep practicing without being afraid of making mistakes; this is one of the best ways to improve.

- Because language conveys technical expertise to some extent in North America, learn the technical words that people use in your field. Find a native English speaker who will take the time to discuss this with you; use sketches, diagrams, and pictures to ensure that you understand all these technical terms. Use them repeatedly until they become second nature.

- Latin Americans and Latin Europeans may learn to refrain from starting to speak before others have finished saying what they have to say.

- Do not attempt to use slang and idiomatic expressions until you are comfortable with the language. You may use them in the wrong situation, which may backfire on you.

Context

Both high- and low-context people can take many steps in order to bridge the gap between their respective approaches, as described in Exhibit 4.5.

Time Orientation and Horizon

The best way of bridging this difference is fairly straightforward: People who are past-oriented should focus on the future when working with future-oriented people, and vice versa. This is easier said than done, however, but it is well worth the effort because much can be learned from one another in this situation, as discussed in the next section.

Feedback

As in the case of manager–employee relationships, feedback between people who have different feedback scales needs to be handled with care to avoid unwittingly offending others.

Exhibit 4.5

Steps that low-context people can take to communicate more effectively with high-context people, and vice versa.

	Low-Context People Communicating with High-Context People	High-Context People Communicating with Low-Context People
Space	• Express your discomfort in words rather than by stepping back. Whenever possible, accept their incursions in your comfort zone. • Initiate physical contact (handshakes, embraces, etc.) when you can. Receive physical contact as positive.	• Refrain from coming too close. Give low-context people space. • Avoid physical contact. Apologize when it takes place.
Time	• Learn to pick up the phone and "just" call or to walk to someone and ask them "just one question." • Accept interruptions and disruptions of schedules when they occur. • If you want something to be discussed, invite the key people for a meal outside of the office. • Learn to connect topics during meetings and conversations. • Be ready to extend the meeting until the conversation runs out of steam.	• Schedule events, meetings, telephone conversations, etc. • Make more of an effort to follow the schedule. • If you want something to be discussed, make sure it is on the meeting agenda. • Refrain from walking to someone's office to ask "just one question" and from jumping from one topic to another related topic. • Be ready to wrap up at the appointed time.
Information	• Refer to the existing situation more indirectly. You do not need to spell background information out. • Identify the people who can best act as sources of information on specific topics and consult them when you need new information.	• Provide more background information at the beginning of the meeting or presentation. • Learn to look for information in written format (library or Internet searches).

Relationship	
	• Keep the relationship alive by sending small e-mail messages from time to time.
	• Build relationships through small talk and gifts; this is the best way to achieve your professional objectives with high-context people. Find out what is important for your high-context counterparts (family, sports, arts, organizational changes, etc.) and inquire regularly about recent developments.
	• In a meeting with new faces, ensure that you are introduced to all participants. Provide details.
	• If there is nothing professional to say, do not say anything. Wait until you have a specific need before calling or sending an e-mail.
	• Focus on the task at hand. Delivering consistently on set objectives is the best way to build relationships with low-context people.
	• In a meeting with new faces, walk up to people and introduce yourself to everyone. Limit this introduction to your name and your company or department. Let people ask for more information.

Communication	
	• Increase your use of gestures and body language.
	• Incorporate the nonverbal message provided by high-context people in your interpretation of the situation.
	• When you have difficulties expressing your emotions about something, consider verbalizing them.
	• "Yes" may mean "I heard you," not "I agree." Do not take "yes" for an answer.
	• Recognize the implicit probability that events will actually take place. Qualifying statements imply different levels of probability. For example, "I will do it," "I may do it," "I might do it," "Maybe I will do it," "Perhaps I will do it," "I would do it (if)," "We will do it," etc. all imply different probabilities. This also applies to double negatives: "It is not impossible" does not carry the same probability as "It is possible."
	• Reduce the amount of gestures and body language communication you use.
	• Make your communication more explicit. Double entendres and indirect messages are likely to be misunderstood by low-context people.
	• Avoid reacting strongly to words or messages that sound blunt to you.
	• Whenever possible, give low-context people an estimate of the probability that what you say is going to happen is actually going to happen.

When providing feedback to people who have a wider neutral zone than you do, you may consider cranking up the volume faster than you normally would, *without reading anything in the lack of response* (this is the difficult part). Monitor continuously for response: If there is none, the feedback recipient may not have understood your point, in which case you may have to restate it more firmly. In extreme cases consider getting some advice from people who understand all the cultures involved, in order to avoid creating an impasse.

When providing feedback to people who have a more narrow neutral zone than you do, you may consider toning down your feedback. The challenge here is that when you "soft-pedal" feedback, you may not have the impression that the person has really understood what you have in mind. Monitor the response in order to ensure that your point did come across.

Expressiveness

The best way of bridging this difference is both straightforward and usually difficult to implement. Neutral people should consider displaying more emotions when working with expressive people. Neutral people generally find that this is easier to do on the positive side: They may consider "letting their hair down" to a greater extent when something positive happens in a joint project or meeting with expressive people.

More important, they should not let the strong emotions, particularly negative emotions, displayed by expressive people throw them off course. When the emotions displayed by expressive participants become overwhelming, neutral participants may consider calling a time-out in order to give everyone, including themselves, some time to reset their emotional gauge. In addition, neutral people should consider the fact that emotions are a piece of data for expressive people. In many cases, this data may need to be discussed objectively for expressive people to feel comfortable with the decisions that need to be made.

Conversely, expressive people need to put a damper on their emotions, particularly those on the negative end of the spectrum. They should also avoid discussing emotions in meetings with neutral people because the chances of losing credibility in their minds are high at that point.

Not expressing emotions can be accomplished easily when communication does not take place in real time, as in the case of written documents and phone messages. Expressive people may consider proofreading their documents once to identify specific words and passages that contain emotions. For example, sentences that start with "I feel" are likely to have a somewhat negative impact on neutral people. Consider rephrasing the sentence and starting it with something like "I believe," "I consider," or "I think" because these expressions do not convey emotions.

The same can be done for voice-mail messages: Some voice-mail message systems allow callers to listen to the message they left and record new ones, which provides an opportunity to edit out emotionally charged comments. When leaving a message on a system that does not offer that feature, expressive people may consider writing down their message before calling so that they have a chance to edit it accordingly.

When communication takes place in real time, checking your emotional responses at the door is not easy. Expressive people who sense that their neutral counterparts are saturating (when neutral people go silent or start agreeing with you after having opposed your points for a while, chances are you have reached that point) should consider backing off and calling for a time-out. Otherwise, they run the risk of winning the battle and losing the war (i.e., people will appear to agree with them, using vague statements, only to end the meeting as fast as possible and reconvene in their absence).

Power Distance

Participative people can bridge the communication gap between themselves and their hierarchical counterparts through the following actions:

- Use titles, last names, and formal greetings until they are invited to switch to first names and informal greetings.

- Focus attention on the highest-ranked person in the room during presentations and address reports and documents to the highest-ranked person who made the request. This person is the official recipient of the document; all others are on the cc (copied to) list.

- Seek the opinion and approval from the highest-ranked person in the room. This will more or less signal the end of the decision-making phase.

- Pay attention to seating arrangements during meetings and business meals to reflect the hierarchy.

- Use "arguments of authority" (i.e., quotes that support specific points and that come from people who are recognized as experts by their hierarchical counterparts).

Conversely, hierarchical people can bridge the communication gap between themselves and their participative counterparts through the following actions:

- Use first names and informal greetings.
- Focus attention relatively equally on everyone in the room during presentations and address reports and documents to everyone.
- Seek support and approval from everyone, rather than from the highest-ranked person.
- Pay less attention to seating arrangements during meetings and business meals.
- Avoid "arguments of authority" because they have usually little weight for participative people.

Risk Tolerance

Risk-averse people who want to communicate more effectively with risk-tolerant people may consider the following steps:

- Include less information in their presentations and reports. In particular, they should provide a short summary up front (in many cases, this is the only part that risk-tolerant readers will read or remember).
- Provide fewer details about the assumptions, definitions, methodology, sources, logic, data, and experiments.
- Focus more attention on the recommendations. These recommendations need to be practical. You may skip collecting some data or running some experiments in order to ensure that your recommendations are acceptable.
- Refrain from asking many detail-oriented questions during the presentations of risk-tolerant people. Instead, ask for references and additional documentation after the presentation.

Risk-tolerant people who want to communicate more effectively with risk-averse people may consider the following steps:

- Dot all the i's and cross all the t's before making a presentation or sending out a report. Look for inconsistencies. In particular, make sure that the units match in your formulas and that the control data is always the same (if it is not, explain why).

- Provide more information in the body of the report or presentation. Your audience will ask for it, so you might as well provide it up front. Include all calculations, sources, experimental methods, and so on in your reports. In your presentations, provide more information on your assumptions, definitions, methodology, sources, logic, data, and experiments.

- Prepare the answers to questions related to your assumptions, methodology, sources, logic, data, and experiments. This will often lead you to collect more data than you think is necessary, but this data is necessary because you will not convince your audience without it.

Individualism

In order to improve communication, people on different sides of the individualistic–collectivistic spectrum may consider various tacks. For instance, individualistic people can try to anticipate and verbalize how their actions and words will affect their collectivistic counterparts. In particular, collectivistic people really appreciate when individualistic people consider the impact of their decisions (whether this decision has to do with product design or organization restructuring) on their work and responsibilities. When giving advice to collectivistic people, individualistic people may try giving that advice from their counterparts' perspective: "I suggest that you . . ." or "You may consider . . ."

Conversely, collectivistic people can try to focus on their own actions. They should refrain from comments that suggest they can place themselves in the shoes of individualistic people and know how they think or feel ("You probably think that . . ." or "If I were you, I would . . ."). They may try to replace these statements with comments that relate to how they personally think or feel ("I experienced a similar situation when . . . and here is what I did"). Collectivistic people may also focus on their own tasks and responsibilities and let their individualistic counterparts worry about the impact of their actions and words on their own areas of responsibilities.

In many cases, collectivistic people refer to "we" without defining who is included in the "we"; to their collectivistic co-workers, this point is obvious—"we" refers to the team, the department, or the company, and they can identify which one from the context. Because their individualistic co-workers are not used to saying "we," they are not used to identifying from the context who "we" represents. To avoid this issue, collectivistic people may consider identifying who "we" is;

conversely, individualistic people may consider asking who "we" represents.

Points To Examine as a Group

The following represents suggestions that people from different cultural backgrounds may consider discussing together in order to improve the effectiveness of their communication as a group. This discussion may take place formally in a meeting (it may be part of the agenda in a low-context group) or informally in a restaurant, as part of a relationship-building meal (in a high-context group).

In order to meet the needs of both high- and low-context group members, these meetings should be designed to build a better understanding and create a better rapport among the people involved as much as to find an actual solution to the problem. For example, in the case of dress code, the group may agree that its dress code will be the dress code in place where the meeting is held, the dress code of the client, or the dress code that corresponds to the corporate culture of the organization.

The key here is the process leading to this agreement: Hierarchical group members may use arguments related to who holds the most power in the group; risk-averse people may ask for extensive information before making a commitment, and low-context members may make blunt statements. These discussions are a trial run, on a small scale, of what the group is likely to go through in later discussions or negotiations. Reaching a decision in a manner that respects everyone's needs and expectations sets a positive tone for future communication.

In these group discussions, people need to explain how they view the standard operating procedure of others and why they do things the way they do. From there, they can look for a common ground. These discussions are often greatly facilitated by the presence of someone who understands what is important to everyone involved and can help find a suitable compromise.

Language

Here are guidelines for the use of languages other than English in English-speaking organizations that the group can use as a starting point for discussion:

- In team situations, people should try to avoid using a language that some team members do not understand because it does not foster team cohesiveness; it clearly makes a distinction between those who understand the language and those who do not.

- Outside of team situations (e.g., in the cafeteria), the use of languages other than English helps non-native English speakers relax and communicate more thoroughly and quickly than in English. When native English speakers show interest in joining the conversation, switching to English is a welcoming gesture; conversely, if that interest is not sustained, switching back to another language is not an excluding gesture.

- Group members should discuss becoming active listeners. When receivers send back their understanding of the message and verify with the sender whether what they understood matches what the sender meant to say, communication can be greatly improved. If the two match, then both know that they have communicated effectively. If not, they have a chance to clarify. The sender will send the same message in a different way (with additional information, more slowly, using different words, etc.) depending on the mismatch.

Part of active listening consists of asking clarifying questions (i.e., questions designed to test the understanding of the listener), such as the following:

- These questions should not be yes or no questions. In particular, "Do you understand what I mean?" does not test the listener's understanding. As long as the listener has understood something, he or she is likely to answer "yes" (this is particularly true in the case of Far Easterners, for whom saying "no" may result in loss of face for the speaker).

- Generic questions do not make good clarifying questions either. Asking something like "What do you think of this idea?" will likely elicit an answer such as "Sounds good to me" if the listener has not really understood what the sender said.

- In some cases, the clarifying question may simply be: "Can you repeat what I just told you in your own words?"

Agreeing on Communication Protocols

Besides language, group members should consider examining certain areas that often lead to cross-cultural misunderstandings. They should reach agreement regarding the following topics:

- Dress code, forms of greeting, use of first or last names, and titles
- Distribution lists (for documents) and invitation lists (for meetings and presentations)
- Time horizons, both looking back (how far back do we consider past events relevant?) and forward (how far into the future should we plan?)
- Who should be copied on messages and meeting minutes—In particular, which managers need to be informed, consulted, or involved in making the decisions that the group needs to make?
- When one team member sends a message to another team member by e-mail, fax, or voicemail, how quickly should they expect a response?
- How far and wide the impact of the group's decisions will be in the organizations—Who needs to be informed, consulted, and involved?
- How much information needs to be gathered and communicated to the group

The group may examine how people are expected to handle situations in which one group member offends another group member unintentionally. This may result from the misinterpretation of gestures, body language, feedback, or emotions when the offender and offendee come from different cultural backgrounds.

One possible approach consists of asking the person who has been offended to describe which behavior offended them (which words, gesture, or reaction did they object to?) and how they interpreted this behavior. Conversely, when people notice that others seem offended, they may ask first if such is the case and, if so, why. This approach is better suited to groups that are on the low end of the context scale.

High-context groups may decide to handle offenses through time-outs and discussions through third parties. A third party then works behind the scenes to help both the offended and the offending parties find a common ground, maybe discuss things offline together, and so on.

Approaches to Multicultural Meetings

In multicultural meetings, the following steps can significantly reduce the frequency and magnitude of misunderstandings (Laroche, 2002):

- *Send prework before the meeting.* Low-context people often appreciate this step because it implies that the meeting has been thought through and should result in concrete outcomes. It also helps people whose English is not fluent look up words in the dictionary, enabling them to follow the conversation more easily.

- *Ensure that everyone has a chance to participate.* In multicultural meetings, Far Easterners wait for an extended pause before they consider speaking; North Americans wait for others to finish speaking; and Latinos often start speaking before others have completed their sentences. As a result, Far Easterners get a disproportionately low fraction of the speaking time. It is important to provide them with the opportunity to contribute to the conversation explicitly rather than wait for them to volunteer information. The team leader or meeting chair should pay particular attention to this point.

- *Repeat and record decisions and corresponding action steps.* Make sure everyone agrees that a decision has been made before writing it down in the minutes. Also ensure that everyone agrees on what the decision is.

- *Follow up on the meeting discussions.* After the meetings, send a draft e-mail of minutes, including what was agreed to and action items resulting from the meeting. Allow for responses, disagreement, edits, and corrections and circulate the changes. In most cases, speed and accuracy are more important than format and presentation; a quick e-mail the next day is better than formal minutes a week later.

What Can You Gain?

Just about everyone has experienced, at one point or another, the waste of time and uselessness of a meeting in which people do not communicate effectively. In this respect, learning to communicate effectively with people of different cultural backgrounds increases the probability that what was decided by everyone was actually agreed by everyone and will actually take place. Tangible progress is an instant reward for effective communication.

In the case of cross-cultural communication, the biggest gain you can make is to learn to adapt your communication style to a greater extent than you would have otherwise. In particular, you may learn to use some of the techniques with people who come from culturally different backgrounds, and then you may use them with everyone more often. You may also learn to balance your communication style with respect to context, time orientation and horizon, feedback, and expressiveness (power distance, risk tolerance, and individualism are described in Chapter 3):

Context

- High-context people may learn to focus on the tasks at hand and to emphasize deliverables and schedules to a greater extent.
- Low-context people may learn to emphasize relationships and the importance of building rapport with others to a greater extent.

Time Orientation and Horizon

- People oriented toward the future may learn to take the past into consideration in order to avoid repeating the mistakes of the past.
- People oriented toward the past may learn to focus more on the future and on ways to improve it, rather than continuously focusing on something that is gone and will never come back.
- People oriented toward the long term may learn to think of quicker gains and not plan for contingencies that have a low probability of occurrence.
- People oriented toward the short term may learn to think of the longer term and not let major issues brew until they become open crises.

Feedback

- People may learn to adjust the intensity of their feedback to the receptiveness of the feedback target and make it stronger or softer depending on how that feedback is received.

Expressiveness

- People may learn to modulate their expressiveness (both the amount of emotions displayed and the rate of change in emotions) to the surrounding people. Expressive people may learn to keep their emotions in check, while neutral people may learn to show and talk about them to a greater extent.

The techniques and approaches you learn to communicate effectively with people from different cultural backgrounds can be used in other circumstances with people from your own culture. In this respect, they may help you communicate with people who "seem to come from another planet" (this may include your in-laws!).

Special Case of Global Teams

As discussed in the previous chapter, global teams have to contend with both the geographic distance and the time difference among their members. Telecommunication tools enable members to overcome this distance, when they are used properly. Overcoming time difference requires discipline and collaboration within the team. This section examines how to make the best use of telecommunication tools and to deal with time difference.

Time Difference

Communicating with teammates who work in vastly different time zones is significantly more challenging than communicating with teammates who are in close time zones. In this respect, it is much easier for North Americans to work with Latin Americans than with people in the Far East or Eastern Europe, where there is little to no overlap between working hours.

Teams split between time zones that have little overlap in their official working hours need to find a time slot during which team members have a chance to communicate interactively in real time. For example, an IT team with members on the West Coast of the United States and in Western Europe may consider communicating early in the morning West Coast time, which corresponds to the evening in Western Europe. In this case, team members may consider modifying their working hours, either officially or unofficially, in order to increase the overlap in their working days.

When no overlap exists, as in the case of teams split between Japan and the East Coast, communicating interactively is challenging. At that point, some or all team members will need to use their personal time to ensure good communication in the team. In order to create a good team spirit, it is often helpful to ensure that this imposition is shared among team members in a way that everyone recognizes as fair.

The Medium Is the Message

Telecommunication tools are part of the foundation of global teams—a global team cannot operate without them. Over the past few years, several new tools have appeared, providing a wider choice of approaches to communication for global team members. Here is a partial list of communication tools currently available:

- Telephone and telephone conference services
- Videoconferences (from people's desktops or from videoconference rooms)
- Online instant messaging tools (like Sametime™)—These are the professional equivalent of Internet chat rooms.
- Applications that enable people to share documents and collaborate with each other, such as NetMeeting™
- Interactive digital whiteboards, such as Smartboard™
- Permanent, organized archives that enable team members to store documents, such as Global Team Space™
- Web-based presentation tools, such as Contigo™

As Marshall McLuhan said, "the medium is the message." This statement applies to global teams because neutral, individualistic, and/or low-context team members (which would include most Anglo-Saxon North Americans) tend to use noninteractive tools more than their expressive, collectivistic, and/or high-context counterparts.

Noninteractive communication is easy to fit into a schedule and takes a limited amount of time, particularly when you are asking for a specific piece of information. As long as this piece of information is disconnected from other aspects of the project (which is often the case for individualistic people) and does not depend on the context (which is often the case for low-context people), it can easily be provided in that manner. In addition, neutral people are not trying to gauge the emotional state of the person from whom they ask for information, so they do not need to hear the voice of that person to get a "sense of where they are at."

By contrast, expressive, collectivistic, and/or high-context team members tend to prefer using interactive telecommunication tools. For them, the higher the bandwidth the better. Telephone and videoconferences give them the opportunity to gather information about the emotional state of their counterparts and their sense of progress (for expressive people), their nonverbal communication (for high-context people), and the connections between the information provided and the rest of the project (for collectivistic people). This information is not available through e-mail or similar forms of communication.

A good case in point of how the same telecommunication tool can be perceived and used differently by people from different cultural backgrounds is voice-mail. Voice-mail is often used by neutral, individualistic, and/or low-context people as a noninteractive tool. People leave detailed voice-mails, explaining what information they need and what they are going to do with it. They often get in return a voice-mail message that contains the response. The people involved may communicate by voice-mail without actually talking to one another.

In many cases, expressive, collectivistic, and/or high-context team members tend to use voice-mail in a different manner: In most cases, they leave a message along the lines of: "Hi, it's so-and-so, call me when you have a chance." They may leave several voice-mail messages in the same day. High-context people who know each other well may only say: "Hi, it's me. I need to talk to you." The person listening to the message is expected to recognize the caller from his or her voice (this affirms the relationship between the two because you cannot recognize the voice of a stranger). They are also expected to determine how urgently their response is needed from the tone of voice and the frequency of the messages the person has left.

In global teams, misunderstandings are common. Neutral, individualistic, and/or low-context team members find the voice-mail messages left in their voice-mail box by their expressive, collectivistic, and/or high-context counterparts too frequent, uninformative, and, sometimes, irritating. Because they do not know what the caller wants, they do not know how long the conversation they are likely to have with that person will last when they call back, so they cannot schedule it easily. As a result, it tends to slip in the priority order. On the other side, the expressive, collectivistic, and/or high-context caller is not getting the information he or she needs, leading him or her to leave more messages or to attempt to communicate through other media. At that point, the caller may conclude that getting information and communicating with such teammates is not worth the effort, thereby starting the communication breakdown process.

In the reverse situation, expressive, collectivistic, and/or high-context team members find the voice-mail messages left in their voice-mail box by their neutral, individualistic, and/or low-context counterparts uninformative. Because they do not contain the information they need to answer the question, they are likely to call back to ask for this information to give what they consider a proper response. This may lead to a long telephone conversation that low-context people do not appreciate—they expected to do something else during that time. At that point, low-context team members may conclude that getting information and communicating with such teammates is not worth the effort, thereby starting the communication breakdown process.

Using the Right Tool in the Right Way

Within the range of tools available to global teams, some are better suited for some form of communication than others. Exhibit 4.6 describes the advantages and challenges associated with each category of telecommunication tool and provides some tips on how to best use them.

Summary

Communication among people from different cultural backgrounds can lead to serious misunderstandings for several reasons:

- Issues may arise from verbal and nonverbal message misinterpretation. This can come from the fact that some of the people involved may speak English as a second language or may speak a different version of English. This may also result from different rules of conversation: You are expected to give time to people to think in the Far East, to speak one at a time in North America and in Northern Europe, and to show understanding by speaking together in Latin Europe and Latin America. Gestures and communication through diagrams may also result in misunderstandings.

- The large spatial distance and the scheduled and compartmentalized approach to communication of low-context people confuse high-context people. The short spatial distance and the encompassing and parallel approach to communication of high-context people equally confuse low-context people.

- Past-oriented people look at future-oriented people as repeating history's mistakes, whereas future-oriented people see past-oriented people as stuck in a rut. Differences in time horizon also create misunderstandings when short-term and long-term people are planning together.

- Differences in feedback scales can lead to people either offending others unintentionally or not getting their point across.

- Expressive people often overwhelm neutral people when they express strong negative emotions about the probability of success of the project. Conversely, expressive people consider that neutral

Exhibit 4.6

The advantages and challenges of each type of telecommunication tool and suggestions for communication protocols with these tools.

Tool	Advantages	Challenges	Best Practices
Telephone conference	• Useful to share information, catch up with one another, clarify misunderstandings. • Provides tone of voice (emotional context).	• Need to find a common time in people's schedules. • Body language and gestures are not communicated. • Difficult to work collaboratively on a document.	• Forward material to be discussed ahead of time; refer to material as you speak. • Make sure that everyone knows who is attending at each location. • Avoid background noises and side conversations; mute your side when your location is not talking. • Come closer to the microphone when speaking and announce who you are ("This is Claudia speaking").
Online instant messaging tools	• Best suited for quick, one-liner questions. • You can determine whether the person you want to talk to is online or not. • You can send messages to several people at the same time.	• Difficult to work collaboratively on a document. • Working with several people concurrently requires strong discipline from everyone involved. • Body language, tone of voice, and gestures are not communicated.	• Respect the online status of individuals. • Wait for people to finish typing their sentence before starting to type. When several people type and read at the same time, the discussion becomes rapidly difficult to follow. • Indicate when you are done typing and expect a response by typing "over" or something equivalent. • Use manners comparable to oral communication (say "hello" and "bye").

Continued

Exhibit 4.6 *Continued*

Tool	Advantages	Challenges	Best Practices
Microsoft NetMeeting™	• Large amounts of information can be shared visually. • Several people can work collaboratively on one document.	• Requires high-speed connections; otherwise, delays make the session difficult. • Only one person can modify the document at any given time.	• Use video or telephone conference in parallel for maximum effectiveness. • When presenting to others, ensure that everyone can see the specific part of the document you are referring to. • When working collaboratively, ensure that meeting documents are shared and that everyone has a chance to provide input (if appropriate). • Agree on procedure for taking and giving control of document when working collaboratively.
Digital white board	• Everyone involved can enter and edit information at the same time. This ability makes this tool useful for brainstorming sessions. • Text can be edited by circling and underlining, which enables people's creativity.	• Requires videoconference equipment. • White board takes over video communication, therefore eliminating the visual contact with other participants.	• Share the final result with everyone. • Use block letters for clarity. • Agree on input and edition process (When do we write something new? When do we edit existing text?).

	Advantages	Disadvantages	Guidelines
Videoconference	• Communicates nonverbal messages (gestures, some body language, tone of voice). • Enables participants to combine several modes of communication (words, nonverbal, drawings, etc.), which helps overcome fluency issues.	• Requires video equipment. • It is not always easy to establish a connection and to keep it going—videoconferences are prone to technical problems. • When there are more than three locations, the image often switches back and forth between locations, which can be difficult to follow. • People may be less comfortable because others are watching them.	• Ensure that the connection is there before the actual start time of the conference. • Give people time to finish their sentences. Because of time delay, leave a blank before starting to speak. • Forward material to be discussed ahead of time; refer to material as you speak. • Make sure that everyone has been introduced or has introduced oneself to everyone else before starting. • Avoid background noises and side conversations; mute your side when your location is not talking. • Come closer to the microphone when speaking. • Agree on a protocol for who speaks next (raising hands, having someone facilitate and decide who goes next, etc.). • Finish speaking by saying "over" or something equivalent to mean "I'm finished—someone else's turn."
Shared team intranet space	• Encourages the sharing of ideas and documents. • Contributes to creating a team spirit. • Helps bring new team members on-board. • Progress can be documented and monitored.	• Requires extensive discipline from team members in order to be really useful.	• Ensure that the team space is maintained properly. • Ensure that everyone knows both how to post information and how to retrieve information. • Agree on what information should be posted and what should not be. • Agree on the frequency of updates.

Continued

Exhibit 4.6

Continued

Tool	Advantages	Challenges	Best Practices
Web-based presentation tools	• Enables interactive communication with audience (questions and answers, in particular). • Can be recorded for future uses. • Enables simultaneous presentation to large audiences in several locations.	• No visual connection between audience and presenter. • Requires appropriate equipment. • Requires discipline from participants to keep communication orderly.	• Agree on protocol for questions and answers. Are people in the audience expected to ask questions at the end or during the presentation? Should people other than the speaker mute their sides? • Forward presentation material to be discussed ahead of time; refer to material as you speak. • Ensure that the connection is there before the actual start time of the presentation. • Avoid background noises and side conversations in the presenter's location. • Presenter and people asking questions need to come close to the microphone when speaking and announce who they are ("This is Claudia speaking"). When several locations are involved, people asking questions need to say in which location they are.

people do not understand the gravity of the situation when they remain composed in the face of adversity.

- Hierarchical people tend to consider that participative people do not show proper respect for management, whereas participative people expect hierarchical people to de-emphasize hierarchical differences among the people involved.

- Risk-tolerant people consider that risk-averse people spend too much time on assumptions, definitions, methodology, sources, logic, data, and experiments and not enough on recommendations and next steps. Conversely, risk-averse people tend to consider that risk-tolerant people are not sufficiently thorough in their communication.

- Individualistic people focus on themselves, whereas collectivistic people focus on others, leading to a serious imbalance in the communication.

For each potential issue, people can take many small steps, either individually or as a group. Group discussions, particularly when they are facilitated by people who have experienced the types of issues that the group may face, can be invaluable in setting ground rules that everyone can agree upon. This is particularly important in the case of global teams because distance and time difference represent additional hurdles to communication within the team. In that case, using the right telecommunication tool can make a major difference to the team's progress.

References

Axtell, R.E., and Fornwald, M. 1998. *Gestures: The do's and taboos of body language around the world.* New York: John Wiley & Sons.

Boyle, J.D., and Laroche, L.F. 2000. Going to Japan for business? Zutphen, The Netherlands: *Valve World*, June, pp. 46–50.

Clauss, L., and Laroche, L.F. 2001. Succeed in business in Germany and Switzerland, *Chemical Engineering Progress*, November, pp. 88–92.

Gercik, P. 1996. *On track with the Japanese.* New York: Kodansha America, pp. 28–35.

Hall, E.T. 1987. *Hidden differences: Doing business with the Japanese.* Garden City, NY: Anchor Press/Doubleday.

Hall, E.T. 1983. *The dance of life.* Garden City, NY: Anchor Press/Doubleday.

Hall, E.T. 1977. *Beyond culture.* Garden City, NY: Anchor Press/Doubleday.

Hall, E.T., and Reed Hall, M. 1990. *Understanding cultural differences: Germans, French and Americans.* Yarmouth, ME: Intercultural Press, pp. 10–12.

Harris, P.R., and Moran, R.T. 1999. *Managing cultural differences: Leadership strategies for a new world of business*, 5th ed. Woburn, MA: Butterworth–Heinemann, p. 25.

Laroche, L.F., and Mercer Bing, C. 2001. Technology, protocol keep global teams going without face-to-face meetings, *Canadian HR Reporter*, October 22, pp. 17–19

Malinowicz, N., and Laroche, L.F. 2001. Doing business in Latin America. Zutphen, The Netherlands: *Stainless Steel World*, March, pp. 54–58.

Morrison, T., Conaway, W.A., and Bordon, G.A. 1995. *Kiss, bow or shake hands: How to do business in 60 countries*. Holbrook, MA: Adams Media.

Ricks, D.A. 1999. *Blunders in international business*, 3rd ed. Oxford, United Kingdom: Blackwell.

Trompenaars, A., and Hampden-Turner, C. 1998. *Riding the waves of culture: Understanding diversity in global business*, 2nd ed. New York: McGraw-Hill, pp. 70–80, 113.

Career
Management

During a conference for French students studying in the United States organized by the French consulate, the Vice-President of the Research and Development Department of a large French chemical company made an extensive presentation on the career prospects open to chemists and chemical engineers in his organization. He talked in particular about the dual managerial/technical ladder and the importance given to technical experts in his organization. After his presentation, he sat down next to me and said: "Anyway, the technical ladder is for those who cannot manage people."

—French engineering student in the United States

People's motivations and career aspirations vary significantly. This is true within a given culture, but it is even more true when you consider different cultures. This chapter examines how career management (including rewards, recognition, and promotions) is handled differently in different cultures. It starts with a description of the most common cross-cultural issues related to career management, followed by an analysis of the dynamics that lead to these issues. This analysis becomes the basis for the recommendations and suggestions provided in the next section. This chapter focuses on New North Americans as they manage their careers in North American organizations; it is also designed to help North American managers and human resources (HR) professionals advise their New North American colleagues.

What Are the Signs of Cross-Cultural Career Management Issues?

As in the case of manager–employee relationships and teamwork, cross-cultural misunderstandings related to career management are usually interpreted differently by New North Americans and by their North American managers and HR colleagues.

New North American Perspective

Some New North American employees experience the following:

- A position at the next level has opened and, even though they think they are the most qualified for the job, they do not get the promotion. Instead, one of their colleagues, whom they consider to be less qualified than they are, is promoted. That person may end up being their manager, adding insult to injury.

- Their contributions are not appreciated for what they are worth. They have accomplished a great deal for the organization (they may have designed and implemented new processes that saved millions of dollars), and yet they are still at the bottom of the ladder.

- When they apply for positions in other parts of the organization or in other organizations, for which they consider themselves to be qualified, they find out that they are not even considered for these positions.

- When they are looking for a better job, they find that their North American colleagues do not provide them with the help they would expect to receive from people who come from the same cultural background as they do.

North American Perspective

Some of the managers and HR professionals who work with New North American employees experience the following:

- A position at the next level has opened and the best candidate got the job. They do not understand why one of the New North American employees seems to think that he or she was suited for that position; the reality is that he or she did not even come close to the person who got the promotion. There was no contest.

- Some New North American employees who have been given many forms of recognition appear continuously dissatisfied and comment about a lack of recognition.

- Some New North American employees apply for transfers within the organization that do not make any sense (the two positions are totally unrelated and the transfer is way too big of a jump). They may also apply for positions for which they are not qualified.

- Some New North Americans appear to expect that managers can do miracles. For example, they appear to expect management to be able to create positions for themselves or one of their relatives.

What Is Going On?

Managing your career is never a simple task; managing your career in an environment that operates according to unwritten rules that you do not know is especially difficult, particularly when you are not aware that these rules are different from those you were brought up with. This is the dilemma faced by many immigrants when they manage their careers in North American organizations.

Who is responsible for your career? For most North Americans, the answer to this question is obvious: *Everyone is personally responsible for his or her own career.* Although it is relatively easy to achieve consensus in North America on this point, this answer is not universal; the North American answer is characteristic of an individualistic and low power-distance culture.

In others cultures, someone's career is determined to a much greater extent by other people. The organization and its management play a critical role in the case of collectivistic and hierarchical cultures. In hierarchical cultures, people consider that, to first order, *their managers* are responsible for their career.

When New North Americans expect their organizations or their managers to take care of their careers, they often find that the result does not match their expectations. At the same time, their managers consider that their New North American employees do not fully utilize their potential. This section examines how career management is handled in different parts of the world and how these differences affect the careers of New North Americans in North American organizations.

Promotions

In this section, promotion is considered in the managerial sense of the word (i.e., it corresponds to an increase in responsibilities and number of direct and indirect reports). Promotions on the technical ladder (i.e., when someone reaches a higher level of technical expertise and is recognized accordingly) are considered as a form of recognition; as such, they are examined in the next section.

What is needed to get a promotion varies significantly from culture to culture. When New North American technical professionals work toward a promotion according to what it takes to succeed in their country of origin, they may not achieve their goals. The path that leads to a promotion depends largely on power distance (power distance is described in detail in Chapter 2). In addition, the criteria used to determine eligibility for a promotion depend on power distance, risk tolerance, individualism, and expressiveness (risk tolerance and individualism are described in detail in Chapter 3, while expressiveness is described in Chapter 4).

Promotion Process

In a participative or mildly hierarchical organization, the path to promotions consists of taking a little bit more responsibility every day while taking good care of one's current responsibilities. As represented in Exhibit 5.1, someone who wants to be promoted is expected to regularly take on some new responsibilities at the next level. He or she *asks* for these responsibilities, by volunteering to be part of one or more task forces or committees or to be part of a new project team. Over time, the range of responsibilities that this person manages moves slowly from one level in the hierarchy to the next. When this person is acknowledged as performing the job at the next level without the title, he or she usually receives a promotion when a new position opens at that level.

As this person acquires new responsibilities at the next level, he or she sheds some responsibilities at the lower end of his or her current level to prevent being overloaded. These responsibilities are usually picked up by someone at the level below who is trying to do the same thing (i.e., take on some additional responsibilities in order to move up in the organization).

In a hierarchical culture, promotion follows a different path, as illustrated by Exhibit 5.2. In this scenario, an employee who is seeking a promotion is expected to excel in his or her current responsibilities. He or she is expected to take good care of the responsibilities assigned

Exhibit 5.1

Responsibilities as a function of time for someone who gets promoted in a participative or mildly hierarchical organization.

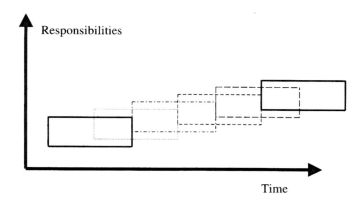

Exhibit 5.2

Responsibilities as a function of time for someone who gets promoted in a hierarchical organization.

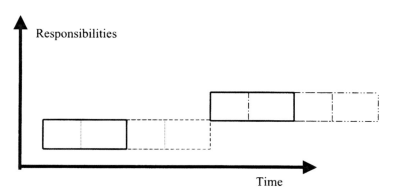

by his or her manager. Over time, his or her managers will notice the quality of the work; when a position at the next level opens, he or she usually receives a promotion. This promotion represents a step change in responsibilities: The person who is promoted trades in one set of responsibilities for another set, at the next level in the organization. The same process may be repeated at the level below, where one person is promoted at the same time and takes on the responsibilities left by the person just promoted.

Qualifications

What people need to do to be promoted depends on power distance, risk tolerance, individualism, and expressiveness. Let's look at each of these factors separately, starting with power distance.

In participative and mildly hierarchical countries, promotion results from taking good care of your current responsibilities and taking on more responsibilities gradually. People generally expect that performance on the job is the primary factor determining promotions.

In hierarchical countries, promotion results from excelling in your current responsibilities. In many cases, this is not the only factor; family background and education, which are expected to play at most a limited role in promotions in North America, may also play an important role in such countries. People who come from the best families or the best universities are expected to achieve more; therefore, they are preferentially given the high-profile projects and assignments. This treatment, in turn, makes them more likely to achieve more and to rise more quickly through the ranks (Trompenaars, 1997).

For example, in Japan, many employees of the famous MITI (Ministry of Industry) are graduates of the University of Tokyo. In France, more than half of the executives of the large French corporations are graduates of the Ecole Polytechnique de Paris. Here is the experience of a retired French engineer who worked for a large French corporation:

> I graduated from what French people would consider a third-rate engineering school. I joined this organization 30 years ago. Past a certain level in this organization, you only find graduates of the Ecole Polytechnique de Paris. I was determined to break this "educational glass ceiling." Over time, I rose through the ranks and came to the point where I was one promotion away from "breaking through." At that point, new rungs started to appear on the ladder: The organizational chart would change, and new levels appeared between this glass ceiling and my current level. In this manner, I could be promoted to the next level without breaking through. This took place a couple of times until I finally made it. Then I could retire.

The impact of risk tolerance can be described in the following manner:

- In risk-averse countries, people need to gather extensive technical knowledge in order to be promoted. Managers in risk-averse cultures are expected to "have at hand precise answers to most of the questions that his or her employees may raise about their work" (Laurent, 1981). As a result, in risk-averse cultures, people are promoted to a much greater extent based on their accumulated technical knowledge, as represented graphically in Exhibit 5.3. In this manner, they are able to face and handle appropriately any new and unexpected situation.

- In risk-tolerant countries, accumulation of technical knowledge is less important for promotions. Interpersonal skills take on more importance, particularly in mildly hierarchical and participative cultures, as shown in Exhibit 5.4. In these cultures, managers cannot simply impose their decisions on their employees, so they need to have the ability to influence or convince them of going in the direction they have in mind.

On the technical side, risk-averse cultures tend to value theory over experiments, and people who are good at mathematics often have an edge in such cultures. By contrast, hands-on engineers and scientists have the inside track in risk-tolerant cultures.

Exhibit 5.3

In risk-averse countries, people who are promoted tend to come from the shaded areas: They usually have better than average technical skills, while their interpersonal skills may not matter as much.

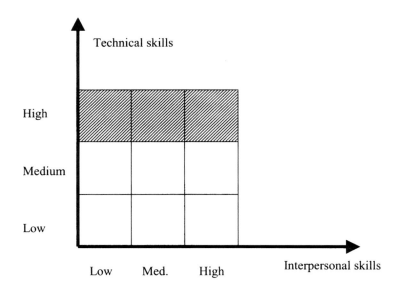

Exhibit 5.4

In risk-tolerant countries, people who are promoted tend to come from the shaded areas: They usually have either better than average technical or interpersonal skills.

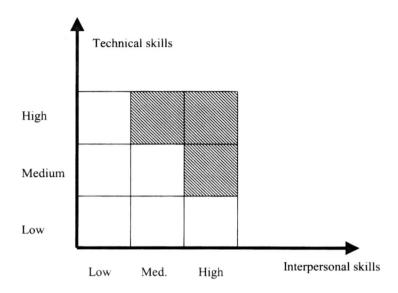

Here is the impact of individualism:

- In individualistic cultures, people tend to become specialists. Within teams and task forces, they are expected to take good care of their own areas of responsibilities.

- By contrast, in collectivistic countries, people are expected to understand how their work affects the work of others. Generalists tend to be more valued in collectivistic cultures.

In addition, collectivistic people tend to be more attached to their organization than are individualistic people—in the case of Japanese people working for large corporations, this is an important part of their own identity. Showing loyalty to the organization (by refraining from criticizing it in front of outsiders and by defending it when outsiders criticize it, for example) plays a significant positive role in promotions in collectivistic organizations, whereas the importance of this behavior is much lower in individualistic organizations.

Seniority is also a factor for promotion in collectivistic organizations because belonging to the group and being able to understand how the whole organization operates and can be influenced are important attributes of a good manager in such a system. It tends to be less of a factor in individualistic organizations.

Finally, expressiveness also needs to be taken into consideration:

- In expressive cultures, managers show and are expected to show a wide range of emotions in the workplace.
- In neutral cultures, managers show and are expected to show a narrow range of emotions in the same circumstances.

Coming to North America

When people immigrate to North America as adults, they bring with them their mental map of the world. In particular, they have already learned how one gets ahead in their home country. Some learn quickly that the way to get ahead in North America is not the same as in their home country. For others, this mental shift takes more time. For a while, they project onto the North American society the rules of their own culture and behave accordingly; in particular, they may have expectations and approaches to career management that may not fit the North American workplace.

For example, they may work hard to obtain a promotion with little result because they invest their time and energy in areas that are not valued by their North American colleagues and managers. In the following situations, these efforts may go against the expectations of their North American colleagues and managers:

Some people from collectivistic cultures may not understand how people who have less seniority than they do in the organization are promoted ahead of them. They may also be confused by the behavior of some of their North American colleagues, which they perceive as demonstrating a lack of loyalty to the organization. They are also surprised by the lack of response of management in such situations. Finally, they may not grasp that their ability to understand the interactions between parts of projects or between parts of the organization may not be as valued as they think it should be and how people who are specialized may be promoted ahead of them.

Some people from risk-averse cultures may expect that promotion is the result of the accumulation of technical knowledge. They may therefore be continuously upgrading their technical skills. When they consistently achieve high levels of technical expertise, they may not understand why they are not given the promotion they consider they deserve. In Exhibit 5.5, these people are in the upper left corner of the technical/interpersonal skills space and are continuously trying to

Exhibit 5.5

Some people coming from risk-averse cultures may be trying to increase their technical skills in order to be promoted (*solid arrow*), whereas they would have a better chance of achieving this objective by working on their interpersonal skills (*dashed arrow*).

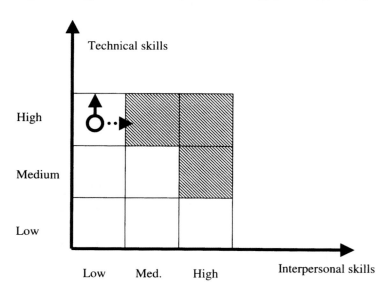

increase their technical skills, whereas the path for promotion for them consists of working on their interpersonal skills.

Some people from hierarchical cultures expect promotions to be the result of excelling in their current position. They expect and wait for their managers to assign them to new projects or teams. For them, taking the initiative and becoming part of new initiatives without being instructed by their managers to do so would represent a big risk. If their manager does not approve, they have made a commitment for which their manager will not let them make time, so they will have to do the new task in addition to their regular responsibilities. To prevent stretching themselves too thin, they do not volunteer for new responsibilities, new committees, or task forces; they may even turn these opportunities down. They will wait for their managers to tell them to participate, while their managers are waiting for them to volunteer and ask to participate. In this situation, they see themselves as doing a great job—truly excelling in their current responsibilities—and do not understand why people who are not doing as well in their responsibilities are getting ahead of them.

Finally, some New North Americans from expressive cultures may show negative emotions that may be acceptable from managers in their home country while being considered beyond the range of emotions that North American managers may show in the workplace. When this occurs, these people are often considered unsuitable for managerial positions because North American managers are expected to remain composed at all times.

In many cases, these situations evolve in the following manner: New North American employees consider that their contributions are undervalued. In their minds, they are doing better than their peers; this may well be true when they use the performance criteria applied in their home country to measure themselves against their colleagues. Yet, they see that some of their colleagues, whom they consider as lower performers, get ahead of them. This may generate confusion, as well as some bitterness and resentment. Depending on their past experiences and the current circumstances, they may interpret this situation as a sign of discrimination. When this happens repeatedly, they may consider looking for another job in another organization—one that would recognize their contributions adequately.

Their North American managers, colleagues, and the HR professionals in their organization are often confused by the situation. As far as they are concerned, the promotion process was fair—the best person got the job. In their minds, the complaints that these New North American employees voice have no foundation because these people clearly have not shown that they are ready for this promotion. For example, they may not have the necessary interpersonal skills, or they clearly display a lack of initiative that would not be compatible with increased managerial responsibilities.

Another situation that leads to significant misunderstandings is the case of some New North Americans who come from hierarchical countries and who may expect to be fast-tracked for reasons that would apply in their home country but do not apply in North America. This is particularly the case when these people are selected to take part in high-potential employee programs (i.e., programs designed to help employees with high potential develop more rapidly) because the implications of such programs may be different:

- In North America, participants are recognized as having high potential. They are given an opportunity that they are expected to seize. Participants are responsible for making use of this opportunity in their work.

- In hierarchical countries, being sent to such a program implies that the person is now on the fast track; promotions are expected to follow rapidly.

When they are not given a promotion within a few months of participating in such a program, some New North Americans may consider that the corporation is giving them mixed messages; this problem does not exist in the minds of their North American managers and HR colleagues.

Lateral Moves

In many large organizations, lateral moves are encouraged as a way for employees to get a better understanding of the organization as a whole, its operations, its departments, and their interactions. Lateral moves are handled differently in different parts of the world:

- In North America, people who make lateral moves from one department to another often start again at the bottom of the ladder of the new department. For example, someone who has climbed a couple of rungs and manages a significant group in the Customer Service Department goes back to an entry-level position when he or she moves into the Sales Department. The experience this person has gained in other parts of the company is considered useful only to the extent that it enables him or her to get the job. People are expected to move back up the hierarchy of the second department quickly—usually more quickly than people who start in the organization at a comparable level without prior working experience.

- In France, people who make lateral moves keep their hierarchical level. For example, someone who has climbed a couple of rungs and manages a significant group in the Customer Service Department will be given a somewhat equivalent managerial role when he or she moves into the Sales Department. The managerial experience this person has gained in other parts of the organization and his or her knowledge of how the organization operates as a whole are considered applicable in the second department.

- In Japan, new recruits in large corporations often go through an extensive training program at the beginning of their career (this program may last as long as two years), during which they rotate through positions in many departments. In this manner, they gain a detailed understanding of the organization, its operations, and the interactions among the various departments.

Because collectivistic people see organizations as an interconnected set of departments and teams, they often have a better understanding of these interconnections than do individualistic people. As a result, they may consider that they are ready for lateral moves that individualistic people would consider unthinkable, like going from Research to Sales. They may also expect to keep their hierarchical rank in a lateral move. Obviously, these expectations are likely to make little sense when they are transferred and applied to the North American workplace.

Moving On

The speed and ease with which people can move from one organization to the next may be different. They depend on both the status of the job market (you can find another job more quickly in an employee's market than in an employer's market) and on people's risk tolerance:

- Canada and the United States are somewhere in the middle on the risk-tolerance scale. Here, people change organizations from time to time. No negative stigma is associated with changing organizations. Interviewers may start asking questions of candidates who have changed organizations too frequently (say, more than once every couple of years); at that point, they may wonder about their stability.

- People in Hong Kong show much tolerance to risk. They tend to change jobs more frequently than North Americans. This was particularly true before 1997; during the early 1990s, someone could find eight positions in a week without really trying. Employees who had achieved something significant—something that would look good on their resumes—would start looking for a new position within a few weeks if they were not given a raise or a bonus for delivering these results. People in Hong Kong still change positions quickly by North American standards.

- French people are significantly less risk-tolerant than North Americans and therefore tend to change positions less frequently. Many French people would prefer working for large corporations or for the government, because this implies a high level of job security, than for a startup organization. For many French people, the potential gains (e.g., stock options, growth) associated with startups are not worth the additional risks.

- Japan has a low score on the risk-tolerance scale. In Japan, employees of the large corporations are expected to work for that corporation until they retire. Changing corporations in Japan tends to be seen negatively; for example, a Canadian engineer leaving a Japanese–Canadian joint venture received several e-mails from his Japanese colleagues that expressed either incomprehension or shock.

Pay and Raises

The concept of "pay-for-performance" is deeply rooted in the North American culture, and many North American organizations apply this principle in various ways. Note, however, that this concept is not universal:

- During the Communist era, there was essentially no correlation between pay and performance in Eastern Europe and Indochina. The salary of a plumber was essentially the same, no matter how skilled he or she was.

- A few years after India gained independence, the national railroad company had a small surplus and management decided to give some of that surplus back to employees. Then the question came: Who will get what? Management decided to give a one-time bonus to poor performers as a way to motivate them to perform more. Management considered that good performers were getting a lot of satisfaction from getting the job well done, so they did not need any additional incentive.

With the end of Communism, the idea that pay and performance should be positively correlated is becoming more and more widely accepted around the world. There remain, however, important differences in how this concept is applied; in this respect, differences in individualism, power distance, and risk tolerance often show up in the compensation scheme used by organizations in different countries.

In individualistic countries, as in the U.S. and Canada, "performance" is often considered to be the individual's performance. People receive raises based on their personal contribution. By contrast, people in collectivistic countries tend to receive raises based on the performance of the whole team. This difference is in line with the different concepts of teams that individualistic and collectivistic cultures have. For New North Americans, getting used to this modus operandi is tantamount to getting used to the way teams operate in North America.

Power distance also plays an important role in compensation schemes. In mildly hierarchical and participative countries, an employee may be paid more than his or her manager (this situation is more common in sales, where the salary, bonus, and commission received by a sales representative may exceed the compensation of his or her sales manager). This situation is unheard of in a hierarchical culture. Managers are always expected to make more than the people who report to them. This difference of approach to pay can be a challenge to hierarchical New North Americans, who may have difficulties accepting that someone who is hierarchically in a lower position than they are is making more money than they do. In turn, if they go and talk to their managers or the HR department, their complaint is likely to baffle the person they talk to. As far as this person is concerned, everything is the way it should be, so where is the problem?

Finally, compensation schemes are usually heavily dependent on the risk tolerance of the employees that the organization is trying to attract. In risk-tolerant countries, people look forward to commissions and bonuses, as it gives them the opportunity to earn more. In risk-averse countries, the average employee shuns the corresponding unpredictability of their income. As a result, they tend to prefer compensation schemes with little to no commission—the lower the variability of their income, the better. Some multinational companies take this point into consideration when designing the commission plan for their sales representatives: The variable portion of a sales rep's income may be higher in risk-tolerant countries than in risk-averse countries. As in the case of power distance, when risk-averse New North Americans are placed in situations where their income is significantly more variable than they are used to, they may be quite uncomfortable with the situation. In particular, they are likely to experience a significant amount of stress. Again, talking to their managers or HR department representatives will only compound the problem in most cases; as far as these people are concerned, the compensation scheme is doing what it was designed to do; that is, entice people to be more productive.

Rewards and Recognition

Some forms of recognition that are common in North America are either not used or have a different meaning in other parts of the world. This may make them ineffective for some New North Americans because they may not understand the extent to which their work is appreciated. In particular, difficulties are likely to arise when what is given means much more or much less to the person who receives the reward:

- When the reward means less to the person who receives it than to the person who gives it, the person who receives it feels unappreciated.

- When the reward means much more to the recipient than to the giver, the recipient may overestimate his or her status and position in the company.

As in the case of promotions, misunderstandings are more likely with people coming from countries that are significantly different from North America on the power-distance scale. For example, many technical organizations around the world have dual ladders, with a technical stream and a managerial stream; the difference between the two ladders may be more or less important depending on power distance:

- In participative and mildly hierarchical cultures like the United States and Canada, the technical stream is highly valued. People on the technical side of the ladder report to managers at a level higher than them, and their inputs are highly considered. They are given perks and benefits on par with the managerial counterparts. In mildly hierarchical cultures, a manager can trump a technical expert when push comes to shove; this is not as likely in a participative culture.
- In hierarchical countries, the technical ladder is not valued nearly as much as the managerial ladder, as the anecdote presented at the beginning of this chapter demonstrates. The most common measure of success in hierarchical cultures is the power you have, as measured by the number of people who report to you and by your rank in the organization.

Issues may arise when people who come from hierarchical countries do not recognize awards granted for technical excellence as "real" rewards. To them, these awards are nice, but a promotion up the managerial ladder would represent a much more substantial form of recognition. When these people have outstanding technical skills and poor interpersonal skills (i.e., they are located in the upper left corner in Exhibit 5.5), the direction of their careers may be problematic:

- Their managers may be gently nudging them toward the technical ladder, with the idea that they could climb this ladder quickly.
- They may see themselves as prime candidates for a promotion on the managerial ladder because in their cultures technical expertise is a more important factor in promotions. They do not want to climb the technical ladder because the corresponding rewards do not mean much to them.

In addition, people's accomplishments tend to be celebrated in more subdued ways in participative and mildly hierarchical cultures than in hierarchical cultures. The result is similar to what happens when someone with a large neutral zone is given positive feedback that is not strong enough: The recognition provided may not be recognized for what it is. Here are three examples.

- In a research center, everyone may be entitled to attend one conference per year. The importance of the conference (small or major event) and the location (local or in a desirable, distant location) tend to depend on the status of the researcher and may be considered as recognition by management.

- Being first to receive a powerful portable computer may not feel like a reward to some New North Americans, even though it may be considered as such by their colleagues.

- Having an individual office with a window may not be valuable to New North Americans, particularly if they come from a collectivistic culture; yet, it may be a form of recognition in their organization.

Aligning with Corporate Values

Many North American organizations have created corporate value statements that are expected to provide guidance to employees about the way they should conduct business as members of the organization. For example, Johnson & Johnson has its Credo, Procter & Gamble has its Success Actions for Winning, and so on.

One of the challenges faced by New North American employees in North American organizations is the fact that their interpretation of these corporate value statements may not be the intended meaning. Many such statements are phrased in general terms, which often include implicitly North American professional values. For example, a statement like "We want to be leaders in all that we do and we want to be a company of leaders that take risks and embrace change" may not be interpreted as it was intended by New North Americans for several reasons.

The concept of leadership is cultural. In hierarchical countries, where the number of direct and indirect employees is an important measure of power, being a leader and being a manager are essentially synonymous. In essence, in hierarchical countries, people who are not in managerial positions cannot be leaders.

As discussed in Chapter 3, the amount of risk that people can take comfortably varies from culture to culture. Someone from Hong Kong may take this corporate value statement to heart and start taking risks that will be beyond what his or her North American colleagues consider reasonable.

Change is viewed positively in North America. "New and improved" is one of the most common phrases used on product packages. The idea that change is positive is not universal; in cultures that are more oriented toward the past, traditions are more highly valued. For example, high-tech French companies will often refer to their "tradition of innovation."

It's Not What You Know, It's Who You Know

In the United States and Canada, one of the most important avenues for networking is to be active in professional associations (see Appendix D for more details on North American technical professional associations). As a result, American and Canadian professional associations have developed into large organizations with significant memberships. Both membership and active participation in these associations are often mentioned on North American resumes. Networking is done differently in other parts of the world.

In some countries, one networks primarily along the lines of alumni associations. This is the case in France: French professional associations have comparatively far fewer members than their Canadian or American counterparts. On the other hand, alumni associations organize many events, which are usually well attended. For example, the Annual Ball of the Ecole Polytechnique de Paris gathers on average about 5,000 people, and the Bicentennial Ball (which took place at the Palace of Versailles in 1989) gathered about 20,000 people. Annual alumni events in France play the same role as annual conferences in Canada and the United States.

In countries like Mexico and Saudi Arabia, where family ties play a major role in society's organization, networking is often done along family lines. This means that one attends events organized by important families to which one has connections. For example, a Mexican professional will attend the Annual Ball organized by the Hernandez family. In the case of upper-class families, this event may take place in a spacious villa with large grounds and involve a few hundred to a few thousand people.

There are key differences among cultures in what can be expected from your network. In individualistic cultures, your network is your personal responsibility and property. If your spouse or friends are also technical professionals, they have their own network. When you access the network of an individualistic person, this access will usually be in the form of a name, a phone number, and an e-mail address.

In collectivistic cultures, other members of the same group have significant access to your network, and vice versa. When you access the network of collectivistic people, they are likely to make the introduction themselves, rather than letting you introduce yourself. In this process, they often put their reputation on the line: In essence, they lend credibility to both sides; making an introduction suggests implicitly that both sides should have something in common and that it should be worth their while to get to know one another. The difference in approach to networking is illustrated by the experience of a Canadian engineer working in Mexico:

> I was in the office of my Mexican counterpart when she received a phone call from one of her friends. This friend had just been laid off and was contacting everyone in her network in order to find leads for a new job. My Mexican counterpart told her friend: "Send me your resume. I know a few companies that are likely to need people with your expertise. I will call my contacts there to find out if they are hiring. If they are, I will pass on your resume and arrange a meeting for you."

When collectivistic New North Americans project their expectations of networking onto North America, they may be quite disappointed. People coming from collectivistic cultures view a "Here is the phone number of so-and-so, she may be able to help you" response from North Americans as inadequate—they are not helping to the extent that collectivistic New North Americans think they should. This may happen also to New North Americans coming from hierarchical countries. There, someone in a high-level managerial position is often able to create positions or have a significant influence on who is hired when a position opens up. As a result, networking in hierarchical countries tends to focus on those who have power. Some New North Americans transfer this expectation to the North American workplace, as the experience of a Romanian engineer indicates:

> I had a good relationship with one of my neighbors, who is also Romanian. When he found out that I had a managerial position, he asked me to give his daughter a job. When I explained to him that I could not do that, but I would be happy to take her resume to the HR Department and put in a good word for her, he was quite upset. He thought I was letting him down.

Some New North American technical professionals underestimate the value of being active members of professional associations in North America (see Appendix D) because these professional associations have far less clout and impact in their home countries. Becoming a member of such associations can give them some insights into how people in North America view their professions and approach the management of their careers.

What Can You Do?

In areas like manager–employee relationships and teamwork, being aware of the existence of potential issues and diagnosing them appropriately represents half of the solution. In the case of career management, making people aware of the potential problems and providing them with the information they need to make an informed choice is essentially the whole solution. In the end, everyone is responsible for his or her own career in North America, including New North Americans. This chapter examines ways in which organizations can provide this information to New North American employees, their managers, and HR colleagues, as well as ways these people can get the information on their own.

What New North Americans Can Do

For most new North American technical professionals, the challenge consists in understanding how careers are managed in North America and how they can achieve their own professional objectives. The following steps may be helpful in this process:

1. *Identify professional objectives.* This point may not be as obvious as it may seem, particularly to those who come from hierarchical and collectivistic cultures, because the organization and its management may have had much of a say in the management of their careers before they came to North America. Some may need to learn what "managing their career" means. For example, rather than waiting for management to point them toward interesting projects, they may consider telling their managers what makes a project interesting to them. They may also need to learn to voice their desire to be part of new task forces or project teams when these are in the early stages of formation (stage 1 or 2): "Speak up now or forever hold your peace." In most cases, once the team

has been put together, "the train has left the station" and it is too late to join.

2. *Understand what managers expect from them.* What do they need to do in order to obtain a promotion or a raise? Such a discussion may be part of the Performance Appraisal process. This discussion is likely to be more effective when both employees and managers use specific examples in order to inform one another of their respective approaches and expectations.

3. *Understand the corporate value statement.* Discussing the corporate value statement with someone in the HR department in order to understand what these values mean in concrete situations can help New North Americans acclimate to the values of North American culture.

4. *Understand the compensation scheme of your organization.* A discussion with someone in the HR department will help you to understand how it works, what is valued, and what is required to obtain raises.

5. *Obtain a mentor.* Many New North Americans find that having a mentor can make a significant difference in their understanding of the North American workplace and in the management of their career. Ideally, mentors should understand both the North American culture and the culture from which the person they are mentoring comes from. Some New North Americans achieve this combination by talking to several people—some North Americans, some coming from the same cultural background as they do.

6. *Seek out career counseling or training.* Some organizations provide access to career management professionals or coaches, either directly or through their employee assistance programs. New North American employees may consider taking advantage of such offerings; for best results, they should select professionals who understand the unique challenges they face in the North American workplace.

What Organizations Can Do

For organizations, the challenge consists of ensuring fairness in the promotion, reward, and recognition processes while considering the unique challenges faced by New North Americans. In this respect, providing them, their managers, and HR professionals with information about these unique challenges and the benefits that the organization as a whole may derive from dealing with them effectively can create the necessary awareness. Effective formats for conveying this information include the following:

- Workshops that are delivered by either internal or external resources—These workshops should cover the career management process in the organization, explain the values of the organization, and examine behaviors and actions that are required for advancement in the organization, using specific examples for best communication.

- Individual coaching sessions provided by career management professionals who understand these issues.

- Mentorship programs set up within the organization—These can be particularly effective because mentors can provide advice that is specific to the organization.

What Can You Gain?

Both organizations and individuals have much to gain from good career management practices. On the organization's side, the benefits are as follows:

- *Increased retention of skills.* Some New North Americans may leave the organization thinking that their skills are not properly recognized. When these people have valuable technical skills, their departure can create a void that may be difficult to replace. In this respect, an ounce of prevention may well be worth a pound of cure.

- *Increased employee effectiveness.* When New North American employees understand what they need to do in order to achieve their career goals, their motivation and their effectiveness increase.

On the employee's side, the benefits are as follows:

- *Increased motivation and morale.* New North American employees can align their actions with their professional objectives and go for them.

- *Increased effectiveness.* New North American employees can see that their actions yield the results they expected. This, in turn, may motivate them to invest more in their careers.

Summary

The best approach to career management is culture-specific; however, this point is not always immediately apparent to New North American technical professionals when they work in North American organizations. Promotions, compensation, rewards and recognition, and lateral moves are handled differently in North America and in other parts of the world. Ensuring that New North Americans understand both explicit and implicit rules of the North American workplace can help them manage their careers in a way that is beneficial to both employees and organizations.

References

Laurent, A. 1981. Matrix organizations and Latin cultures, *International Studies of Management and Organizations*, 10(4):101–104.

Sears, W.H., and Tamulionyte-Lentz, A. 2001. *Succeeding in business in Central and Eastern Europe: a guide to cultures, markets, and practices*, Woburn, MA: Butterworth–Heinemann.

Simons, G. 2002. *Eurodiversity: cultural considerations and business success in Western Europe*, Oxford, UK: Butterworth–Heinemann.

Trompenaars, A., and Hampden-Turner, C. 1998. *Riding the waves of culture: Understanding diversity in global business*, 2nd ed. New York: McGraw-Hill, pp. 105–122.

Looking Ahead

I was on a flight of a Latin European airline. I asked a flight attendant if I could meet the pilot. He came back a few minutes later and said "Sure, go ahead"—this was before 9/11. I introduced myself to the pilot and the co-pilot. We started a conversation and, after a few minutes, the pilot asked me if I wanted to drink something. I gladly accepted his offer. He then called a flight attendant and asked her to bring a bottle of champagne, so that we could toast to our camaraderie. I was floored; my airline had a very strict zero-tolerance policy for alcohol. Clearly, his airline had a different approach.

—Senior American pilot working for a U.S. airline

As this book demonstrates, cultural differences have an impact on technical professionals today. This impact is significant, and it is often misunderstood. In most cases, differences in values and approaches lead initially to additional challenges that require special attention; in particular, misunderstandings create rework and inefficiencies. Once these challenges are overcome, cultural differences often lead to synergies that can be beneficial for the individuals involved and for their organizations.

Cultural Differences in the Future

This is the situation today. What will it be in the future? Several factors point toward some convergence of world business cultures:

- Over time, some of the *visible* cultural differences tend to diminish in importance, as people around the world get used to wearing similar clothes and to eating food coming from other parts of the world. The worldwide successes of companies like Coca-Cola, McDonald's, Nestle, Club Med, BMW, Sony, and Heineken (and the list goes on) point to the increased acceptability of similar products and services around the world.

- More and more businesspeople around the world are learning to speak English, making worldwide communication easier and enabling the creation of more global teams.

- The history of the United States and Canada shows that many waves of immigrants have been integrated into the mainstream culture.

- Multinational corporations have created their own organizational cultures that tend to transcend borders and cultural differences.

- The fall of the Berlin Wall and the end of communism as a worldwide political force point to the adoption of the capitalist system and its market-oriented values around the world.

- New telecommunications and transport technologies have made and continue to make interactions among culturally different people more common. As culturally different people interact together, they influence and learn from one another.

Other factors point to either a status quo or even a divergence:

- Some of the products and companies that are successful globally are successful because they adapt to local market expectations. For example, wine and beer are offered in Euro Disney restaurants, whereas they are not on the menu of Disney's North American theme parks. Nescafe™, the leading product of Nestle, is sold in more than 1,000 combinations of packaging, sizes, labels, and so on around the world.

- There is a big step between eating sushi or hamburgers and understanding how Japanese or North Americans think. While the visible cultural differences are easily identified and understood (Far Easterners who immigrate to North America quickly learn to shake hands, if they did not already know), some *invisible* cultural differences are resilient. Hall (1990) describes his research with Hispanics living in New Mexico for generations—they were the "sixth- or seventh-generation descendants of the original Spanish families who settled in North America in the early seventeenth century":

> Despite constant contact with Anglo-Saxon Americans for well over a hundred years, most of these Hispanics have remained polychronic. In three summers of interviewing we never once achieved our scheduled goal of five interviews each week for each interviewer. We were lucky to have two or three. Interviews in Hispanic homes or offices were constantly interrupted when families came to visit or a friend dropped by. The Hispanics seemed to be juggling half a dozen activities simultaneously, even while the interviews were in progress.

- Learning a language does not mean that one adopts a culture; several cultures share the English language as a result of the political and economic domination of the UK and the United States in recent times. Singapore is a good case in point: Most people in Singapore speak English, yet the Singaporean business culture is different from the North American business culture. Differences between Singapore and North America are well known when it comes to political systems: The Singaporean government has significantly more authority than its North American counterparts.

- Throughout the world, some cultural differences have withstood extensively the test of time. The historic rivalry between France and the UK is well known worldwide and, while the two countries have accomplished much together in recent history, few are predicting that the English and French business cultures are going to merge in the foreseeable future. For example, France is progressively enacting a 35-hour work week, while the UK has implemented many new laws that provide significantly increased flexibility in the labor market. The conflict in Northern Ireland also indicates that some cultural differences may last for a long time even when language is not an issue. The Israeli–Palestinian conflict, the division of Cyprus, and the stalemate on the Indian subcontinent are all reminders that cultural differences are unlikely to go away soon. Closer to home, some groups, like Acadians, have kept their own identity for extended periods.

- The corporate culture of many multinational organizations is often dominated by headquarters. Working for Honda in North America is not the same as working for General Motors in North America, even though both organizations are multinational corporations making and selling the same kind of products.

- The fall of the Berlin Wall did not mark the end of history. Although many former communist countries have adopted the capitalist system, their business culture remains distinctly different from the North American business culture (Sears, 2001).

- Being in frequent contact with people from other cultures does not imply that people know how others think, as differences between airlines and the story of the U.S. pilot traveling on a Latin European flight demonstrate.

Global teams are a good example of how these forces come into play. The mere existence of such teams is a testimony to the power of recent telecommunication and transport advances; these teams cannot operate without e-mail, fax, telephone, and videoconferences, and often require face-to-face meetings. By bringing together culturally different people and giving them the opportunity to learn from one another, global teams are a factor of cultural convergence. In addition, members of a global team are often part of the same organization; their interactions reinforce the corporate culture of this organization.

At the same time, members of global teams work in their own countries; in particular, they are likely to communicate with their local co-workers in their own language rather than English. Subsidiaries of the same multinational company operating in different countries do not operate according to the same procedures; in many cases, local employees and managers adapt these procedures by incorporating some local business practices (this point is an important watch-out for expatriates). In that sense, the interactions among members of a global team are limited to the communication events, so the factors leading to convergence have a limited chance to operate. So where does this take us? Will there be a single, universal business culture at some point in the future, as Isaac Asimov described in some of his novels? Only time will tell. However, it appears rather safe to say that whatever convergence results will take place in a long-term future; deep cultural changes tend to be measured in generations. In that sense, cultural differences will be with us for a while.

Learning from Others

Because cultural differences are here to stay in the short term and because they significantly affect the work of technical professionals, organizations in general and employees in particular can benefit by learning how to deal with cultural differences effectively. This need is strong in the case of New North Americans; their careers will usually suffer extensively if they do not learn how to communicate and work effectively with others in a North American context. The need is also strong for North Americans working with culturally different people, either in North America or on global teams.

To the suggestions contained in previous chapters, which go a long way toward this goal, can be added the following recommendations, which are more general in nature. These are designed to foster an attitude that is receptive to cultural differences, rather than address a specific category of misunderstanding. Some recommendations apply to almost everyone:

- Do not make derogatory statements about someone else's country. This is like criticizing someone's family; you rarely gain anything in the process.

- As much as possible, avoid reacting to statements that sound to you like a comparison between countries in which your country is viewed negatively. The comparison may not have been intended.

- Patience is certainly a virtue when it comes to cross-cultural business. It often helps prevent small incidents and misunderstandings from becoming major issues.

- Ask questions in order to understand your counterparts' country and culture, both at work and outside. Understanding the country's history, geography, political system, educational system, and current challenges can go a long way toward building bridges with culturally different colleagues.

- When someone from a culturally different background than yours does or says something that appears either strange or negative to you, check whether your interpretation of these actions or words is correct. The best approach is to check with the person who did or said it because this gives them a chance to clarify their intentions. If this is not possible, clarify with someone who understands that cultural background.

- Avoid "off-the-cuff" remarks. These remarks (like the comment made by the French VP of R&D while sitting down, mentioned at the beginning of Chapter 5) are often read as revealing your true thoughts and feelings. If your remarks imply something other than what you want to communicate to your culturally different counterparts, they are likely to remember only the meaning communicated by these remarks.

New North Americans may consider the following:

- "When in Rome, do as the Romans do." Learn how North Americans would do the work you have to do, so that you can do it in a way that makes sense to the people around you.

- When you have a new idea about doing something differently that is based on an approach that is common in your country of origin, beware of telling your North American co-workers something that sounds like "In my country, we do it this way." People may read into it a competition between countries—in these competitions, nobody wins. One way to have your North American colleagues accept your suggestion is to first show them that you can do it well their way, then do it your way. At that point, results should speak for themselves.

- Learn about North America and the people who live there. In particular, learn enough about North American sports, movies, and TV series to be able to understand the references that people often make in everyday conversations.

- Ask questions to understand how things work in North America, how North Americans handle various situations. Listen to the answers and make sure you interpret and understand the answers you get from the respondent's cultural perspective rather than from your own cultural perspective.

- Make use of continuing education, training, coaching, and mentoring programs offered by your organization. Even if you were excellent in an area back home, take courses in North America, so that you can understand how it is done here. For example, if you were excellent at making presentations in your home country, consider taking presentation courses in North America.

- Do not be afraid to start at the bottom of the ladder. Although this may feel like a major step backward, you can move up relatively quickly. You may have to do things that you would not have had to do in your home country (work night shifts, for example, or organize the company's summer barbecue), but sticking to the job at hand will usually enable you to move up quickly.

North Americans may consider the following:

- Ask your New North American colleagues how they would handle similar situations back home. You may learn something in the process.

- Become mentors/coaches for New North Americans, which will help you and them learn about one another.

Rewards

There are significant rewards for learning to deal effectively wit cultural differences: personal growth, new opportunities, new solu tions to existing problems, and so on. These rewards may go all th way to the creation of new product lines, new businesses, and the lik In this respect, the North American dream is still alive, and New Nort Americans can make significant contributions to large corporations c create new ones. Here are two well-known Canadian examples:

- Magna International Inc., an automotive parts supplier, whic was founded by Frank Stronach, a New Canadian born in Au tria. Magna had sales of US$10.5 billion in 2000 and employ approximately 63,000 people around the world.
- ATI Technologies Inc., a manufacturer of graphic silicon chip which was founded by K. Y Ho, a New Canadian from Hor Kong. In 2001, ATI had sales of slightly more than US$1 billic and employs approximately 1,900 people around the world.

In Canada, 27 of the 100 richest people are New Canadian according to the magazine *Profit*. New North Americans have much contribute to North American organizations. I hope this book hel you and your organization benefit from this tremendous potential.

Summary

In the long run, it is difficult to determine whether globalization w result in the creation of a single business culture or not. What can l said with a high degree of confidence is that cultural differences w continue to exist and make their presence felt in the world of technic professionals for the next 30 years. There is therefore a strong ince tive for all technical professionals who work closely with cultural different colleagues to learn how to overcome the challenges related cultural differences and to reap the benefits of these differences.

References

Hall, E.T., and Reed Hall, M. 1990. *Understanding cultural differenc Germans, French and Americans.* Yarmouth, ME: Intercultural Press, p 21–22.

Katsioloudes, M.I. 2002. *Global strategic planning: cultural perspectives for profit or non-profit organizations,* Woburn, MA: Butterworth–Heinemann.

Sears, W., and Tamulionyte-Lentz, A. 2001. *Succeeding in business in Central and Eastern Europe: A guide to cultures, markets, and practices.* Woburn, MA: Butterworth–Heinemann.

Appendix A

Advice for Diversity Trainers and HR Managers

Throughout their formal education and their careers, technical professionals tend to focus on physical systems and the laws that govern them. They seek to understand these laws in order to use them to their advantage by designing, building, and operating systems that do what they want them to do. They continuously create new systems that do more with less (sometimes a lot more with a little less, other times a little more with a lot less). Their daily activities are full of numbers, data, experiments, and equipment.

By contrast, diversity trainers and HR managers tend to focus on people and the interactions among them. Their primary goal is to get these people to work together effectively, regardless of their race, religion, gender, sexual orientation, cultural background, and so on.

Because of these differences, interactions between these people are not always as smooth as they could be. In particular, technical professionals attend cultural diversity training sessions with some reluctance, for several reasons:

- The laws of physics do not change from country to country. In addition, technical curricula emphasize an objective and scientific approach that is expected to be constant. In this context, they expect the role of cultural differences to play little to no role in their work. They do not see the real need for such training.

Part of this appendix was first published in the Spring 2001 issue of the *Profiles in Diversity Journal* and is reprinted with its permission.

- Many technical professionals consider soft skills in general and interpersonal skills in particular as secondary to technical skills, so they would rather further their technical skills than attend a cultural diversity training session.

In order to work effectively with technical professionals, diversity trainers and HR managers need to address these issues at the outset of the training session to the satisfaction of their audiences. This appendix examines what they can do to communicate more effectively with audiences made of technical professionals.

Needs

The need for cross-cultural training varies significantly with the complexity of the tasks performed by technical professionals. Cultural differences (as well as other differences, like personality) play a limited role in simple tasks, such as operating machinery, running experiments according to a predetermined protocol, or entering data in a database. These tasks are characterized by the fact that they require either limited interaction between people or interactions that follow a predetermined script. Such tasks are easier to automate than more complex, interactive tasks. When technical professionals think of these tasks as major components of their jobs, it is obvious to them that differences between people have little to no impact on their work.

As the tasks become increasingly complex, differences between people have an increasing impact on the outcome. For example, as described in Chapter 3, the approach to solving complex technical problems depends partly on the cultural backgrounds of the people involved. Cultural differences have a bigger impact on technical professionals involved in designing consumer products because a perfectly functional product may be a failure in the marketplace for several reasons (e.g., if consumers do not understand how it works).

Differences among people have an even larger impact on technical professionals involved in work processes that include extensive human interactions. As their careers unfold, the work of technical professionals has more and more impact on people throughout the organization. As we saw in this book, this situation is particularly true for those who move into managerial or sales positions. This is also true for technical professionals who move up the technical ladder: An important part of their responsibilities consists then in providing technical advice and leadership to senior management.

In technical organizations that employ many New North Amer icans, the usefulness of cross-cultural training is often underesti mated. This is not the only issue that diversity trainers and HR managers face when providing cross-cultural training to technica professionals. They also need to adapt the training contents and approach to this specific audience.

Training for Technical Professionals

In order to reach their audience effectively, trainers adapt thei training styles to the learning style of participants. Here are some o the issues that commonly arise when technical people attend a cultura diversity training session (suggestions on how to best circumvent thes problems are provided in the next section):

- Technical professionals tend to view engineering and science a serious business. Training activities that are called "games" ma not be well received because of the playful label.

- Technical professionals are trained to analyze information and look for hidden information. As a result, training activities where the actual objective is either different from the stated objective o not stated may miss their mark. For example, when playing th Barnga card game, technical professionals are analyzing the gam and trying to understand why the rules were taken away at som point.

- Technical professionals may also run the activity proposed by th trainer in their heads (performing a "thought experiment") an not actually do it physically.

- For technical professionals, qualitative information has littl value relative to quantitative information. In science and engi neering, qualitative information is used only to justify the nee for more research in a specific area.

- Technical professionals spend a significant fraction of thei careers analyzing quantitative data. As a result, they examine analyze, and dissect any quantitative information presented in a training session. For the data to be accepted, technical profes sionals often need to know, in a fair amount of detail, how th data were collected. In their minds, they will then assess whethe the data collection is in line with the conclusions that the stud purported to draw and whether the data are consistent. If eithe of these two elements is not clearly demonstrated by the traine few of the conclusions drawn from the data will be considered valid.

- Although technical professionals have an extensive understanding of physical processes, they often have a limited understanding of human processes and group dynamics—more limited than many trainers assume. As a result, some training programs require participants to perform tasks (such as "creating a contract between them" or "working on team issues") that are beyond their capabilities.

- When technical professionals look at HR data, they tend to over-analyze this data (i.e., look at differences between two numbers and think of reasons why this difference might exist), whereas this difference is considered meaningless by HR professionals. In this respect, keep in mind that the precision and accuracy that can be achieved in science and engineering is generally much higher than the precision and accuracy that can be achieved in social sciences.

Suggestions for Diversity Trainers and HR Managers

To improve the effectiveness of their training sessions and to communicate better with technical professionals, diversity trainers and HR managers may consider the following:

- Label "games" as activities; this may increase the receptiveness of technical professionals.

- Avoid training activities where the objective is not the stated objective or where there is no objective at all.

- Before a training session, discuss with a technical professional whether the activities you have in mind may be approached as "thought experiments." If they might be, determine what additional benefit there is by doing it physically rather than mentally, and provide your audience with that information if they start doing the activity in their heads. Keep in mind that "it will be fun" may not qualify as a valid reason to them for doing it physically.

- Whenever possible, support the points you want to make during a training session with quantitative evidence.

- For technical professionals to accept the data you are presenting, they need to know how the data have been collected and how it supports the conclusions you are trying to make. If you experience difficulties on this point, discuss your data with some technical professionals to understand where your logic stops making sense to them. In some cases, the issue may be more a question of the way you present it than the data or methodology itself.

- When you are asking technical professionals to work on human processes, create contracts between themselves, or any such activity that assumes a fair amount of knowledge about interpersonal and group interactions, monitor their progress closely. You may need to facilitate this particular part of the session (as opposed to letting them run it) and explain how to do it.

- Explain what is a meaningful difference in the data you present.

- Whenever possible, use pictures, diagrams, and sketches to illustrate your points. Engineers and scientists use drawings extensively to communicate about their work and will usually respond positively to such illustrations. You may want to run new visuals by some technical professionals to ensure that they make sense to them.

Reference

Laroche, L.F. 2001. Pushing a rope: Providing cultural diversity training to technical people, *Profiles in Diversity Journal*, Spring 30–31.

Demographics of
New North Americans

Immigration has always played a major role in the history of Canada and the United States. For both countries, immigration remains an important source of population and skills. In both countries, immigration is an important topic and receives significant attention from the federal government. In particular, both countries have either a ministry (Citizenship and Immigration Canada) or an agency (Immigration and Naturalization Services) specifically to regulate immigration. In both countries, immigrants can become citizens in a relatively short period: three years in Canada, five years in the United States. The North American approach to immigration can be contrasted to the approach in place in other developed countries:

- In France, immigration is managed by the Ministère de l'Intérieur (i.e., the ministry in charge of police and customs). It takes 10 years of residence for immigrants to become French citizens.

- Germany has a large population of *Gastarbeiter* (guest workers), with a large fraction of these coming from Turkey. Only a small minority of these guest workers has acquired German citizenship. German citizenship is primarily obtained by birth: You are German because one of your parents is German, not because you were born on German soil (Nees, 2000).

- Japanese citizenship is also acquired by blood. There are very few cases of people becoming Japanese citizens.

Immigration and Naturalization

The following are some differences between the United States and Canada in their specific approaches to immigration and naturalization

- U.S. immigration law gives preferential immigration status to persons with a close family relationship with a U.S. citizen or legal permanent resident; then come persons with needed skill and refugees. For example, the maximum number of visa allowed to be issued in 1998 was 366,000: that is, 226,000 (62%) for family-sponsored immigrants and 140,000 (38% for employment-based immigrants. Between 1991 and 1996 6,146,200 immigrants entered the United States; this represent approximately 2.5 percent of the total U.S. population. In 1998 the United States received 660,500 immigrants.

- Canadian immigration law is based on a point system that give preferential immigration status to persons who can quickly make professional contributions to the Canadian labor market. In this system, immigration applicants are given a number of points for having achieved higher levels of formal education (doctorate or master's degrees), speaking one of the two official language (English or French), having some work experience, and being between the ages of 21 and 44. Applicants who reach the man dated minimum requirement are accepted in Canada; since 1991 approximately 60 percent of immigrants were accepted based on their skills. Between 1991 and 1996, 1,039,000 immigrant entered Canada; this represents approximately 3.7 percent of the total Canadian population. In 2001, Canada received 252,08 immigrants.

- With respect to citizenship, the key difference between the two countries is that becoming an American citizen requires abandoning one's original citizenship, whereas this is not required to become Canadian.

Countries of Origin

Canada and the United States do not draw from the same pools of immigrants, as demonstrated by Exhibit B.1. The United State receives a higher percentage of its immigrants from Mexico, Central America, and the Caribbean than Canada, whereas Canada receives a higher percentage of its immigrants from Asia.

Exhibit B.1

The leading countries of immigrants entering Canada and the United States between 1991 and 1996.

Country of Origin	Number of Immigrants Entering Canada	Percentage
Hong Kong	108,915	10.5
People's Republic of China	87,875	8.5
India	71,335	6.9
Philippines	71,325	6.9
Sri Lanka	44,235	4.3
Poland	36,965	3.6
Taiwan	32,140	3.1
Vietnam	32,060	3.1
U.S.	29,020	2.8
U.K.	25,425	2.4
Total	**1,038,995**	**100.0**

Country of Origin	Number of Immigrants Entering the U.S.	Percentage
Mexico	1,651,400	26.9
Philippines	348,500	5.7
Vietnam	317,800	5.2
People's Republic of China	268,700	4.4
Dominican Republic	258,100	4.2
India	238,500	3.9
El Salvador	147,700	2.4
Poland	130,200	2.1
Haiti	114,400	1.9
Korea	114,100	1.9
Jamaica	109,800	1.8
Total	**6,146,200**	**100.0**

Skills

As Exhibit B.2 illustrates, New Canadians tend to have, on average, significantly more formal education than the rest of the population at large; this exhibit also shows that New Canadians are more often unemployed. These unemployment figures do not take into consideration the significant number of New Canadians who are underemployed (engineers driving taxis or operating dry cleaning businesses). Comparable data for the United States is not available from the U.S. Census Bureau.

Exhibit B.2

Education and unemployment rate for New Canadians aged between 21 and 44, who arrived in Canada between 1991 and 1996 (1996 data).

	Men	Women
Recent immigrants who hold a university degree	36%	31%
Canadians who hold a university degree	18%	20%
Unemployment rate among recent immigrants	29%	49%
Unemployment rate among Canadians	9.7%	9.5%

At the same time, New Canadians occupy many positions in the natural and applied sciences. For example, they represented 46 percent of aerospace engineers, 39 percent of chemists, and 38 percent of computer engineers. Recent immigrants alone (i.e., immigrants who arrived in Canada within the last five years) accounted for 11 percent of all computer engineers in 1996.

References

1996 Census: Immigration and Citizenship. 1997. Ottawa, ON: Statistics Canada. www.statscan.ca/Daily/English/971104/d971104.htm

Statistical Abstract of the United States: 2001. Washington, DC: U.S. Census Bureau. www.census.gov/prod/2002pubs/01statab/pop.pdf

Nees, G. 2000. *Germany: Unraveling an enigma.* Yarmouth, MA: Intercultural Press, p. 154.

A Cross-Cultural Look at Technical Education

Throughout the world, people attempt to teach their children what they think their children will need in order to operate effectively in society and have successful lives. At the individual level, parents teach their kids things like proper manners, how to handle conflicts with others, and so on. Some of this education is done explicitly, but most of it is done by example (i.e., children modeling their behavior after the behavior of their parents).

At the societal level, people in a given country set up their educational system to provide students with the tools they will need to do their jobs later on. Because different cultures have different ideas of what skills technical professionals need in order to be successful at solving technical problems and managing organizations, technical education curricula vary significantly from country to country.

This point often comes as a surprise to some technical professionals. To illustrate this point, this appendix compares the mechanical engineering curricula in a few universities in Canada, the United States, France, and Mexico. There are key differences in the education of engineers that have an impact later in their professional activities. This comparison does not suggest that one curriculum is better than another; however, it does suggest that engineers are not all made out

---

Part of this appendix was first published in the February 2001 issues of *Stainless Steel World* and *Valve World* and is reprinted with its permission.

of the same cloth. As Chapter 3 indicates, these differences can be used synergistically in multicultural teams.

This appendix compares the mechanical engineering curricula of the following universities:

- The University of Waterloo and McGill University, located respectively in Waterloo, Ontario, and Montreal, Quebec
- The California Institute of Technology (Caltech), Massachusetts Institute of Technology (MIT), and Stanford University, located respectively in Pasadena, California; Cambridge, Massachusetts; and Palo Alto, California in the United States
- L'École Polytechnique de Paris in Palaiseau, France
- The Tecnologico de Monterrey, Instituto Tecnologico de Saltillo, and Instituto Tecnologico de Tijuana, located respectively in Monterrey, Saltillo, and Tijuana, in Mexico

This comparison is based on the information obtained from the websites of these universities, as posted in April and December 2000.

Theory Versus Practice

The French and Mexican education systems for engineers tend to emphasize theory, whereas the Canadian and American systems include more time for practice. As we saw in Chapter 3, France and Mexico are risk-averse countries, where theory tends to be highly valued. By contrast, the United States and Canada are more risk-tolerant; pragmatic approaches appeal more to such cultures.

This difference is reflected in the relative amount of time spent, on average, in university classes versus time spent on internships, as shown in Exhibit C.1. These percentages are based on the number of weeks spent in university versus the number of weeks spent in internships or on extended vacations (which are considered suitable for summer jobs). French and Mexican students spend more time in class than their Canadian and American counterparts in order to learn more from their professors.

The Latin preference for theory over practice is also reflected in the fact that French and Mexican engineering students spend more time in the classroom and less time in laboratories than do Canadian and American students, as shown in Exhibit C.2.

Exhibit C.1

Relative amount of time spent in class versus outside the university in internships.

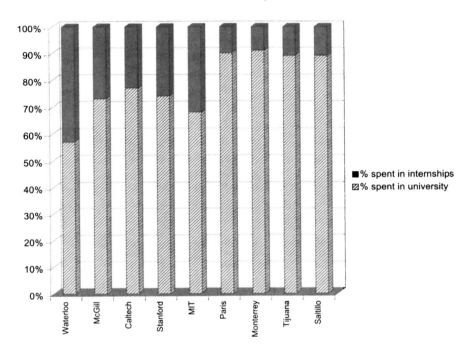

Engineering Versus Arts and Sciences

The range of subjects that mechanical engineering students study varies widely in the four countries (see Exhibit C.3). The Canadian and French universities considered in this study are at opposite ends of the spectrum with respect to the concentration of credits in engineering, versus other subject areas. The percentage of credits allocated to engineering courses varies from 21 percent at the École Polytechnique de Paris to 64 percent at the University of Waterloo.

Each country tends to approach engineering education differently. Here are some of the key differences:

- In Canada, undergraduate engineering degree programs are accredited for licensing purposes. Specific guidelines stipulate the number and content of engineering courses. As a result,

Exhibit C.2

Percentage of time spent in classrooms versus laboratories.

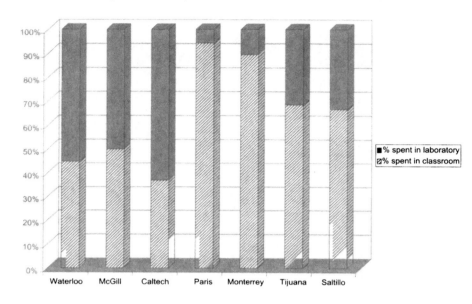

Exhibit C.3

Percentage of the total number of credits needed in each field.

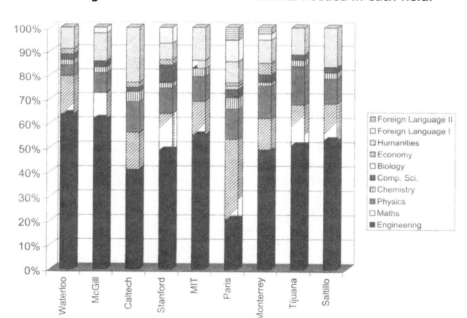

variations among engineering schools are not as significant as they are in other countries. Because the best Canadian students (honors program students) are encouraged to specialize, the percentage of courses allocated to engineering in honors programs is higher than the percentage of courses allocated to engineering in regular programs.

- In the United States, where national engineering standards provide more latitude, engineering faculties have more discretion in choosing what topics should be part of their curricula. As a result, variations in the content of engineering programs are more significant in the United States than they are in Canada. For instance, the percentage of credits allocated to chemistry and humanities can vary widely from one university to the next.

- Some Mexican universities are emulating the curriculum of American universities. For example, the Tecnologico de Monterrey is aiming to be the "MIT of Latin America."

- French students are encouraged to have a wide breadth of scientific and technical interests, rather than to specialize in one area. Engineering students at L'École Polytechnique de Paris, who are considered to be the best French students (admission to this institution is based on a countrywide competition), are expected to study a broad range of scientific topics from a mathematic point of view. These students actually take three times more mathematics courses and half as many engineering courses as Canadian engineering students. In addition, mechanical engineering students at L'École Polytechnique de Paris take courses in electrical, chemical, and mechanical engineering.

This difference in educational approach comes from different emphases: In France, the best students are encouraged to learn a little about a lot of subjects because major breakthroughs are expected to come from people who apply ideas and concepts from one scientific field to another. In Canada, the best students are encouraged to concentrate on one area within their field because major improvements come from experts who know specific processes or topics inside out and can apply their knowledge to a wide range of situations.

Reference

Laroche, L.F. 2001. What makes an engineer an engineer? *Stainless Steel World*, February, pp. 46–48.

Appendix D

Technical Professional Associations

For some New North American technical professionals, the large number of North American professional associations, the importance that they seem to have, and their seemingly overlapping scopes can be a source of confusion. For example, as a chemical engineer working in Ontario in the plastics industry, I could become a member of the following associations:

- The Canadian Society of Chemical Engineers (CSChE)
- The American Institute of Chemical Engineers (AIChE); this association includes many members outside the United States (in particular, it has an active chapter in Alberta).
- The association of Professional Engineers of Ontario (PEO)
- The Ontario Society of Professional Engineers (OSPE)
- The Society of Plastics Engineers (SPE)

This list does not include alumni associations, which are not specific to technical professionals. For many New North Americans, the question becomes: Which one(s) should they join? This appendix is meant to shed some light on this question.

A key difference to remember when discussing professional associations is the strong, positive connotation of the word *professional* in North America. North Americans tend to value greatly being a professional and behaving professionally. In this respect, one of the worst comments that can be made about someone is that his or her conduct (or behavior) is unprofessional; this is a strong, negative statement. The desire to be recognized as professionals is strong (e.g., career coaches are called career management professionals, human resources specialists are called HR professionals, etc.).

The Lay of the Land

Professional associations in the United States and Canada can be grouped according to the following four criteria:

- *Professional field.* There are associations for every category of technical professionals, from architects to zoologists. Membership in these associations (which include the CSChE and the AIChE) is primarily a function of the degree one has obtained and the work that one does.

- *Industrial sector.* Technical professionals working in the same industrial sector have created specific associations. The SPE and the Society of Automotive Engineers are two examples of these associations.

- *Geographic/regulatory associations.* In North America, unlike in many other parts of the world, some technical professions are regulated. For example, engineering, geology, and geophysics are regulated in many U.S. states and Canadian provinces. This means that state or provincial governments have passed laws that are designed to safeguard the public and that determine the following:
  - Criteria for obtaining a "professional designation" (P.E., P.Eng., or Ing. in the case of professional engineers working in the United States, English Canada, and Quebec, respectively); In most cases, obtaining a professional designation requires passing some examinations (some jurisdictions have technical examinations, others have law and ethics examinations, while some have both) and becoming a member of these associations. Some professional associations also have continuing education requirements.
  - The scope of activities for which a professional designation is explicitly required; for example, someone cannot legally work as an engineer in Ontario without being a professional engineer or working under the supervision of a professional engineer.

○ Disciplining mechanisms so that complaints about the actions or behaviors of some of these professionals can be handled effectively.

There are some differences between the United States and Canada in that respect. For example, engineering is entirely regulated in Canada, whereas only certain areas of engineering are regulated in the United States. This difference can be significant for some New North Americans, like software engineers. In Canada, they are expected to obtain their professional designations (i.e., become members of the corresponding provincial association of engineers).

- *Advocacy associations.* Most associations act as advocates for their members and represent them to federal, provincial, and state governments. In some cases, the advocacy function is dissociated from the regulatory function, as in the case of engineers of Ontario: The OSPE is an advocacy association, while PEO is a regulatory association.

In many cases, there are both American and Canadian associations; for example, chemists in the United States may join the American Chemical Society, while Canadian chemists may join the Chemical Institute of Canada. Many American professional associations have chapters in other countries (e.g., the AIChE has chapters in Alberta, Saudi Arabia, and Belgium/the Netherlands); as a result, some Canadian technical professionals are members of both Canadian and American associations.

Some associations have formed groups of associations. For example, the AIChE, CSChE, and their Mexican counterpart have formed a North American Association of Chemical Engineers. Similarly, state and provincial professional engineering associations have federal representatives that lobby the U.S. and Canadian federal governments on behalf of their members. In most cases, individuals cannot join these associations directly—they need to join through their local associations.

To Join or Not to Join

Here are some of the services many professional associations offer:

- *Networking opportunities*, often in the form of events (e.g., dinners, dances, golf tournaments)

- *Continuing education.* This can be done formally (with classroom or online courses) or informally (through breakfast or lunch presentations, visits of facilities of particular interest to members, etc.).
- *Publications.* Most associations publish magazines or newsletters that are distributed specifically to their members.
- *Conferences*
- *Job search support.* These associations often receive job postings specific to their members; they also often offer some assistance to their members (publication of a "Job wanted" ad in their magazine, specific information, etc.).
- *Representation* of their members in front of state, provincial, or federal governments
- *Buying guides* and, in some cases, *discounts* on technical books and products that are commonly used by their members
- *Salary surveys* that help members determine where they are relative to their peers in terms of compensation

For New North American technical professionals, becoming members of professional associations offers additional benefits:

- In the case of regulatory associations, they may expand significantly the range of opportunities that are available to them.
- They have a chance to create a network of people who work in similar technical areas and who are established in these fields. These people can make them aware of opportunities that outsiders to the field would not know about.

In the experience of many New North Americans who have lived and worked in North America for several years, becoming active members of professional associations has a beneficial impact on their careers. Being active (i.e., attending meetings, participating in meeting) is important because this is when the networking takes place.

So, how do New North American technical professionals choose the association(s) that is (are) right for them? In case of regulatory associations, the answer is usually simple: If your area of expertise falls within the regulated area, you should become a member. Otherwise, your career opportunities are automatically more limited.

In the case of nonregulatory associations, shop around. Most associations welcome nonmembers at their events; the only difference is that they usually charge them a slightly higher fee than that for members. By attending a few events of several different associations in which it would make sense for you to become a member, you will have a chance to determine which association(s) work(s) best for you. Do not hesitate to ask questions related to your area of interest; for example, if your interest in joining is related to continuing education, ask about the courses they offer, the corresponding fees, and so on. Such questions are considered perfectly normal in North American associations.

Glossary of North American Idioms and Sports Phrases

General Expressions

Loose cannon: Cannons that are not attached to the ground and therefore fire every time in a different and, more important, unpredictable direction, making them dangerous for anyone near them.

Shooting from the hip: Make a decision, with limited analysis. When drawing a gun from its gun holder, people shoot faster if they shoot from the hip (with the gun at hip level) rather than bringing their gun to eye level and aiming, but their accuracy is lower.

When the rubber hits the road: When things start moving.

To tune someone out: To stop listening to that person.

To ruffle someone's feathers: To irritate someone; to do something that they do not appreciate and would like you to stop.

To pass the buck: To avoid taking responsibility by letting someone else make a decision or be blamed for a mistake rather than taking that decision or being blamed oneself.

To be caught between a rock and a hard place: To be stuck in an unpleasant and difficult situation.

We will cross that bridge when we come to it: We will deal with this event when it occurs.

Examination in camera: Examination behind closed doors (as opposed to a public examination that everyone can attend). In camera does not mean that the examination will be taped.

To have a field day: To enjoy a situation thoroughly, like elementary school students going on a field trip.

To start off on the wrong foot: To start in a way that does not work well, like dancers who start on the wrong foot and end up tripping or stepping on each other's toes.

To bring people up to speed: To give people the necessary background information.

To let one's hair down: To show one's true feelings (or to relax).

To put a damper on something: To tone down, from the damper that is used to put out a fire.

To run something by someone: To ask this person to review your work.

Speak up now or forever hold your peace: If you have something to say, say it now. This is your last chance; after that, you are expected to refrain from commenting on this issue. This expression is used in wedding vows to the guests present.

Baseball Expressions

To cover all the bases: To have a plan for all contingencies.

To be far out in left field: To make no sense at all.

To be in the right ballpark: To be of the right order of magnitude.

Ballpark figure: Rough estimate.

To hit a home run: To achieve something significant.

To bat 1,000: To have a perfect record.

Three strikes, and you're out: Making the same mistake three times will have negative consequences.

To go to bat for someone: To take a personal risk for that person.

To take one for the team: To make a sacrifice for the team.

To touch base: To call someone to see how things are going.

To step up to the plate: To get ready to do something challenging.

To pull a fast one on someone: To surprise this person with an unexpected action (usually has a negative connotation).

To throw a curve ball: To ask someone to do something difficult.

It's out of my league: I am not qualified to do this.

This is an entirely different ball game: This has nothing to do with what we were discussing before.

Football Expressions

To punt: To give up.

To fumble: To make a mistake.

To drop the ball: To forget to complete a task.

Two down, three to go: We have completed two tasks and we still have three to take care of (comes from the yardage required to gain field position).

To do an end run around someone: To complete a task without getting that person involved.

To call a time out: To ask for a break.

Monday morning (armchair) quarterbacking: Commenting on a project after the fact, from a safe distance.

Kick-off: Starting point.

To score a touchdown: To be successful.

To throw a long bomb (Hail Mary): To put all your resources into a single, big project and hope for the best.

To do one for the gipper (coach): To do it one more time.

To run interference: To prevent other people from looking into something.

Other Sports Expressions

To cross the blue line: To enter enemy/competitor territory.

To pass the baton: To hand a task or project off to someone else.

To have the inside track: To have an advantage over others.

To level the playing field: To give everyone equal chances, equal opportunities.

In the long run: In a distant future.

Index

About the Author

Dr. Lionel Laroche, P.Eng., is a cross-cultural trainer and consultant who facilitates workshops specifically designed for technical professionals. In this book, he makes use of his 15 years of international engineering experience, during which he has worked with people from over 50 countries. He has worked in eight different countries (France, Germany, Italy, Belgium, Denmark, the Netherlands, Canada, and the United States) for several multinational companies, including Xerox, Procter & Gamble, British Petroleum, and Jeumont-Schneider. In particular, he has worked as a member of multinational project teams on several assignments, including:

- The licensing of a new polymerization process worldwide
- The development of a single new feminine hygiene product for several continents
- The development of complex supply chains spanning several countries in different continents

Over the past five years, Dr. Laroche has provided cross-cultural training, coaching, and consulting services to over 1000 people in seven countries (Canada, the U.S., Mexico, Peru, France, Belgium, and China).

He is the author of over 80 publications examining the impact of cultural differences on business in general and technical functions (engineering, science, and software) in particular. His publications have appeared in over 20 trade magazines published in seven countries (Canada, U.S., U.K., Netherlands, France, Mexico, and Australia).

Dr. Laroche has made numerous invited presentations in a number of conferences and venues, including the 27th Annual Conference for Insurance Companies organized by the Royal Bank of Canada, and the 2000 Summer Diversity Institute organized by the University of Calgary. Recently, he has been invited to make several presentations on the impact of cultural differences in business by the Canadian Chamber of Commerce in Mexico, the Canadian Chamber of Commerce in Peru, the Swedish-Canadian Chamber of Commerce, and the International Trade Club of Toronto.

Born in France, Dr. Laroche obtained his Diplôme d'Ingénieur Polytechnicien from the Ecole Polytechnique de Paris and his Ph.D. in Chemical Engineering from the California Institute of Technology in Pasadena, California.

/

CPSIA information can be obtained at www.ICGtesting.com
Printed in the USA
BVOW062034031111

275102BV00001B/25/P